THE DIDACHE

THE EPISTLE OF BARNABAS

THE EPISTLES AND THE MARTYRDOM
OF ST. POLYCARP

THE FRAGMENTS OF PAPIAS

THE EPISTLE TO DIOGNETUS

Ancient Christian Writers

THE WORKS OF THE FATHERS IN TRANSLATION

EDITED BY

JOHANNES QUASTEN, S. T. D.
*Professor of Ancient Church History
and Christian Archaeology*

JOSEPH C. PLUMPE, Ph. D.
*Associate Professor of New Testament
Greek and Ecclesiastical Latin*

The Catholic University of America
Washington, D. C.

No. 6

THE DIDACHE
THE EPISTLE OF BARNABAS
THE EPISTLES AND THE MARTYRDOM OF ST. POLYCARP
THE FRAGMENTS OF PAPIAS
THE EPISTLE TO DIOGNETUS

NEWLY TRANSLATED AND ANNOTATED

BY

JAMES A. KLEIST, S. J., Ph. D.

Professor of Classical Languages
St. Louis University
St. Louis, Mo.

NEWMAN PRESS

New York, N.Y./Ramsey, N.J.

Imprimi Potest:

Joseph P. Zuercher, S.J.
Provincialis

Nihil Obstat:

Johannes Quasten, S.T.D.
Censor Deputatus

Imprimatur:

Patricius A. O'Boyle, D.D.
Archiepiscopus Washingtonensis
die 2 Junii 1948

Library of Congress
Catalog Card Number: 78-62453

ISBN: 0-8091-0247-1

PUBLISHED BY PAULIST PRESS
Editorial Office: 1865 Broadway, New York, N.Y. 10023
Business Office: 545 Island Road, Ramsey, N.J. 07446

PRINTED AND BOUND IN THE UNITED STATES OF AMERICA

CONTENTS

THE DIDACHE

OR

THE TEACHING OF THE TWELVE APOSTLES

INTRODUCTION

The *Didache*, or *The Teaching of the Twelve Apostles*, has been hailed as the most important patristic find in the latter half of the nineteenth century. The manuscript, dated 1056, was discovered, together with other valuable early writings, by the Orthodox Metropolitan Bryennios at Constantinople in 1873 and published by him ten years later.[1]

The *Didache* purports to be an instruction based on sayings of the Lord and given by the Twelve Apostles to pagans who wished to become Christians. Part I (1-6) is an epitome of Christian morality, suited to pagan candidates for baptism. This catechetical section inculcates, under the form of The Way of Life and The Way of Death, the practice of Christian virtue and enumerates the vices to be shunned. Its starting point is the double commandment of the love of God and of neighbor, and the Golden Rule in its negative wording. Part II (7-10) is a ritual or liturgical summary. It explains the rite of baptism (7) both by immersion and by aspersion (infusion); the Christian practice of fasting and prayer (8); the prayers to be used at the private or domestic celebration of the Eucharist (9 and 10). Part III (11-15), the canonical section, broadly outlines Church organization and Church life. It distinguishes three classes of Church officials (11): "apostles" or itinerant missionaries; "prophets" or men speaking in ecstasy; "teachers" or catechists. It lays down principles (12) for according or refusing hospitality to travelling brethren, and urges the support of prophets (13). It

3

makes reference to the regular Sunday observance (14),
and gives rules for proper behavior toward bishops and
deacons (15). Presbyters are not explicitly mentioned.[2] The
treatise closes with an exhortation (16) to take life seriously
in view of the impending Judgment and the end of the
world. Christian dogma is not imparted as such, but is, of
course, implied in several precepts.

Where was the *Didache* composed? Some of its statements
(13) seem to suppose a small town or rural community; but
we are still left to conjecture whether a Syrian (or Pales-
tinian) or Egyptian provenance is the more likely. The
former is suggested by the hint of a possible lack of running
water needed for baptism (7.2); by the warning against " the
hypocrites " (the Jews, no doubt) in 8.1 and 2; by the mention of the grain scattered on the hills (10.4). Other considerations favor Egypt as the place of composition: the
testimony of Clement of Alexandria (*Strom.* 1. 20. 100. 4),
the popularity of the *Didache* in Egypt, the finds of Greco-
Coptic papyri, etc.

The date of composition is a warmly debated problem.
While some scholars are ready to fix it somewhere in the
first century, there are others that move it down into the
third. The *Didache* as we know it, that is, consisting of six-
teen chapters, need not be the work of any one man and
the result of one well-considered plan, but is perhaps a
fusion of two (or even three) little tracts, each of which
serves a definite purpose and may have its own date of composition. At all events, the injunctions given in Ch. 7 regarding the proper way of baptizing seems to be addressed
to pagans that have just been baptized, since they are told
how to instruct and baptize others. On the other hand, the
section on the Eucharistic prayers takes the presence of un-

baptized persons at the Eucharistic meal for granted. Other problems arise from the possibility of literary dependence. There are obvious points of contact with other early documents, notably the *Epistle of Barnabas* (*Did.* 1-6: *Barn.* 18-20), and the Latin *Doctrina duodecim apostolorum.* But there can be no doubt that certain writings that have to do with Church liturgy and Church law (*Didascalia, Apostolic Church Order,* Book 7 of the *Apostolic Constitutions*) are indebted to the *Didache.*[2]

There are, however, certain facts that invite pondering. Antioch, that important Syrian centre of paganism, was evangelized in 42 or 43. St. Paul conducted his first missionary tour between 45 and 48. That, then, was the time when the problem of catechizing pagans came to the fore and pressed for a solution. In 49 or 50, the Apostolic Council looked into the matter and laid down its well-known decrees (Acts 15. 28 ff.). We are sure, therefore, that about this time some more or less uniform method of catechizing pagans was worked out. Now, it is noteworthy that the very title of the *Didache* connects at least the first tract in one way or another with " the Twelve Apostles," and it is not rash to conclude that it was their method of catechizing that found its way into the *Didache.* When this happened we do not know; but since the *Didache* offers a somewhat modified form of the Apostolic decree (see 6. 2 and 3), some time must have elapsed between the year 50 and the date of composition. If we allow the space of a whole decade to have intervened between the two events, we reach the year 60, and it is impossible to disprove the statement of some scholars that the *Didache* was written, if not in whole, at least in part, between 60 and 70. Others prefer the period between 70 and 80, while still others cling to the following decade, 80-90. It should, therefore, be admitted that we have a thoroughly conservative, and altogether reliable, estimate in the statement of many leading scholars that the *Didache* was written " before the end of the first century."

This reasoning is strengthened by a consideration of the contents of the *Didache*. Judged by the internal evidence of language and subject matter, it is undoubtedly of great antiquity.[4] Every detail points in this direction. For instance, the organization of the Church is still primitive and reminiscent of Eph. 4. 11 and 1 Cor. 12. 28; charismatic leaders of the Church are still prominent (11. 3 ff. and especially 13.3); the presbyterate is not yet mentioned as an office distinct from that of bishops and deacons, although St. Clement's letter to the Corinthians, penned about 96, makes mention of " bishops, presbyters, and deacons "; finally, baptism is still conferred in streams.

On the other hand, these indications of primitiveness are offset by others that seem to exclude the Apostolic Age as the time of composition.[5] The validity of baptism by infusion or aspersion is already recognized (7.3); there is a touch of anti-Semitic bias apparent in the condemnation of certain Jewish practices (8. 1, 2); the authority of the " prophets " needs to be supported, which shows that an abuse of the charismatic gifts had already set in (10. 7; 11. 7, 11; 13.1); finally, " church orders " (a sort of reflective stocktaking of ecclesiatical usage), of which the *Didache* is an example, as a rule require a certain length of time for their development. However, one further significant indication of early composition remains.

The chief interest—and great puzzle—of the *Didache* is in its Eucharistic Chapters 9 and 10. The author does not describe the celebration of the Eucharist which he has in mind (cf. Rom. 16. 5); but in furnishing prayers to be used at such a celebration, he gives several indications which allow us to see how he wanted the prayers to be fitted in. It should now be observed that not a few scholars postulate a number of transpositions in the text as necessary for making it intelligible.[6] But transpositions are a violent tampering with the text as handed down, and *an effort to let it tell its own story should be welcomed.*

"Regarding the Eucharist." This is the first intimation of the theme of Chapters 9 and 10. We are surprised to find the cup mentioned before the bread. We remember, however, that a cup is also mentioned before the bread in Luke 22. 17-19. The prayers which follow make no reference to the Body and Blood of Jesus Christ, unless, perhaps, the expressions "the Vine of David" (9.2) and "the broken bread" (9.3) were designedly chosen as convenient substitutes.

We are now at the end of § 4, and rightly suppose that, since the grace-before-meals is finished, the company present is understood to begin the meal. This the Didachist does not state in so many words, but in 10.1 we find that all the participants have had their fill of food. It is certain, then, that a meal was taken at the end of § 4. In § 5, during or at the end of the meal, the unbaptized are warned not to partake "of *your* Eucharist," that is, not of this Christian "offering of thanks." It is certain, therefore, that the repast, for which 9. 2-4 prescribes the grace to be said, was an ordinary community meal. Whether it is called *agape* or by any other name has no bearing on the problem before us.

When this meal is over, at the end of 9.5, the uninitiated either leave the room (or, perhaps, the Christians retire to an "upper room": cf. Mark 14. 15) or, at least, step aside while Mass is said in their presence, and do not receive Holy Communion. In the light of the Church's later practice the former supposition is the more probable, since catechumens were allowed to attend the Mass of the Catechumens (consisting of prayers, songs, readings, and sermons), but were barred from the Mass of the Faithful.

At the beginning of Ch. 10 we are told that all the members of the group have had their fill of food. This means that the prayers in 9.2-4 were for all a preparation for the common meal, and for the Christians a preparation also for Holy Communion. It is now clear why those prayers make no indubitable reference to the Body and Blood of Christ. The reason for this silence, or, better, for the veiled language of the prayers, is given by the Didachist himself: "Do not give to dogs what is sacred" (9.5). In their original context (Matt. 7.6) these words of Our Lord are a general injunction not to divulge (much less, to give) to infidels what is sacred to Christians. Are they not the forerunner of the later *disciplina arcani?* Pliny's report to the emperor Trajan confirms our impression.[7] Spies had been sent out to investigate the strange behavior of the Christians at their services; but all they were able to ascertain was that they ate *cibum promiscuum et innoxium,* "just ordinary and harmless food." They saw that bread and wine were given to the communicants, but were unable to learn that they were the Body and Blood of Christ.

In 10. 2-5 the grace-after-meals is of a very solemn character. Again, there is no explicit reference to the *mysterium fidei.* The reason for this is again the presence of unbaptized, who have either not left the room, although they abstained from Holy Communion, or else have returned to join the group in their thanksgiving. For them, then, these prayers are a thanksgiving for their common meal, while for the Christians they are a way of thanking God both for the ordinary food and for the Eucharist. To the latter the sacramental nature of the second meal was evident from the outset and was, moreover, intimated by such expressions as " spiritual food and drink " and " eternal life " as well as by " the Holy Vine of David " in 9.2.

The text in 10.6 comes at first as a real surprise to the modern reader. But if we bear in mind that the early Christians were actually yearning for " the end of the world " and the παρουσία or coming of the glorified Christ, we have no trouble in explaining " Grace " as but another name of Christ. That the celebration of the Eucharist was deemed a suitable moment for that yearning is at once clear if we know that through Holy Communion the glorified Christ is actually " coming " into the hearts of the faithful. This explains the rapturous joy with which the Christians hailed His final coming by two well-known eschatological texts, " Hosanna to the God of David " and " Marana tha." It follows immediately that the intervening sentence, " If anyone is holy, etc.," shares the eschatological character of the context. When the glorious Christ returns to take His elect home with Him to the Father (John 14.3), then " whoever is holy," that is, " a Christian," may confidently come forward to meet Him; but if anyone is not a Christian, " let him be converted" and become a Christian.[8] Thus the much-discussed imperative ἐρχέσθω is an encouragement to the Christians in the group to persevere in the faith, and to the unbaptized an exhortation to submit to baptism.

A word should here be said about a possible alternative to the interpretation just given. It might be said that Mass was not said and Holy Communion not given at the end of

9.5, but that as soon as the unbaptized have withdrawn, a new set of prayers is provided in 10.2-5 by way of preparation for Holy Communion, which is given to the faithful in 10.6. But there arise several awkwardnesses if this view is the correct one. It is awkward that again no mention is made of the Body and Blood of Christ although the participants are Christians. One might, of coure, say that this tract of the *Didache*, like all the rest, was intended for circulation among the pagans, and so the *disciplina arcani* forbade any specific reference to the *mysterium*. Another inconvenience would be the presence of unbaptized persons, implied in the exhortation to "conversion." One might say that the word "holy" is here taken in the narrower sense of "being in the state of grace" and the verb which regularly means "to be converted" is taken to mean "to be sorry for one's sins and thereby recover the state of grace." Even so it seems awkward to explain the words "Let Grace come and *the world pass away*" as an invitation to come forward and receive Holy Communion.

These and other possibilities must be given due weight; but, at all events, it should be perfectly clear that either the explanation preferred above or its alternative has an advantage over any interpretation that is *based on a disruption of the text*. It is the historian's duty to interpret a given text as it stands, without first remodelling it to suit preconceived notions. The necessity of rearranging the Eucharistic prayers has not been proved and should, therefore, be flatly denied.

But, it will be asked, is not all the available literary evidence against this interpretation? [9] Yes and no. If we admit an early date of composition, all the evidence is in favor of it; if we insist on a late date,[10] we have to face a mass of conjectures and hypotheses. Supposing, then, with many schol-

ars, that the *Didache* came into existence " before the end of
the first century," we need do no more than bring its statements into harmony with the New Testament. From the
longer text in Luke 22. 17-19 and from 1 Cor. 11. 17 ff. it
appears that the Last Supper was patterned on a Jewish feast
in which a cup opened the meal.[11] This tallies with the
Didache account, which puts the cup before the bread. In
the Synoptics and St. Paul, of course, the bread-and-wine
order is brought out distinctly after the mention of the cup;
but this need not upset us, for there the meal described is
strictly Eucharistic, while that of the *Didache* in 9 is common. Three passages in the Acts (2. 42; 2. 46-47; 20. 7-12)
which speak of " the breaking of the bread," throw no light
on our problem. As to 1 Cor., it is " clear beyond doubt
that we are here in the presence of a common meal united
to the Eucharist. And it is clear that the Eucharist does not
precede the meal." [12] So far, then, as the New Testament is
concerned, " we are in a position to conclude definitely *both
the existence of an ordinary community meal in the primitive
Church and its union with the Eucharist.*" [13] This is all the
evidence with which we have to reckon to understand the
Eucharistic practice of the primitive pre-Pauline Church at
Jerusalem; and this evidence is for, and not against, the
explanation given above. To admit its value, all we need is
to bring ourselves to rest satisfied with an early date of composition for the *Didache*, or at least for the central section
dealing with the Eucharist.

It is true that the practice of one common thanksgiving for
an ordinary meal and the Eucharist is not attested; but an
argumentum ex silentio is not necessarily decisive, least of all
in the field of early Christian literature, where the sources
flow scantily enough. In point of fact, however, both Matt.

26. 20 and Mark 14. 26 do testify that, before Jesus and the Apostles left the upper room, "they chanted a hymn of thanks." This was, no doubt, the Hallel, intended to render thanks to God for the paschal non-sacramental supper and all the blessings which it signified; but, at least in the mind of Christ, was it not *also* a thanksgiving for the Eucharist which concluded the paschal meal? The Apostles at the time may not have been aware of this combination; but later, when the leaders of the young Church were assembled at Jerusalem for several years after the Ascension, and considered ways and means of carrying out the Lord's behest, "Do *this* in commemoration of me," would they not spontaneously think of the paschal supper as the most suitable, if not the only, pattern to be followed? If so, they arranged for a joyous meal (by whatever name they called it) and joined to it the celebration of the Eucharist as a fitting climax. This is what the Lord Himself had done.[14] This, too, is the situation which the Didachist had in mind when he penned the prayers to be said at this private or domestic form of holding the Eucharist.

Being, then, in all probability the oldest extant non-canonical literature, the *Didache* brings us to the point where the New Testament ends, if we except the writings of St. John. In it, as in the New Testament, the odor of the Old is still strongly perceptible. Its chapters on Church organization are still reminiscent of the primitive conditions met with in St. Paul. All through it we seem to hear the "Apostles" speak to us, as the title indicates. A point of special interest to the modern reader is the fact that the opening chapters are "the earliest form of catechetical instruction in the Church" outside the New Testament, which may well have furnished "the general matter of catechesis" for St. Augustine's *First Catechetical Instruction*.[15] In making converts from paganism, the early Church followed two methods, both of which are illustrated in the Apostolic Fathers. The *Epistle to Diognetus* shows how she approached the educated pagans, the pagan intelligentsia. In speaking to the ordinary run of men, she states authoritatively what is to be done, what is to be shunned. That here the main stress falls on outward actions is natural. But outward performance is not the whole of Christianity. The love of God and the neighbor is enforced at the outset, is, in fact, made the starting point for all that follows; perfection is represented as the goal of Christian life; almsgiving and works of charity are encouraged; not only certain outward actions, but such inward springs of action as anger, lust, presumption, are forbidden; faith in God is implied in the rite of baptism; fear of God and hope in God are necessary states of mind in a Christian; the Eucharistic prayers, though expressed in veiled language, are highly spiritual; the ordinary happenings of life are ennobled by faith in God's Providence. The early catechist was, therefore, not content with mere cataloguing of vices and virtues, but aimed from the start at fostering in the new converts a spirituality unknown to them before. That this was but a first step to a deeper initiation in the mysteries of Christianity is clear from the Ignatian letters and from the *Epistle to Diognetus*.

The *Codex Hierosolymitanus*, discovered by Bryennios, contains the only known manuscript of the *Didache* in its present form. However, to a very considerable extent textual control is possible because of the presence of a varied auxiliary tradition. Thus, a large part of the *Didache* was incorporated into patristic writings and early Church manuals, notably the *Epistle of Barnabas*. The Oxyrhynchus Papyri have yielded two valuable fragments (1. 3-4 and 2. 7-3. 2). The six first chapters have survived in a Latin translation (?) of the third century; and a number of passages have been preserved in Coptic, Arabic, Ethiopic, and Georgian documents.

⸱   ⸱   ⸱

The text used for this translation is that of Theodor Klauser, *Doctrina duodecim apostolorum. Barnabae epistula* (Flor. Patr. 1, Bonn 1940).

Among the numerous translations into modern languages the following call for special mention:

Bigg, C., *The Doctrine of the Twelve Apostles* (with new intro. and rev. notes by A. J. Maclean, Society for Promoting Christian Knowledge, London 1922).

Bosio, G., *I Padri apostolici* 1 (Corona Patrum Salesiana, ser. graeca 7, Turin 1940) 1-59.

Hemmer, H.—Oger, G.—Laurent, A., *Les Pères apostoliques* 1 (Textes et documents 5, 2nd ed., Paris 1926) 1-29.

Hennecke, E., *Neutestamentliche Apokryphen* (2nd ed., Tübingen 1924) 555-65.

Lake, K., *The Apostolic Fathers* 1 (Loeb Classical Library, London 1912) 305-33.

Lightfoot, J. B., *The Apostolic Fathers* (ed. by J. R. Harmer. London 1898) 213-42.

Zeller, F., *Die apostolischen Väter* (Bibliothek der Kirchenväter 35, Munich 1918) 1-16.

TEACHING OF THE TWELVE APOSTLES [1]

AN INSTRUCTION OF THE LORD GIVEN TO THE HEATHEN BY THE TWELVE APOSTLES

1. Two Ways there are,[2] one of Life and one of Death, and there is a great difference between the Two Ways.

2 Now, the Way of Life is this: *first, love the God who made you; secondly, your neighbor as yourself:* [3] do not do to another *what you do not wish* to be done to yourself.[4]

3 The lesson of these words is as follows: *bless those that curse you,* and *pray for your enemies;* besides, fast *for those that persecute you. For what thanks do you deserve when you love those that love you? Do not the heathen do as much?* For your part, *love those that hate you;* [5] in fact, have no enemy.[6] 4 *Abstain from gratifying the carnal* [and bodily] [7] *impulses.*[8] When anyone gives you a blow *on the right cheek, turn to him the other as well,* and *be perfect;*[9] when *anyone forces you to go one mile with him, go two with him;* when anyone takes *your cloak* away, give *him your coat also;* [10] when anyone robs you of *your property, demand no return.*[11] You really cannot do it.[12] 5 *Give to anyone that asks you, and demand no return;* [13] the Father wants His own bounties to be shared with all. Happy the giver who complies with the commandment, for he goes unpunished. Trouble is in store for the receiver: if someone who is in need receives, he will go unpunished; but he who is not in need will have to stand trial as to why and for what

purpose he received; and, if he is thrown into prison, he will be questioned about his conduct, and *will not be released from that place until he has paid the last penny.*[14] 6 However, in this regard, there is also a word of Scripture: *Let your alms sweat in your hands until you find out to whom to give.*[15]

2. A further commandment of the Teaching:[16] 2 *Do not murder; do not commit adultery*; do not practice pederasty; do not fornicate; *do not steal*; do not deal in magic; do not practice sorcery; do not kill a fetus by abortion, or commit infanticide. *Do not covet your neighbor's goods.* 3 *Do not perjure yourself; do not bear false witness*;[17] do not calumniate; do not bear malice. 4 Do not be double-minded or double-tongued, for a double tongue is *a deadly snare.*[18] 5 Your speech must not be false or meaningless, but made good by action. 6 Do not be covetous, or rapacious, or hypocritical,[19] or malicious, or arrogant. Do not have designs upon your neighbor. 7 Hate no man; but correct some, pray for others, for still others sacrifice your life as a proof of your love.[20]

3. My child,[21] shun evil of any kind and everything resembling it. 2 Do not be prone to anger, for anger leads to murder. Do not be fanatical,[22] not quarrelsome, not hot-tempered; for all these things beget murder. 3 My child, do not be lustful, for lust leads to fornication. Do not be foul-mouthed or give free rein to your eyes; for all these things beget adultery. 4 My child, do not be an augur,[23] because it leads to idolatry. Do not be an enchanter, not an astrologer, not an expiator, and do not wish to see ⟨and hear⟩ these things; for they all beget idolatry. 5 My child, do not be a liar, for lying leads to theft. Do not be a lover of money, or a vain pretender.[24] All these things beget

thievery. 6 My child, do not be a grumbler,²⁵ because it
leads to blasphemy; or self-willed, or evil-minded. All these
things beget blasphemy.

7 On the contrary, be gentle, for *the gentle will inherit
the land.*²⁶ 8 Be long-suffering, and merciful, and guileless,
and quiet,²⁷ and good, and *with trembling treasure* forever
the instructions you have received. 9 Do not carry your head
high, or open your heart to presumption. Do not be on
intimate terms with the mighty,²⁸ but associate with holy and
lowly folk. 10 Accept as blessings the casualties that befall
you, assured that nothing happens without God.

4. My child, day and night *remember him who preaches
God's word to you,*²⁹ and honor him as the Lord, for where
His lordship is spoken of, there is the Lord. 2 Seek daily
contact with the saints to be refreshed by their discourses.
3 Do not start a schism, but pacify contending parties. *Be
just in your judgment:* ³⁰ make no distinction between man
and man when correcting transgressions. 4 Do not waver in
your decision.³¹

5 Do not be one that opens his hands to receive, but shuts
them when it comes to giving. 6 If you have means at your
disposal, pay a ransom for your sins.³² 7 Do not hesitate to
give, and do not give in a grumbling mood. You will find
out who is the good Rewarder. 8 Do not turn away from the
needy; rather, share everything with your brother, and do
not say: "It is private property." ³³ If you are sharers in
what is imperishable, how much more so in the things that
perish!

9 Do not withdraw your hand from your son or your
daughter, but from their youth teach them the fear of God.³⁴
10 Do not, when embittered, give orders to your slave, male

or female, for they hope in the same God; otherwise, they might lose the fear of God, who is the Master of both of you. He surely is not coming to call [35] with an eye to rank and station in life; no, He comes to those whom the Spirit has prepared. 11 But you, slaves, be submissive to your masters as to God's image [36] in reverence and fear.

12 Abhor all sham [37] and whatever is not pleasing to the Lord. 13 Do not by any means neglect the *commandments of the Lord,* but *hold fast* to the traditions, *neither adding nor subtracting anything.*[38] 14 In church confess your sins,[39] and do not come to your prayer with a guilty conscience.

Such is the Way of Life.

5. The Way of Death is this. First of all, it is wicked and altogether accursed: *murders, adulteries,* lustful desires, *fornications, thefts, idolatries,* magical arts, *sorceries,* robberies, *false testimonies,* hypocrisy, duplicity, *fraud, pride, malice,* surliness, *covetousness,* foul talk, jealousy, rashness, haughtiness, *false pretensions,* ⟨the lack of the fear of God⟩.[40] 2 It is the way of persecutors of the good, haters of the truth, lovers of falsehood; of men ignorant of the reward for right living, not *devoted to what is good*[41] or to just judgment, intent upon not what is good but what is evil; of strangers to gentleness and patient endurance; of *men who love vanities,* and *fee hunters;*[42] of men that have no heart for the poor, are not concerned about the oppressed, do not know their Maker; *of murderers of children,*[43] destroyers of God's image; of men that turn away from the needy, oppress the afflicted, act as counsels for the rich, are unjust judges of the poor—in a word, of men steeped in sin. Children, may you be preserved from all this!

6. See *that no man leads you astray*[44] from this Way of the Teaching, since any other teaching takes you away from God. 2 Surely, if you are able to bear the Lord's yoke in its entirety,[45] you will be perfect; if you are not able, then do what you can. 3 And in the matter of food, do what you can stand; but be scrupulously on your guard against meat offered to idols; for that is a worship of dead gods.[46]

7. Regarding baptism. Baptize as follows: [47] after first explaining all these points, *baptize in the name of the Father and of the Son and of the Holy Spirit*, in running water.[48] 2 But if you have no running water, baptize in other water; and if you cannot in cold, then in warm. 3 But if you have neither,[49] pour water on the head three times *in the name of the Father and of the Son and of the Holy Spirit*. 4 Before the baptism, let the baptizer and the candidate for baptism fast, as well as any others that are able. Require the candidate to fast one or two days previously.[50]

8. Your *fasts* should not coincide with those of *the hypocrites*.[51] They fast on Mondays and Tuesdays; you should fast on Wednesdays and Fridays. 2 And do not *pray as the hypocrites do*.[52] but pray as the Lord has commanded in the Gospel:

> *Our Father, who art in heaven; hallowed be Thy name; Thy kingdom come; Thy will be done on earth as it is in heaven; give us this day our daily bread, and forgive us our debts as we also forgive our debtors; and lead us not into temptation, but deliver us from evil;* for Thine is the power and the glory for evermore.

3 Say this prayer three times a day.[53]

9.　Regarding the Eucharist.[54] Give thanks as follows: 2 First, concerning the cup:

> " We give Thee thanks, Our Father,
> for the Holy Vine of David [55] Thy servant,
> which Thou hast made known to us
> through Jesus, Thy Servant." [56]

> " To Thee be the glory for evermore."

3 Next, concerning the broken bread: [57]

> " We give Thee thanks, Our Father,
> for the life and knowledge [58]
> which Thou hast made known to us
> through Jesus, Thy Servant."

> " To Thee be the glory for evermore."

4 " As this broken bread was scattered over the hills
and then, when gathered, became one mass,[59]
so may Thy Church be gathered
from the ends of the earth into Thy Kingdom." [60]

> " For Thine is the glory and the power
> through Jesus Christ for evermore."

5 Let no one eat and drink of your Eucharist but those baptized in the name of the Lord; to this, too, the saying of the Lord is applicable: *Do not give to dogs what is sacred.*[61]

10.　After you have taken your fill of food, give thanks as follows:

> 2 " We give Thee thanks, O Holy Father,
> for Thy holy name
> which Thou hast enshrined [62] in our hearts,
> and for the knowledge and faith and immortality

which Thou hast made known to us
through Jesus, Thy Servant."

"To Thee be the glory for evermore."

3 "Thou, Lord Almighty,
hast created all things [63] for the sake of Thy name
and hast given food and drink for men to enjoy,
that they may give thanks to Thee;
but to us Thou hast vouchsafed spiritual food and
    drink and eternal life
through ⟨Jesus⟩, Thy Servant."

4 "Above all, we give Thee thanks
because Thou art mighty."

"To Thee be the glory for evermore."

5 "Remember,[64] O Lord, Thy Church:
deliver her from all evil,
perfect her in Thy love,
and *from the four winds assemble* her,[65] the sanctified,
    in Thy kingdom
which Thou hast prepared for her."

"For Thine is the power and the glory for evermore."

6 "May Grace come, and this world pass away!" [66]
"*Hosanna to the God of David!*" [67]
"If anyone is holy, let him advance; if anyone is
not, let him be converted. *Marana tha!*" [68]
"Amen."

7 But permit the prophets to give thanks as much as they
desire.[69]

11. Accordingly, when an itinerant teaches you all that has just been said, welcome him. 2 But should the teacher himself be a turncoat and teach a different doctrine so as to undermine (this teaching), do not listen to him. But if he promotes holiness and knowledge of the Lord, welcome him as the Lord.

3 Now, as regards the apostles and prophets,[70] act strictly according to the precept of the Gospel.[71] 4 Upon his arrival every apostle must be welcomed as the Lord; 5 but he must not stay except one day.[72] In case of necessity, however, he may stay the next day also; but if he stays three days, he is a false prophet. 6 At his departure the apostle must receive nothing except food to last till the next night's lodging; but if he asks for money, he is a false prophet.[73]

7 Moreover, if any prophet speaks in ecstasy,[74] do not test him or entertain any doubts; for *any sin may be forgiven,* but this sin *cannot be forgiven.* 8 However, not everyone speaking in ecstasy is a prophet, except he has the ways of the Lord about him.[75] So by their ways must the true and the false prophet be distinguished. 9 No prophet who in an ecstasy orders the table spread,[76] must partake of it; otherwise, he is a false prophet. 10 Any prophet that teaches the truth, yet does not live up to his teaching,[77] is a false prophet. 11 When a prophet, once approved as genuine, does something by way of symbolizing the Church in an earthly manner,[78] yet does not instruct others to do all that he himself is doing, he is not liable to your judgment, for his judgment rests with God. After all, the Prophets of old acted in the same manner. 12 But if anyone says in ecstasy, " Give me money," or something else, you must not listen to him.[79] However, should

he tell you to give something for others who are in need, let no one condemn him.

12. Anyone *coming in the name of the Lord* [80] must be welcomed; but, after that, test him and find out—you will of course use your discretion either for or against him. [81] 2 If the arrival is a transient visitor, assist him as much as you can, but he may not stay with you more than two days, or, if necessary, three. 3 But if he intends to settle among you, then, in case he is a craftsman, let him work for his living; [82] 4 if he has no trade or craft, use your judgment in providing for him, so that a follower of Christ will not live idle in your midst. 5 But if he is not satisfied with this arrangement, he is a Christmonger. [83] Be on your guard against such people.

13. Every genuine prophet who is willing to settle among you *is entitled to his support.* 2 Likewise, every genuine teacher is, like *a laborer, entitled to his support.* [84] 3 Therefore, take all first fruits of vintage and harvest, of cattle and sheep, and give these first fruits to the prophets; [85] for they are your high priests. 4 But if you have no prophet, give them to the poor. 5 When you bake bread, take the first loaf and give it according to the commandment. 6 Likewise, when you open a fresh jar of wine or oil, take the first draught and give it to the prophets. 7 Of money and cloth and any other possession, first set aside a portion according to your discretion and give it according to the commandment.

14. On the Lord's own day, [86] assemble in common to break bread and offer thanks; [87] but first confess your sins, so that your sacrifice may be pure. 2 However, no one quarreling with his brother may join your meeting until they are reconciled; [88] your sacrifice must not be defiled. 3 For here we have the saying of the Lord: [89] *In every place and time offer me a pure sacrifice; for I am a mighty King, says the Lord; and my name spreads terror among the nations.*

15. Accordingly,[90] elect for yourselves bishops and deacons,[91] men who are an honor to the Lord, of gentle disposition, not attached to money, honest and well-tried;[92] for they, too, render you the sacred service of the prophets and teachers.[93] 2 Do not, then, despise them; after all, they are your dignitaries together with the prophets and teachers.[94]

3 Furthermore, correct one another, not in anger, but in composure, as you have it in the Gospel;[95] and when anyone offends his neighbor, let no one speak with him—in fact, he should not even be talked about by you [96]—until he has made amends. 4 As regards your prayers and alms and your whole conduct, do exactly as you have it in the Gospel of Our Lord.[97]

16. *Watch* over your life; *your lamps* must not go out, nor *your loins* be ungirded; on the contrary, *be ready. You do not know the hour in which Our Lord is coming.*[98] 2 Assemble in great numbers,[99] intent upon what concerns your souls. Surely, of no use will your lifelong faith be to you if you are not perfected at the end of time.[100] 3 For in the last days [101] the false prophets and corrupters will come in swarms; the sheep will turn into wolves, and love will turn into hate. 4 When lawlessness is on the increase, men will hate and persecute and betray one another;[102] and then the Deceiver of this world will appear, claiming to be the Son of God, and give *striking exhibitions of power;*[103] the earth will be given over into his hands, and he will perpetrate outrages such as have never taken place since the world began. 5 Then humankind will undergo the fiery test,[104] and *many will lose their faith* and perish; but *those who stand firm* in their faith will be saved by none other than the Accursed. 6 *And then the proofs* of the truth *will appear;* [105] the first proof, an opening in the heavens; [106] the next proof, *the sounding of the trumpet;* and the third, the resurrection of the dead—7 not of all indeed, but in accordance with the saying: *The Lord will come and all the saints with Him.* 8 *Finally,* the world *will behold* the Lord *riding the clouds in the sky.*[107]

THE EPISTLE OF BARNABAS

INTRODUCTION

We do not know who the author of the *Epistle of Barnabas* is, or when and where he wrote, or to what specific group of Christian readers he addressed his words of warning. Nor is the meaning of some allusions to his time beyond all doubt.[1] One thing is certain: it is only from this epistle that we learn the interesting fact that between the destruction of Jerusalem in the year 70 and the second catastrophe in Hadrian's time, Judaism, which had been a disturber of peace from earliest times, raised its head so high as to become a grave danger to a certain Christian community.

The Epistle falls into two parts. Part I (1-17) is predominantly speculative or doctrinal, though interwoven with exhortations; Part II (18-21) is professedly a manual of Christian morality, shot through, however, with bits of doctrinal explanation.

After offering cordial greetings to his "sons and daughters," the author says in substance: You are to be congratulated on your extraordinary spiritual endowments. They will stand you in good stead in meeting the heavy demands God is making on you at this time. For me it is a joy to contribute to your success by strengthening your faith. This I hope to accomplish by perfecting your knowledge of the Old Testament (1). The world is in an evil plight. Be watchful. A better understanding of the Mosaic Law, which the Jews misread from the start, will enable you to escape the wiles of Satan. God was not pleased with the sacrifice of bulls and goats. The sacrifice He desires is that of a contrite heart

(2). Nor was He pleased with the kind of fasting practiced by the Jews. The fast He cares for is abstention from every form of injustice and the practice of charity. His intentions in giving the Law were indicated in its very wording (3). The present crisis calls for careful study. The final stumbling block, foretold by the Prophets, has at last appeared. Be on your guard against the dangerous slogan, "Their covenant is ours also." Moses received the covenant, but the Jews lost it. Hold fast to what you possess. Do away with idle speculations. Be spiritual temples dedicated to God (4). It was for our salvation that Jesus appeared in the flesh and shed His blood (5). The Incarnation and the Passion of Jesus were foretold. Through them we are redeemed from our sins (6). The scapegoat cursed and driven into the desert was a type of Jesus (7). The offering of a heifer and the sprinkling of the people with hyssop was an image of the suffering Christ. The Jews did not understand God's intention in prescribing these ceremonies (8). We do understand it because God circumcised our ears and hearts. The circumcision prescribed to Abraham has been abolished. In reality it was a mystery looking forward to Jesus (9). The rulings discriminating between foods were not meant to be taken literally. They conveyed a spiritual lesson (10). God also enlightened us about the baptismal water (11). The Cross of Christ, too, was prefigured by various incidents in Jewish history (12). It follows that the Covenant with the Chosen People was intended for us rather than the Jews (13). We are its rightful heirs. The mediator of old was the servant Moses; our Mediator is Jesus, the Son of God (14). The laws regulating the Sabbath were misinterpreted by the Jews. The true Sabbath is the day of eternity, "the eighth day" or epoch, which we commemorate, in advance, by our Sunday services (15). The Jews erred egregiously in regard to the Temple. The true worship of God is not bound up with the Temple at Jerusalem. God dwells in our hearts. We are God's spiritual temple. This temple is to be built " in splendor " (16).

After two brief chapters of transition (17 and 18) Barnabas exhorts his readers to a Christian life under the form of The Two Ways known to us from the *Didache*. Since the date of the latter is before the end of the first century, and Barnabas most probably wrote between 117 and 132, this section of his Epistle is indebted to the *Didache*, unless both writings depend on a common source.[2] In terms reminiscent of the opening chapter, the author closes with a fervent appeal to his " children of love and peace."

The *Epistle of Barnabas* is a homily on the mistaken Judaistic conception of the Old Testament. But what special purpose could be served by an abstract discussion of Judaism? No Christian who had read the Gospels and the *Epistle to the Hebrews* could be ignorant of the relation of the Old Covenant to the New. Obviously, the serious tone of the writer, his sharp warning against an actual and acute temptation, and, above all, the implication that the faith of the Christian community was in danger, stamp the letter as a timely tract of practical and immediate urgency. Scholars have therefore tried to discover an event in the history of the Jewish people that was able to create the conditions here taken for granted. No certainty regarding the purpose of this letter has as yet been reached, but a theory is gaining ground in recent years which fixes the date of composition definitely within Hadrian's time, between 117 and 138.

In contrast to Trajan who had dealt most severely with the Jews, Hadrian inaugurated, somewhere between 117, the year of his accession to the throne, and the beginning of the Bar Kochba insurrection in 132, a more lenient policy in dealing with the refractory nation. This, it may be imagined, was an event of the greatest significance to the Jews, which kindled their nationalistic aspirations to such intensity that they entertained hopes for the rebuilding of the Temple and, in consequence, the revival of the old religion. If this view is correct, the reader of the Epistle has a clue to not a few of its otherwise puzzling statements. It will explain, in particular, the nature of the temptation, the stumbling block suddenly thrown into the lives of a certain Jewish-Christian community. The Jews would, of course, at all times be ready to launch a propaganda that was sure to find a fertile soil in the hearts and minds of Christians of Jewish descent. We know that they found it difficult to realize that the new religion was the death of the old. They found it even more difficult to acknowledge the futility of dallying with certain old Jewish customs that had endeared themselves to them before their conversion.[3] Even the destruction of Jerusalem in the year 70, which in the eyes of the more thoughtful meant a complete " annihilation " of their religious hopes,[4] was not altogether able to stifle a desire for emancipation from Roman oppression that was kept burning by insurrectionist leaders. Christ's prophecy came true: " Let someone else come in his own name, and you will give him a hearty welcome " (John 5. 43). And really, how could God's solemn covenant with the Chosen People ever be rendered null and void! Ideas such as this were, it would seem, current among Judaistic Christians somewhere in Palestine or Egypt at the supposed date of this letter, and strong enough to alarm its writer.

His identity may perhaps never be discovered. There is

nothing against supposing that his name actually was Barnabas. It is generally agreed, however, that he was not the
Apostle of the same name. No Apostle could have brushed
the Mosaic Law aside as a deception of an evil spirit. That
he was an Alexandrian is plausibly inferred from his exces-
sive fondness for the allegorical method of interpreting the
Scriptures. Strangely enough, Clement of Alexandria attributes the letter to the Apostle. The *Codex Sinaiticus* of the
fourth century places it directly after the *Apocalypse* and
before the *Shepherd* of Hermas. Origen calls it a Catholic
Epistle; Eusebius reckons it among the disputed, and Jerome
includes it among the apocryphal, writings. Judged by its
matter and form, the author was no intellectual giant. The
diction lacks elegance.

The writer's uncomplimentary attitude toward the Old
Testament is generally considered a fatal objection to an
Apostolic origin of the *Epistle of Barnabas*. Almost all
scholars take him to mean that the Mosaic Law had no
validity from the outset. But there are those who judge him
more leniently [5] and say that his apparently sweeping expressions should rather be interpreted as a vigorous way of saying
that the Law did not have the importance attributed to it by
the Jews. We may perhaps compare the New Testament
way of making negative statements which are obviously not
meant to be flat denials. In 1 John 3. 18, for instance, " Let
us *not* love in word and speech, but in deed and in truth,"
the particle οὐ means " not simply," or " not exclusively."
It is a rhetorical way of making an emphatic assertion. But
there is a further consideration that may exonerate Barnabas.
The Mosaic Law was by itself unable to confer upon the
Jews the necessary spiritual power to live up to its enactments
(Heb. 10. 1). And so, since the Jews from the start errone-

ously regarded it as self-sufficient, instead of preparing the way for the more perfect law of Christ, from which it drew its power to sanctify men, the author may be taken as wishing to stress this inherent weakness of the Jewish ceremonies, without really denying the temporary validity of the injunctions as such.[6] But be this as it may, the Church has never included the *Epistle of Barnabas* among her canonical writings.

Probably few modern readers will warm to the *Epistle of Barnabas*. Its general topic is not one of wide appeal. Our religious life is not threatened by a revival of Judaism. The minutiae of the Jewish ceremonial Law are little more than antiquarian lore to us. The wealth of detail with which they are presented is apt to kill the reader's interest. And yet, may we not take a wider view, and see in the struggle of the community here addressed a mirror of what is happening on a more formidable scale in our midst today? Today, too, *the times are evil and the Agent is in the ascendant.* Barnabas's "sons and daughters" were face to face with the temptation to fall back into Judaism. In recent times we are witnessing an insidious onslaught upon all revealed religion. Judaism, after all, reveres the one true God; but to fall a prey to certain isms and ideologies of modern times would mean complete religious bankruptcy. Viewed in this broader light, the Epistle has not a few points of attraction; and if the reader is wary enough to "pay close attention," he will find sentences or phrases here and there that are strikingly to the point even today. Again, for the historian it is interesting to see that, when an attack threatened the faith of the infant Church— or, possibly, was no more than "in the air"—there were churchmen at hand who scented the danger and sounded the alarm. Barnabas's tendency to allegorize is distasteful to us, but it stresses the needful lesson that, in observing outward rites and ceremonies, it is *the spirit* that *vivifies*.

As the topic of the Epistle is not devoid of interest, so the personality of the writer is not devoid of charm. The relation between him and his readers is that of a loving father and " children of love." He strikes a warm, human tone whenever he forgets, for the moment, his role of exegete, and we believe him when he speaks of the " keen delight " he had experienced when visiting the community. And then, that affectionate way he has of speaking of Jesus Christ—" the Beloved Jesus "! He may—or may not!—have erred in his conception of the Old Testament; in zeal for the true religion he takes rank with Clement of Rome, Ignatius of Antioch, and Polycarp of Smyrna. At all events, the early Church thought highly of its Barnabas—whoever he was.

By way of collateral reading, the first item to suggest itself is the *Epistle to the Hebrews*. The general theme is the same: the Old Covenant was a preparation for the New. But the purpose of *Hebrews* is to set forth the all-surpassing dignity of Jesus Christ, the High Priest of the new dispensation; Barnabas argues that, since the Old Testament was a type of the New, no Christian can, without shipwreck of his faith, clutch at the shadows now that the reality has appeared. A comparison of the two epistles throws no light on the authorship of the *Epistle of Barnabas*; but there is a tradition that *Hebrews*, which expresses the ideas of St. Paul, owes its literary form to someone associated with him, and that this man was none other than the Apostle Barnabas.[7] Was this, perhaps, the reason why the present Epistle was ascribed by some to St. Paul's faithful co-worker?

Other pieces of collateral reading are St. Stephen's speech before the Sanhedrin (Acts 7. 1-53); Our Lord's Sermon on the Mount (Matt. 5. 17 ff.); Chapters 1-8 of the *Didache*; Chapters 3 and 4 of the *Epistle to Diognetus*; Justin's *Dialogus*, and Tertullian's *Adversus Iudaeos*.

Besides several Greek manuscripts and some Latin versions of portions of this Epistle, our two independent texts are the *Codex Sinaiticus* and the *Codex Hierosolymitanus*. The former, written in the early fourth century and discovered in two parts by Tischendorf in 1844 and 1859, contains the Epistle along with the entire New Testament, Hermas, and the *Didache*. The latter manuscript, written in 1056, was discovered by the Orthodox Metropolitan Bryennios in 1873 and published for the first time in 1883.[8]

The text used for the present translation is that of T. Klauser, *Doctrina duodecim apostolorum. Barnabae epistula* (Flor. Patr. 1, Bonn 1940).

Other modern translations of note are contained in the following works:

Bosio, G., *I Padri apostolici* 1 (Corona Patrum Salesiana, ser. graeca 7, Turin 1940) 253-347.

Hemmer, H.—Oger, G.—Laurent, A., *Les Pères apostoliques* 1 (Textes et documents 5, 2nd ed., Paris 1926) 30-101.

Lake, K., *The Apostolic Fathers* 1 (Loeb Classical Library, London 1912) 335-409.

Lightfoot, J. B., *The Apostolic Fathers* (ed. by J. R. Harmer, London 1898) 267-88.

Thieme, K., *Kirche und Synagoge* (Kreuzritterbücherei 3, Olten 1944) 13-65.

Veil, H., in E. Hennecke's *Neutestamentliche Apokryphen* (2nd. ed., Tübingen 1924) 503-18.

Zeller, F., *Die apostolischen Väter* (Bibliothek der Kirchenväter 35, Munich 1918) 71-105.

THE EPISTLE OF BARNABAS

1. Sons and daughters: [1] My best wishes to you for peace in the name of the Lord who has loved us!

2 Great, indeed, and generous are God's gifts of justification [2] bestowed upon you! And so I am exceedingly, in fact beyond all measure, cheered as I think of your happy and glorious endowments. [3] So deeply implanted is the gift of the Spirit that has been graciously vouchsafed to you! 3 For the same reason I congratulate myself all the more on my own hope of salvation, because I really witness in your community an outpouring upon you of the Spirit from the wealth of the Lord's fountainhead. [4] Such keen delight, on your account, has my longed-for sight of you afforded me!

4 Now, I am convinced, and indeed fully conscious, of the fact that, since I spoke among you, [5] I have gained much experience, because my travelling companion on the road to holiness has been the Lord. And so I, too, am altogether constrained to love you more than myself. [6] Surely, great faith and love, *resting on the hope of* His *life*, [7] are at home among you. 5 Accordingly, it occurs to me that, if I should interest myself about you and share with you some portion of what I have received, my ministering to such spiritual persons would bring me a reward. I am taking pains, therefore, to send you a brief message, so that in addition to your faith you may also possess perfect knowledge. [8]

6 To begin with, there are three propositions of the Lord:

the hope of life [9] is the first and last of our faith; holiness [10] is the first and last of the Judgment; love which radiates genuine happiness is the testimony of a holy life.

7 The fact is, the Master [11] has made known to us through the Prophets the past and the present, and given us a fore-taste of the future; and so, when we see these things one by one becoming actual fact just as He has said, we ought to be all the more generous and inspired in our effort to advance in the fear of Him. 8 But I will—not in the capacity of a teacher,[12] but as one of you—suggest a few things to cheer you in the present situation.

2. Well, then, *the times are evil* [13] and the Agent is in the ascendant, and so we ought to watch over ourselves and search into the just demands of the Lord. 2 The auxiliaries of our faith are fear and patient endurance; our allies are long-suffering and self-control; 3 and therefore, as long as these remain intact in all that concerns the Lord, wisdom, understanding, insight, and knowledge will be happy to join their company.

4 We certainly have the revelation He made to us through all the Prophets [14] to this effect: He needs neither sacrifices nor whole burnt offerings nor oblations. On one occasion He declared: 5 *What is the multitude of your sacrifices to me? says the Lord. I am surfeited with whole burnt offerings! I take no pleasure in fat of lambs or blood of bulls and goats, or in your coming to appear before me! Who, in fact, has required these things at your hands? You shall tread my court no more! When you offer wheaten flour, it is in vain; incense is an abomination to me; your new moons and Sabbaths I disdain.* [15] 6 These things, then, He has superseded; [16] it was intended that the New Law of Our Lord Jesus Christ

should dispense with yoke and compulsion, and that its oblation should not be a man-made one.[17] 7 Another time He says to them: *Did I enjoin your fathers, on leaving the land of Egypt, to offer me whole burnt offerings and sacrifices? 8 No! This is what I enjoined on them:* [18] *Let none of you feel resentment in his heart against his neighbor, and take no pleasure in perjury.*[19] 9 Since, then, we are not devoid of understanding, we ought to appreciate our Father's kindly purpose. He speaks to us from a desire that we should find out how we are to approach Him without going astray as they did.[20] 10 To us, therefore, He speaks as follows: *A sacrifice pleasing to the Lord is a broken spirit: an aroma pleasing to the Lord is a heart that glorifies its Maker.*[21] Hence it is our duty, brethren, to be scrupulously exact in the matter of salvation; otherwise the Evil One will cause error to creep in stealthily and hurl us off the path that leads to our life.

3. Again, therefore, He speaks to them about these matters: [22] *Why, I ask, do you fast, says the Lord, so that today your clamorous voice may be heard? Not that is the fast with which I am pleased, says the Lord; not with the man who chastises himself; 2 and if you bend your neck like a hoop and put on sackcloth and make yourselves a bed of ashes— not even that should you call an acceptable fast. 3* But to us He says: *Behold, this is the fast with which I am pleased, says the Lord: destroy every unjust bond; untie the knots of extorted contracts; set the oppressed at liberty, and tear up every unjust promissory note. Break your bread to feed the hungry, and when you see one naked, clothe him; take into your home the homeless; and when you see one who is lowly, do not despise him, neither shall any of your own flesh and*

blood. 4 *Then your light will burst like the break of day;
then your healing will speedily blossom forth; then holiness
will be your vanguard, and the splendor of God will, like a
rear guard, compass you about.* 5 *Then you will cry out and
God will hear you, and while you are yet speaking He will
say: " Behold, I am here! "—provided, that is, you do away
with imprisonment, with violence, and with muttering
speech; from your heart you must give your bread to the
hungry and compassionate an afflicted soul.*[23] 6 It follows,
then, brethren, that the Long-suffering One looked forward
to the time when the people, prepared in His Beloved,[24]
would possess unadulterated faith, and so He instructed us in
advance about everything. He did not want us to suffer
shipwreck by being, as it were, proselyted to their Law.

4. We must, then, carefully study the present situation [25]
and find out the means of our salvation. Therefore let us
shun absolutely any kind of evildoing, or evildoing will get
the better of us. Let us scorn the error of the present time,
and we shall be loved in the time to come. 2 Do not let us
indulge our natural appetites; otherwise they will without
let or hindrance conform to the ways of sinners and reprobates, and we shall be just like them. 3 The final stumbling
block has appeared,[26] of which, as Henoch says, the Scripture
speaks. Indeed, it was for this reason that the Master has
shortened the epochs and eras: He wants His Beloved to
make haste and enter upon His inheritance! 4 The Prophet
voices the same thought: *Ten kingdoms will hold sway upon
the earth, and after a little while a king will rise and at one
blow humble three of the kings.*[27] 5 Daniel has similar
things to say on the same subject: *And I saw the fourth
beast—wicked and strong and more ferocious than all the*

other beasts of the sea, and how ten horns budded out from it, and out of these a small horn, a side-growth, and how this one subdued, at one blow, three large horns.[28] 6 Here, then, is something for you to understand.

Being one of you and loving you both individually and collectively more than myself, I urge this further counsel on you: keep watch over yourselves now [29] and do not imitate certain people by heaping sin after sin upon yourselves and saying: " Their covenant is ours also." 7 Ours, indeed; but in the end they lost it [30] without more ado when Moses had already received it. For the Scripture says: *And Moses was on the mountain fasting forty days and forty nights, and he received from the Lord the covenant—tables of stone inscribed by the finger of the Lord's hand.*[31] 8 But they turned to idols and lost it. For the Lord says as follows: *Moses, Moses, descend in haste; your people, which you led out of Egypt, has broken the Law.*[32] Moses understood: he flung the two tables out of his hands, and their covenant was shattered, that the covenant of the beloved Jesus might be sealed in our heart [33] through the hope which the faith in Him holds out. 9 I should wish to write to you at great length, though not as your teacher; but my chief concern is to write as your humble servant,[34] as becomes one who is anxious that we should sacrifice nothing of what we possess. Let us, then, be on our guard in these latter days.[35] Surely, of no use will the whole span of our lifelong faith be to us if we do not, here and now in this era of lawlessness, and amidst the seductions yet to come, take a firm stand as becomes children of God. 10 In order, then, that the Black One [36] may not find a loophole, let us give a wide berth to all idle speculations; [37] let us utterly detest the practices of the Wicked Way. Do not shut yourselves up and court solitude [38] as though your justification were already assured. On the contrary, attend the common meetings and join in discussing what contributes to the common good. 11 For the Scripture says: *Ruin awaits those who are wise in their own estimation and prudent in their own conceit.*[39] Let us be spiritual-minded; let us be a finished temple of God! So far as in us lies, *let us cultivate the fear* of God, and strive to observe His commandments so that we find our delight in His ordinances. 12 The Lord *will judge* the world *without partiality.*[40] Everyone will be rewarded according to his conduct: if one is good, his holiness will prepare the way for him; if one is wicked, the wages of his wickedness are in store for him. 13 Let us never rest, on the ground that we have been called,[41] or fall asleep in our sins; may the wicked Ruler never gain power over us and force us away from the kingdom of the Lord. 14 And furthermore, consider this, my brethren: since you see that Israel, even after such striking exhibitions of power in its midst, has yet been rejected, let us beware that the Scripture text, *Many are called, yet few are chosen,*[42] may not be verified in us.

5. It is indeed with this purpose in view that the Lord endured to surrender His body to destruction: we are to be sanctified by the remission of sins, that is, through the sprinkling of His blood.[43] 2 For this is what the Scripture says in speaking of Him partly to Israel, and partly to us. It says as follows: *He was wounded because of our iniquities, and languishes because of our sins; by His bruises we were healed; as a sheep He was led to the shambles, and as a lamb that is dumb before its shearer.*[44] 3 Surely, we ought to be exceedingly grateful to the Lord for making clear to us the past,[45] enabling us to act wisely in the present, and not leaving us without discernment in regard to the future. 4 Now, the Scripture says: *Not unjustly are nets spread out for birds.*[46] This means that a man is justly doomed to perish who has knowledge of the Way of Holiness, yet is heading for the Way of Darkness. 5 And another thing, my brethren: if the Lord submitted to suffering for our souls—He, the Lord of the universe, to whom at the foundation of the world God had said, *Let us make man according to our image and likeness*[47]—then how did it happen that He submitted to suffering at the hands of men? Let me tell you. 6 The Prophets, who had received the gift from Him,[48] looked forward to Him in their prophecies; and since it was ordained that *He should manifest Himself in the flesh,*[49] He voluntarily submitted to suffering *that He might destroy death*[50] and establish the truth of the resurrection from the dead. 7 Thus He was to redeem the promise made to the fathers, and—while preparing for Himself the new people—to give proof while still on earth that He would raise Himself from the dead and then judge. 8 And besides, by teaching Israel and giving such wondrous exhibitions of power, He preached and showed His exceedingly great love for it. 9 And when for the purpose of preaching His Gospel He chose His own Apostles from the worst type of sinners[51]—since *it was not His mission to call saints, but sinners*—then it was that He revealed Himself as the Son of God. 10 In fact, had He not come in the flesh, how could men have survived the sight of Him, when at the sight of the sun—His handiwork, which is doomed to perish!—they are unable to look straight at its rays?[52] 11 Surely, then, the Son of God came in the flesh to fill to the brim the measure of the sins of those who had persecuted His Prophets to death.[53] 12 This, therefore, is the reason why He submitted to suffering; for God speaks of the chastisement of His flesh as something due to them: *When*

4 •

they have smitten the shepherd, then the sheep of His flock will perish.[54] 13 But this suffering was due to His own choice. It was ordained that He should suffer on a tree, since the inspired writer attributes to Him the following words: *Save me from the sword,* and, *Pierce my flesh with nails, because bands of evildoers have risen against me.*[55] 14 And again He says: *Behold, I present my back for scourgings, and my cheeks for blows; my face I set as a solid rock.*[56]

6. And when He has obeyed the command,[57] what does He say? *Who wants to quarrel with me? Let him confront me! Who wants to bring me to justice? Let him come near the Servant of the Lord!* 2 *Ruin awaits you! You will all grow old like a garment, and the moth will devour you!*[58] And again, since He was like a strong stone chosen for polishing,[59] the Prophet says: *Behold, into the foundation of Sion will I sink a choice and precious stone—a highly valued cornerstone.*[60] 3 What does He say next? *Whoever believes in Him shall live forever.*[61] Does our hope, then, rest on a stone? God forbid! No, He speaks that way because the Lord has put strength into His body; for He says: *And He set me as a solid rock.*[62] 4 Again the Prophet says: *The very stone which the builders rejected has become the cornerstone.*[63] And again He says: *This is the great and wonderful day which the Lord has made.*[64] 5 I am writing to you in very plain language that you may understand—I, the humble servant of my love for you.[65] 6 And again, what does the Prophet say? *A band of evildoers has encompassed me; they swarmed round me like bees around the honeycomb;* and, *For my garments they cast lots.*[66] 7 Since, then, He was to manifest Himself and suffer in the flesh,[67] the suffering was foretold; for the Prophet denounces Israel: *Perdition*

awaits them: they have framed an evil plot against themselves,
saying: "Let us put the Innocent in chains because He is
troublesome to us." [68]

8 What does the other Prophet, Moses, say to them?
Behold, this is what the Lord God says: "Enter into the
fertile land which the Lord has sworn to give to Abraham,
Isaac, and Jacob, and take possession of it as your inheritance
—a land flowing with milk and honey." [69] 9 Learn now what
an enlightened understanding has to say about it. "Trust,"
it says, "in Jesus, who is to be revealed to you in the flesh."
The "land," which is something passible,[70] means "man,"
since it was out of the earth that Adam was formed. 10 And
what does *into the fertile land, a land flowing with milk and*
honey, mean? Blessed be Our Lord, brethren, who has endowed us with wisdom and understanding of His secrets;
for the Prophet speaks of the Lord in figurative language.
Who will understand but one who is wise and discerning
and loves the Lord? 11 When, therefore, He made us new
by the remission of sins, He made us men of a different
stamp,[71] with the result that we have the soul of little children, as we should have if He were to fashion us anew. 12
For the Scripture speaks of us when He says to the Son:
Let us make man according to our image and likeness; and
let them rule over the beasts on the earth and the birds in
the air and the fish in the sea. And when the Lord saw our
fair creation, He said: *Increase and multiply and fill the*
earth.[72] This is what He said to His Son. 13 I will also
show you how He speaks to us. In these latter days He made
a second creation. The Lord says: *Behold, I make the last*
things like the first.[73] This, then, is what the Prophet announced when he said: *Enter into the land flowing with*
milk and honey, and rule over it. 14 Observe, therefore: we

have been formed anew,[74] as He says through still another Prophet: *Behold, says the Lord, from them*—that is, from those whom the Spirit of the Lord foresaw—*I will take out the hearts of stone and put into them hearts of flesh,*[75] because He was to manifest Himself in the flesh and to dwell in us. 15 Indeed, my brethren, a holy temple,[76] dedicated to the Lord, is this little house, our heart! 16 For the Lord says again: *And where shall I appear before the Lord my God and win praise?*[77] He replies: *Let me give thanks to you in the assembly of my brethren, and in the assembly of the saints will I sing psalms to you.*[78] We, then, are the ones whom He has led into the fertile land. 17 But what does " the milk and honey " mean? It means that, just as a child is kept alive first with milk and then with honey, so we, too, are made alive by the faith in the promised blessing and by the Word;[79] and, once we possess life, we shall rule the land. 18 But He has foretold above: *And let them increase and multiply . . . and rule the fish.* Who, then, is at present in a position to rule over beasts and fish and birds in the air? We must bear in mind, of course, that " to rule " requires authority, that is, asserting one's power by a word of command.[80] 19 Well, since this condition is not verified at present, He has evidently told us when it will be verified—then, namely, when we ourselves are so perfected as to become heirs of the Lord's covenant.

7. You notice, then, children of joy, that the good Lord has revealed everything to us in advance, that we may know to whom a full measure of thanks and praise is due from us. 2 The Son of God, although He is Lord and *Judge of the living and the dead,*[81] underwent suffering, so that His affliction might give us life. Let us, therefore, believe that the Son of God could not suffer except for our sake.

3 Furthermore, when crucified, He was given vinegar and gall to drink.[82] Hear, then, how the priests of the temple had previously made an allusion to this. There is a precept in the Scripture to this effect: *Whoever does not keep this fast shall be cut off from the living.*[83] The Lord gave this commandment because He, too, intended to offer the vessel of His spirit as a sacrifice for our sins and thereby fulfill the type established in the person of Isaac, who was sacrificed on the altar. 4 Now what does He say in the Prophet? *And they shall eat of the goat offered on the day of fasting for the sins of all, and—*pay close attention—*only and all the priests shall eat the inwards unwashed with vinegar.*[84] 5 Why? Because " to me,[85] when I am going to offer my body for the sins of the new people, you will give gall with vinegar to drink: [86] therefore you alone shall eat while the people fast and mourn in sackcloth and ashes." Thus He wanted to show that He had to suffer at their hands.

6 Observe what He commanded: *Take a pair of goats, shapely and like each other, and offer them; and let the priest take the one for a whole burnt sacrifice for sins.* 7 But what are they to do with the other? *The other,* He says, *shall be accursed* [87]—note how Jesus is prefigured by it!—8 *and spit upon it, all of you, stab it, and put scarlet wool about its head; and so let it be driven into the desert.*[88] And when this is done, he whose task it is to carry off the goat, takes it into the desert; there he removes the wool and lays it on the shrub called bramblebush—the same whose fruits we are accustomed to eat when we find them in the field: so sweet are the berries of the bramblebush alone! 9 Now what does this mean? Pay attention: the one is to be placed on the altar, the other to be cursed; and note that the one accursed is wreathed,[89] because on that Day they are going to see Him

wearing the flowing robe of scarlet, and they are going to
say: " Is not this the one whom we once crucified and insulted and stabbed and spat upon? Yes, indeed, this is He
who then declared Himself the Son of God! " 10 And why
is the one " like " the other? The reason why *the goats* were
to be *like each other*, *shapely*, and *of equal build*, is that,
when they see Him coming on that Day, they shall be struck
at the sight of His likeness to the goat.⁹⁰ Observe, then, the
type of Jesus, who was destined to suffer. 11 But what does it
mean that they place the wool among the thornbushes? It
is a type of Jesus, intended for the benefit of the Church:
since a thornbush makes one fear to touch it, it means that
whoever would remove the scarlet wool is bound to suffer
much and cannot secure it except through pain. Just so,
He means, " those who wish to see me and take possession
of my kingdom must possess me through affliction and
suffering." ⁹¹

8. But what do you think is typified by the injunction to
Israel: ⁹² men already grown grey in sin shall offer a heifer,
and slay and burn it; then little boys are to collect the ashes
and put them into vessels, and to tie around a piece of wood
the scarlet wool and hyssop—note here again the type of
the Cross and the scarlet wool!—and with this the boys are
to sprinkle the people one by one, that they may be sanctified by the remission of their sins? 2 Observe how plainly
He speaks to you! ⁹³ The calf is Jesus; the sinners who offer
it are those who brought Him to the slaughter. And now—
gone are the men; gone is the glory of the sinners! 3 The
little boys who did the sprinkling are those who brought us
the good tidings of the forgiveness of sins and the sanctifica-
tion of the heart—those whom He empowered to preach the

Gospel. They were twelve in number to represent the Tribes of Israel, which were twelve.[94] 4 But why are the sprinklers three boys? To represent Abraham, Isaac, and Jacob, since these men were great in the sight of God.[95] 5 And why the wool around the wood? Because the kingdom of Jesus rests on the Wood,[96] and because those who hope in Him will live forever. 6 And why are the wool and the hyssop together? [97] Because in His kingdom there are bound to be foul and evil times, in which we are to be saved; because, moreover, whoever ails through frailty is healed by the foulness of the hyssop. 7 It follows, then, that things like these are plain to us, but were obscure to them,[98] because they did not understand the meaning of the Lord's voice.

9. For again, speaking of ears, He tells how He circumcised our heart. The Lord says in the Prophet: *They but heard with their ears, and at once obeyed me.*[99] And again He says: *With their ears will the far-off hear, and what I did they will understand;* [100] and, *Let your hearts be circumcised.*[101] 2 And again He says: *Listen, Israel; for this is what the Lord your God is saying.*[102] And again the Spirit of the Lord prophesies: *Who is he that would have life forever? With open ear let him listen to the voice of my Servant.*[103] 3 And again He says: *Hear, O heaven, and give ear, O earth, for the Lord has spoken these things to serve as evidence.*[104] And again He says: *Rulers of this race, hear the word of the Lord.* And He says again: *Listen, children, to the voice of one crying in the wilderness.* The conclusion is: He circumcised our ears, that we might hear the Word and believe. 4 But, moreover, the circumcision in which they put their trust has been superseded. In fact, He did not speak of a circumcision to be performed in the flesh; [105]

no, they went against the commandment, being deluded by a bad angel. 5 He says to them: *This is what the Lord your God says*—and herein I find a commandment: *Do not sow among thorns; circumcise yourselves to please the Lord.* What does He mean? *Circumcise your hard-heartedness, and do not stiffen your necks.*[106] And hear again: *Behold, says the Lord, all the heathen lack the circumcision of the foreskin; but this people lacks the circumcision of the heart.*[107] 6 But you will say: " And yet, the people underwent circumcision as a seal! "[108] Well, every Syrian and Arab and all the idol-worshipping priests were circumcised:[109] does it follow that they, too, are members of their covenant? Why, even the Egyptians employ circumcision! 7 Let me, then, children of love,[109a] give you full and detailed information: Abraham was the first to make use of circumcision, and he circumcised looking forward in spirit to Jesus, after he had received an object lesson in three letters.[110] 8 For it says: *And Abraham circumcised eighteen and three hundred men of his household.*[111] What, then, was the knowledge imparted to him? Notice that it first says " ten and eight," and then, in a separate phrase, " three hundred." As to the " ten and eight ": " ten " = **I**, " eight " = **H**. There you have **IESUS**. But since the Cross, prefigured by a **T**, was to be the source of grace, it adds the "three hundred."[112] It therefore points to Jesus in two letters, and to the Cross in the one. 9 He who put in us the implanted gift[113] of His teaching, well understands. No one has received from me a more reliable explanation; but I know you are entitled to it.

10. As to what Moses said: *You shall eat neither swine, nor eagle, nor hawk, nor crow, nor any fish that has no scales on it,*[114] he received, rightly understood, three moral precepts;

2 for the Lord still further says to them in *Deuteronomy*: *And I will set forth to this people my just demands.*[115] Therefore, there is no such divine command as " do not eat "; no, Moses spoke in a spiritual sense. 3 Consequently, speaking of " swine," he meant this: Do not associate with such people as resemble swine, that is, people who forget the Lord when they revel in plenty, but know the Lord very well when they are in want—just as a swine, while feeding, takes no notice of its owner, but grunts when it is hungry and, after receiving food, is silent again. 4 *You shall eat neither eagle, nor hawk, nor kite, nor crow.* Do not, He means, associate with, or resemble, such people as do not know how to obtain their food by sweat and labor, but, in their disregard for law, plunder other people's property. While walking about in seeming simplicity of heart, they watch sharply whom they may rob to satisfy their greed—just as these birds alone do not provide their own food, but, sitting idle, look for a chance to devour the flesh of others—the mischievous pest they are! 5 *And you shall eat,* He says, *neither lamprey, nor polypus, nor cuttle-fish.* Do not, he means, associate with, or resemble, such persons as are impious in the extreme and as good as condemned to death—just as these fish alone are condemned to swim in the deep: they do not swim up and down like the rest, but house at the bottom of the sea below.[116] 6 But furthermore: *You shall not eat the hare.*[117] Why? Do not, he means, be a pederast or like such people, because the hare grows a new anus every year, and their number is proportionate to its years.[118] 7 But *neither shall you eat the hyena.*[119] Do not, he means, be an adulterer or seducer, or like people of that stamp. Why? Because this animal changes its sex every year, and is now male, now female. 8 But he also abhorred *the weasel.*[120] Rightly so. Do not, he means, be like those

who, we learn, through lecherousness do with their mouth what is forbidden; and do not associate with debauched women, who with their mouth do what is forbidden; for this animal conceives through the mouth. 9 Concerning food, then, Moses received three moral precepts and spoke, as I have shown, in a spiritual sense; [121] but the people, carnal-minded as they were, accepted them as referring to real food. 10 Regarding the same three moral precepts, David received enlightenment and says accordingly: *Blessed the man that does not follow the counsel of godless men* [122]—just as those fish move about in the dark deep of the sea; *or enter on the sinners' path*—just as those who under the mask of the fear of the Lord sin like swine; *or sit in the company of pestiferous men*—just as birds sit waiting for prey. Now you are fully enlightened about the use of foods also! 11 Again Moses says: *Eat of every cloven-hoofed and ruminant animal.*[1-3] Why does he name them? Because when they receive food, they acknowledge their feeder, and when they rest after feeding, they are apparently pleased with him. How neatly he expressed the sense of the commandment! What, then, does he mean? Associate with those who fear the Lord, with those who meditate on the precise sense of the words they have heard, with those who have the Lord's commandments on their lips and observe them, with those who realize that meditation is a labor of joy and therefore ruminate on the Word of the Lord. But why " the cloven-hoofed "? Because the good man not only sojourns in this world, but also awaits the holy eternity. You see what an excellent lawgiver Moses was! 12 Alas, how could those people grasp and understand these things? But we rightly understand and explain the commandments in the sense which the Lord intended. He circumcised our ears and hearts for this very purpose that we might understand things like these.

11. Let us now inquire whether the Lord took pains to hint in advance at the water and the Cross. Regarding the water, the Scripture says that Israel will not accept the baptism which brings forgiveness of sins, but will fabricate something to suit its own fancy.[124] 2 For the Prophet says: *Be startled, O heaven, and shudder even more, O earth! This people has perpetrated two crimes: me, the Fountain of life, they have abandoned and dug themselves a cistern of death.*[125] 3 *Is my holy Mount Sinai a barren rock? Truly, you will be like nestlings that flutter about when robbed of their nest.*[126] 4 And again the Prophet says: *I will go before you, and will level mountains, and shatter bronzen gates, and break iron bars; and I will give you hidden, concealed, and invisible treasures. Thus it will become manifest that I am the Lord God.*[127] 5 And: *You shall dwell in a lofty cave of rugged rock, and its water shall never fail; you shall see the King wrapt in glory, and your heart shall meditate on the terror of the Lord.*[128] 6 And again He says in another Prophet: *He who does these things will resemble the tree planted by running waters: it yields its fruit in its season, nor does its leaf fall off; whatever he does will prosper.* 7 *Not so the godless—not so! Like dust they are which the wind whirls off the ground. Therefore the godless will not rise at the Judgment, nor will sinners in the company of the good. The Lord, indeed, approves of the way of the good; but the way of the godless shall end in ruin.*[129] 8 Note how at the same time He describes the water and the Cross. This is what He means: Blessed are those who, fixing their hope on the Cross, have descended into the water; for by the words *in its* *season* He refers to the reward; then, He means, I will pay it. For the present, however, this is what He means by the words *its leaf does not fall*: every word that passes your lips in faith and love will be for many a means of conversion and hope.

9 And again another Prophet says: *And the land of Jacob was praised beyond the rest of the land.*[130] This is what He means: He is glorifying the vessel of His spirit. 10 What else does He say? *And there was a river creeping along to the right, and out of it beautiful trees were rising; and whoever eats of them will live forever.*[131] 11 By this He means that we descend into the water,[132] laden with sins and filth, and then emerge from it bearing fruit, with the fear (of God) in the heart and the hope of Jesus in the soul. And by the words *Whoever eats of them will live forever* He means to say: Whoever hears these words and believes will live forever.

12. He also describes the Cross in another Prophet, who says: *And when will these things be accomplished? The Lord says: "When a tree is felled and rises again, and when blood trickles from the tree."* [133] Once more you have a hint of the Cross and of Him who was to be crucified! 2 Again, when Israel is made war upon by foreigners, He speaks to Moses; [134] and in order to warn them, by means of this very war, that they had been delivered over because of their sins, the Spirit suggests to Moses that he should make a type of the Cross and of Him who was to suffer. He thus intimates that, unless they hope in Him, they will forever be subject to war. Moses, therefore, placed shield upon shield where the fray was thick; and then, standing where he towered above all the rest, he extended his arms. The result was that Israel was again victorious; then, when he lowered them, the

men were again cut down. 3 Why? They were to understand that they could not be saved unless they put their
trust in Him. 4 And again He says in another Prophet: *The
livelong day I extended my arms to a refractory people that
rebelled against my just demands.*[135] 5 And again, to show
that Jesus will have to suffer, and that it is He who will give
life—He whom they will fancy to have destroyed!—Moses
presents another type of Him in the sign given when Israel
was falling in battle: to convince them that they would be
delivered over to death because of their transgressions, the
Lord made every serpent bite them [136] so that they were
perishing (you will recall that the transgression, in the case
of Eve, was occasioned by a serpent). 6 And besides, though
Moses himself had given this commandment: *Neither a
molten nor a graven image shall be your God,*[137] he himself
made one to exhibit a type of Jesus. Moses, therefore, had a
brazen serpent made and erected it conspicuously, and
through a herald's proclamation convened the people. 7 So
when they had assembled, they begged Moses to offer a
prayer for their cure. Then Moses said to them: *If any one
of you,* he said, *has been bitten, let him come to the serpent
attached to the wood and have confidence, in the belief that,
although it is a dead thing, it has yet power to preserve life.
And he will at once be cured.*[138] And so they did. Again you
see in this incident the glory of Jesus, inasmuch as all things
are in Him and for Him.

8 Again, what does Moses say to Jesus, the son of Nave,[139]
to whom—prophet that he was—he had given this name for
the sole reason that the whole people might be informed
that the Father reveals all things concerning His Son Jesus?
9 Moses, then, said to Jesus, the son of Nave, after giving
him this name at the time when he sent him to reconnoitre

the land: *Take a scroll in your hands and write what the Lord is saying: "In the last days the Son of God will destroy, root and all, the house of Amalec."* [140] 10 Behold, there is Jesus again, not a son of man, but the Son of God, though revealed by a type in the flesh. Now, they were going to say that Christ was the Son of David; and so David himself, fearing and comprehending the error of the sinners, prophesied: *The Lord said to my Lord: "Be Thou seated at my right hand, until I make Thy enemies a footstool for Thy feet."* [141] 11 And again Isaias says as follows: *The Lord said to Christ my Lord, whose right hand I uphold, that the nations are to obey Him, and "I will shatter the might of kings."* [142] Note how *David calls Him Lord,* [143] and does not call Him his son.

13. But let us inquire whether our people or the former is the heir, and whether the covenant is intended for us or for them. [144] 2 Hear, then, what the Scripture says about " the people ": *Isaac prayed for Rebecca, his wife, because she was barren. And she conceived.* Next: *And Rebecca went to inquire of the Lord, and the Lord said to her: "Two nations are in your womb and two peoples in your body; one people shall expel the other, and the older shall serve the younger."* 3 You should try to understand who Isaac is and who Rebecca is, and by what means He has pointed out that our people will be greater than the other. 4 In another prophecy Jacob speaks more plainly when he said to his son Joseph: *Behold, the Lord has not deprived me of your sight. Bring me your sons that I may bless them.* [145] 5 And Joseph brought Ephraim and Manasses; but since he wished Manasses to be blessed, because he was the older, he placed him next to the right hand of his father Jacob. But Jacob, enlightened by the Spirit, discerned a type of the people of the future. And what does it say? *Then Jacob crossed his hands and laid his right hand on the head of Ephraim, the second and younger son, and blessed him. And Joseph said to Jacob: "Change your right hand to the head of Manasses, for he is my first-born son." Then Jacob said to Joseph: "I know, my child—I know; but the older must be subject to the younger; just the same, he also shall be blessed."* [146] 6 You see by what means He has ordained that our people shall be first and the heir of the covenant. 7 Consequently, if, in addition to this, our people is also pointed out in the story of Abraham, then we have reached the perfection of our knowledge. What, then, does He say to Abraham when he, the only believer, was accounted justified? *Behold, Abraham, I have appointed you the father of the nations which, though not circumcised, believe in God.* [147]

14. Yes, indeed! But let us see whether the covenant which He had sworn to the fathers to give their people, [148] was actually given. He has given it; but they, owing to their sins, proved unworthy of the favor. 2 For the Prophet says: *And Moses was on Mount Sinai fasting forty days and forty nights, in order to receive the convenant of the Lord, intended for the people. And Moses received from the Lord two tables inscribed by the finger of the Lord's hand in the Spirit;* [149] and after receiving them, Moses intended to take them down and give them to the people; 3 and the Lord said to Moses: "*Moses, Moses, descend in haste; your people, which you led out of Egypt, has broken the Law!*" *And Moses perceived that they had again made themselves molten images; and he flung the tables out of his hands, and the tables of the Lord's covenant were shattered.* [150] 4 Moses received it, but they did not prove themselves worthy.

But how did we receive it? Let me tell you. Moses received it as a servant,[151] but the Lord in person gave it to us in order to make us the people of inheritance by suffering for our sake. 5 He appeared in the flesh, that they might fill up the measure of their sins,[152] and that we might receive the covenant through its destined Heir, the Lord Jesus; in fact, He was appointed for the very purpose of appearing in person and ransoming from darkness our hearts already worn out to death and given over to iniquitous error; and thereby He was to establish among us a covenant by His Word. 6 For the Scripture tells how the Father enjoins Him to ransom us from darkness and prepare for Himself a holy people.[153] 7 This, then, the Prophet says: *I, the Lord your God, have called Thee to establish the right order, and I will take Thee by the hand and strengthen Thee, and I appoint Thee to make a covenant with the race, and to be a Light to the nations: Thou shalt open the eyes of the blind; Thou shalt free the fettered from their shackles and those who sit in darkness from the prison house.*[154] We realize, therefore, from what state we have been redeemed. 8 Again the Prophet says: *Behold, I have appointed Thee a Light to the nations: Thou art to be a Savior as far as the earth extends. Thus says the Lord God, who has redeemed you.*[155] 9 Again the Prophet says: *The Spirit of the Lord is upon me, because He has anointed me to preach the Gospel of grace to the lowly; He sent me to heal the brokenhearted, to announce release to captives, and recovery of sight to the blind; to proclaim a year of grace ordained by the Lord and the time of recompense; to bring comfort to all the sorrowing.*[156]

15. Moreover, the Scripture has also mentioned the Sabbath in the Decalogue, in which He spoke face to face to

Moses on Mount Sinai: *Also keep holy the Sabbath of the Lord, clean of hand and heart.*[157] 2 In another passage He says: *If my children keep the Sabbath, then will I bestow my mercy on them.*[158] 3 He speaks of the Sabbath at the beginning of the Creation: *And God made in six days the works of His hands, and when He had completed them, He rested on the seventh day and sanctified it.*[159] 4 Notice, children, what He means by the words *He completed them in six days*. He means this: in six thousand years the Lord will make an end of all things; for, in His reckoning, the " day " means " a thousand years." He is Himself my witness when He says: *Behold, a day of the Lord is as a thousand years.*[160] Therefore, children, in six days—in the course of six thousand years—all things will be brought to an end. 5 *And He rested on the seventh day.* This is the meaning: when His Son returns, He will put an end to the era of the Lawless One, judge the wicked, and change the sun, the moon, and the stars. Then, on the seventh day, He will properly rest. 6 Furthermore he says: *You shall sanctify it, clean of hand and heart.* Consequently, if anyone is able at present to sanctify, clean of heart, the day on which God has sanctified it, then we are the victims of deception. 7 Consider: we shall, as it appears, properly rest and sanctify it then only when we are able to do so after being ourselves justified and having received the promised blessing; when there is no more iniquity, and all things have been made new by the Lord, then at last shall we be able to sanctify it, because we have first been sanctified ourselves. 8 He further says to them: *Your new moons and Sabbaths I disdain.*[161] Consider what He means: Not the Sabbaths of the present era are acceptable to me, but that which I have appointed to mark the end of the world and to usher in the eighth day, that is,

5 *

the dawn of another world. 9 This, by the way, is the reason why we joyfully celebrate the eighth day—the same day on which Jesus rose from the dead; after which He manifested Himself and went up to heaven.[162]

16. But I will also tell you how those wretches erred in regard to the temple when, instead of putting their trust in their God who had made them, they put it in the building, as if it were the house of God![163] 2 In fact, they almost resembled the heathen in consecrating Him by the temple. But learn how the Lord speaks in superseding it: *Who has measured the heavens with the span of his hand, or the earth with the hollow of his palm? Have not I done it? says the Lord. Heaven is my throne and the earth my footstool. What house can you build for me, or what can be my resting place?*[164] You know that their hope is in vain. 3 Still further He says: *Behold, the destroyers of this temple are the ones that will build it.*[165] 4 This is actually being done. They were waging war, and therefore it was demolished by the enemies; and now the subjects of the enemies are about to build it up again.[166] 5 On the other hand, it has been revealed that the city, the temple, and the people of Israel are doomed! For the Scripture says: *And it will happen in the last days that the Lord will doom to destruction the flock of the pasture and the fold and their watchtower.*[167] And what the Lord says is as good as done.[168]

6 But let us inquire whether there really is a temple of God. There is—there where He Himself says He is building and perfecting it! For the Scripture says: *And really, when the week is coming to an end, a temple of God will be built in splendor in the name of the Lord.*[169] 7 I find, therefore, that there is a temple. How, then, will it be built up in the name

of the Lord? Let me tell you. Before we believed in God,[170] our little house, the heart, was decrepit and infirm, really like a temple built by hand; in fact, it was a nest of idolatry and a haunt of demons, because it was at enmity with God. 8 *It will be built in the name of the Lord.* See to it that the temple of the Lord is built *in splendor!* How? Let me tell you. By receiving the forgiveness of sins and trusting in the Name,[171] we were made new, being created all over again. That is why in our little house—in us—there really dwells God. 9 How? His Word of the faith [172]—His calling us to the promised blessing—the wisdom of His ordinances—the precepts of His teaching—the fact that He personally prophesies in us and personally dwells in us—that He opens to us the door of the temple, that is, our mouth—that He grants us a renewal of spirit—this is what ushers us into the imperishable temple—us, I say, who had been enslaved to death! 10 And in fact,[173] when one is anxious to be saved, one pays no attention to the man, but to Him who dwells and speaks in him, and it is a surprise to him that he has never either heard Him utter such words or had a desire to hear them. This is a spiritual temple which is now being built for God.

17. So far as it was possible to give you a simple explanation,[174] I sincerely trust I have, in keeping with my desire, omitted none of the things that have a bearing on salvation. 2 For if I should write to you concerning things present or yet to come, you would not grasp them, because they are as yet hidden in parables. Let this, then, be enough.

18. Let us now pass on to another kind of knowledge and instruction.[175] There are Two Ways of instruction—as there are two powers—that of Light and that of Darkness. And there is a great difference between the Two Ways: the one is controlled by God's light-bringing angels, the other by angels of Satan. 2 And as the latter is the Ruler of the present era of lawlessness, so the former is Lord from eternity to eternity.

19. The Way of Light, then, is as follows; and whoever desires to make his way to the appointed place must be actively at work. Now, the knowledge granted us to enable us to walk in this way embraces the following points: 2 Love your Maker; reverence your Creator; glorify Him who ransomed you from death; be single of heart and exuberant of spirit; [176] do not associate with such as walk in the Way of Death; abhor everything not pleasing to God; detest every form of hypocrisy; do not by any means neglect the commandments of the Lord. 3 Do not carry your head high, but be ever in a humble frame of mind; do not reach out for personal glory; do not plot evil against your neighbor; do not open your heart to presumption. 4 Do not fornicate; do not commit adultery; do not practice pederasty; do not let the Word of God escape your lips in the presence of any that are impure.[177] Make no distinction between man and man when correcting anyone's transgression. Be gentle, be quiet; with trembling treasure the instructions you have received.[178] Do not bear malice against your brother. 5 Do not waver in your decision.[179] *Do not take the name of the Lord in vain.*[180] Love your neighbor more than yourself. Do not kill a fetus by abortion, or commit infanticide. Do not withdraw your hand from your son or your daughter; but from their youth teach them the fear of God. 6 Do not covet your neighbor's goods; do not be greedy. Do not be on intimate terms with the powerful, but associate with holy and lowly folk. Accept as blessings the casualties that befall you,[181] assured that nothing happens without God. 7 Do not be double-minded or double-tongued, for the double tongue is *a deadly snare.*[182] In reverence and fear be submissive to your masters as representatives of God. Do not when embittered, give orders to your slave, male or female, for they hope in the same God; otherwise, they might lose the fear of God, who is the Master of you both. He surely did not come to call with an eye to rank or station in life;[183] no, He comes to those whom the Spirit has prepared. 8 Share everything with your neighbor, and do not say: " It is private property "; for, if you are sharers in what is imperishable, how much more so in the things that perish! Do not be hasty of tongue, for the tongue is *a deadly snare.* As far as you can, be pure to save your soul. 9 Do not be one that opens his hands to receive, but shuts them when it comes to giving. Love *as the pupil of your eye* [184] anyone that explains to you the Word of the Lord. 10 Day and night remember the Day of Judgment. Seek daily the companionship of the saints. Are you proficient in speaking? Then go to comfort, and endeavor to save, an afflicted soul. Do you work with your hands? Then pay a ransom for your sins. 11 Do not hesitate to give, and do not give in a grumbling mood; you will find out who is your good Rewarder. Hold fast to the traditions, *neither adding nor subtracting anything.*[185] Hate evil incessantly. *Be just in your judgment.*[186] 12 Do not start a schism, but pacify contending parties. Confess your sins. Do not come to prayer with a guilty conscience.

Such is the Way of Light.

20. The Way of the Black One,[187] on the other hand, is crooked and altogether accursed: it is the way to eternal death and punishment. In it is found everything that corrupts the soul of men: idolatry, rashness, the pomp of power, hypocrisy, duplicity, adultery, murder, robbery, pride, lawlessness, deceitfulness, malice, surliness, sorcery, magic, covetousness, want of the fear of God. 2 Here belong persecutors of the good, haters of the truth, lovers of falsehood; men ignorant of the reward for right living, not *devoted to what is good*,[188] or to just judgment; men who neglect widow and orphan, who are on the alert, not because they fear God, but because they are bent on vice; who are utter strangers to gentleness and patient endurance; men *who love vanities*,[189] and *fee hunters*; who have no heart for the poor, take no trouble about the oppressed, are prone to slander, do not know their Maker; *murderers of children*,[190] destroyers of God's image; men who turn away from the needy, oppress the afflicted, act as counsel for the rich, are unjust judges of the poor; in a word—men steeped in sin.

21. To sum up: when one has learned the just demands of the Lord, as contained in the Scriptures, the proper thing is to make them the rule of one's life. Surely, whoever complies with them will reap glory in the kingdom of God; whoever chooses the opposite course with all its works must perish. That is why there is a resurrection, why there is a retribution. 2 I would exhort those who are in better circumstances, if you will accept my well-meant advice: you have in your community [191] persons to whom you can do good; do not miss your opportunity! 3 The day is at hand when all things will perish together with the Evil One. *At hand is the Lord and His recompense.*[192] 4 Again and again I exhort you: be your own good lawgivers; remain your own trusty advisers; [193] away with all hypocrisy! 5 May God, who is Lord over the whole world, grant you wisdom, understanding, insight,

knowledge of His just demands, and patient endurance. 6
Be learners in God's school,[194] studying what the Lord requires of you; and then do it! Thus you will be approved on
Judgment Day. 7 And if there is such a thing as remember-
ing a kindly deed, remember me by pondering what I have
said, so that my heart's desire and my vigils may result in
something good. I ask for this as your favor to myself. 8
As long as the fair vessel is still with you,[195] do not be wanting
to yourselves in any respect; on the contrary, study these
matters continually and carry out every commandment. They
certainly deserve it. 9 For the same reason I have been all
the more anxious to write to you to the best of my ability.
I wanted to cheer you.[196] Farewell, children of love and
peace! May the Lord of glory and of every grace be *with
your spirit!*

Epistle of Barnabas

ST. POLYCARP

THE EPISTLES TO THE PHILIPPIANS

INTRODUCTION

A suitable introduction to St. Polycarp would be to read what his contemporary, St. Ignatius of Antioch, says both to him and about him in the two letters sent to Smyrna shortly after his visit to that city.[1] In fact, acquaintance with these Ignatian letters is necessary if we would fully appreciate Polycarp's *Epistle to the Philippians*. In it Polycarp keeps Ignatius constantly before us, whether in the mention of his name or in the use of some turn of expression peculiar to him.[2] Words familiar to us from Ignatius have a richer flavor when met again in Polycarp. Points of doctrine, stated or implied, as well as lessons in Christian virtue show the same face in both. But we learn more from Ignatius about the early Christian mentality than we do from Polycarp. There is also a decided difference in their style of writing. Ignatius is fiery, abrupt, and impetuous, while Polycarp is calm and sedate, more akin to Clement of Rome. All in all, Polycarp is a happy complement to Ignatius.

Smyrna, the episcopal see of Polycarp, is situated in the centre of the west coast of Asia Minor. Its present interest to us is in the fact that it was visited by Ignatius on his journey to Rome. Polycarp, if he was not perhaps the host of the martyr-saint, at any rate joined the delegates from other Asian Churches in showering kindnesses on him. One of the notable results of this visit was, no doubt, the warm interest taken by Polycarp in the Ignatian epistles,[3] echoes from which are scattered throughout the letter to the Philippians.

After leaving Smyrna, Ignatius was taken northward to Troas, where another respite allowed him to write a letter to Polycarp and one to the Smyrnaeans, in both of which he urged his readers to despatch a messenger—" God's courier," as he says—to Antioch, where in the meantime peace had been restored. A few days later Ignatius crossed over to Neapolis in Macedonia, and from there went to Philippi, where another short stay enabled him to become acquainted with the Philippian community—St. Paul's first Christian settlement on European soil. Since Philippi, a commercial centre on the southern coast of Macedonia, was situated on the Egnatian Way, it was a natural stopping place for travellers from Asia to Italy. It was here that Ignatius was joined by two other Christians bound for Rome to be tried for their faith.

Until quite recently it has been customary to speak of " the Epistle of St. Polycarp to the Philippians." Its genuineness and authenticity have been well established; but critics could not agree on its date of composition. Since there is no attestation of it in contemporary literature, any conclusion that might be reached in regard to its date had to be based on such evidence as the letter itself affords. The story of the many attempts at dating the letter cannot be told in a few words.[4] Suffice it to say that, in the main, two groups of critics have long stood facing each other without a satisfactory adjustment of details. To the one it seemed imperative (13. 2) to assign an early date, that is, shortly after Ignatius's departure from Philippi, somewhere during the closing years of Trajan's reign (before 118); the other was convinced (9. 2) that the letter was written two or three decades later. Now both groups worked out their conflicting views on the tacit assumption that the epistle was penned from start to finish at one and the same time. It is only a little more than a decade ago (1936) that this very assumption was subjected to close scrutiny.[5] It was shown that the supposedly one letter of Polycarp was, in reality, a fusion of two communications despatched at entirely different dates. This two-letter theory separates Ch. 13 (with, or without, the postscript in 14)—" the Covering Note " which accompanied the batch of Ignatian letters sent by Polycarp to the Philippians—from the rest of the letter, " the Crisis Letter," that is, Chapters 1-12, which were written at some later time in answer to a wish of the Philippians for an exhortation on Christian life in general and, no doubt, a word of counsel in a crisis that had come upon their community.

The subjoined analysis both of " the covering note " and of " the letter " is based upon this theory, which in all essentials is here accepted as the last word on this long-standing controversy.

Soon after Ignatius's departure from their city, the Philippians sent a letter of congratulation, destined for the Church at Antioch, to Polycarp, asking him to forward it through a messenger of his own. Polycarp expresses his readiness to comply with the request. The bearer of his note also brought with him a bundle of Ignatian letters which the Philippians had asked for. The closing sentence leaves no doubt that, at the time of writing, Ignatius had not yet reached Rome or, at any rate, that no news concerning his martyrdom had as yet arrived at Philippi. Since Ignatius visited Smyrna late in August, it follows that Polycarp's note probably was penned some time in September of the same year.

Twenty years or so later (about A. D. 135),[6] the Philippians informed Polycarp of the joy they had experienced in welcoming Ignatius and his fellow prisoners during their stay in the city. Polycarp seizes upon this expression of joy as a fitting starting point for his admonitions. It was an old literary convention that, before censure is administered or caution advised, there must be praise.[7] Polycarp therefore praises the Philippians for the faith they had so strikingly exhibited in honoring the martyrs, and at once proceeds to exhort them to maintain a reputation they had acquired even in the days of St. Paul. Remain loyal to your faith, he says in substance, and show your loyalty by making God's commandments your rule of life. This is the gist of all that follows. The special counsels that are yet given are, some of them, so general as to suit any Christians anywhere in the world. In regular Ignatian style, Polycarp has a word to say about the proper conduct of Christian wives, of widows, of deacons, of presbyters, of young men and young women. We notice, however, that certain key words recur again and again. The two points singled out for special insistence are purity of faith and the need of shunning avarice as the root of all evils.

As to avarice, Polycarp leaves us in no uncertainty about his meaning. A certain presbyter of the Philippian community and his wife had given grave scandal by some dishonest financial transaction, the nature of which is not disclosed. We also know what it was that threatened the purity of their faith. It has been shown that the earlier stages of Marcion's doctrinal errors fit best into the picture presented by the epistle.[8] Marcion was in Macedonia at the time and doubtless propagated his Docetic heresy, which denied the reality of the Incarnation and consequently destroyed the fruits of the Passion and death of Christ.

In exhorting his readers, Polycarp draws largely on Holy Scripture.[9] The bulk of his quotations is from St. Paul—the founder of the Philippian community—and the *First Epistle of St. Peter.* A strong appeal to the conscience of the Philippians introduces the remaining part of his exhortations: remember, he says, the great " lesson in holiness," [10] that is, the teaching that a Christian, to be a true disciple of Christ, must be ready to imitate Christ's patient endurance " to the limit," and sacrifice his life in His service. The time was not far off when he practiced what he preached.

In his letter to a friend, a certain Florinus, a disciple of Polycarp, Irenaeus makes mention of several letters written by their former teacher.[11] The one addressed to the Philippians is alone extant. The loss of this correspondence is sincerely regretted by students of early Christianity, for Polycarp must have been in a position to answer many questions concerning " a group of problems, each in its own way fundamental, to which Polycarp was probably better qualified than any other man that ever lived to give authoritative solutions." [12] St. Jerome says that the letter to the Philippians was read *in conventu Asiae* down to his own day.

The question of the date of Polycarp's birth is involved in the practically hopeless controversy over an obscure passage in the *Martyrdom,* where he states that he has been serving his King for six and eighty years.[13] This means that he had been a Christian for that length of time. He became a Christian by baptism; but was he baptized in his infancy or later in life? And if his parents were Jews or pagans, how old was he at his conversion? A similar doubt hangs over the date of his martyrdom, even though February 23, 155 (or February 22, 156) is generally accepted as the most probable.[14] Nor are we much helped by the fact that Polycarp went to Rome to confer with Pope Anicetus not long before his martyrdom—perhaps about the year 154; for while it is not likely for a man almost one hundred years old to undertake the hardships of such a journey, still the possibility of his doing so cannot be simply brushed aside.

The text of this epistle has come down in a somewhat carelessly made Latin version, consisting of fourteen chapters. It was first printed in Paris as early as 1498 by Jacobus Faber Stapulensis.[15]

The Greek text is preserved in nine manuscripts, all of which break off at the end of chapter 9 and are immediately followed by a section from the Epistle of Barnabas. They therefore derive from a manuscript that was itself a copy. Chapters 9 and 13 (without the last sentence) are also preserved in Eusebius, *Hist. eccl.* 3. 36. 13 and 14. The Greek text was printed for the first time by Peter Halloix at Douai in 1633.

✶   ✶   ✶

The text used for this translation is that of F. X. Funk, revised by K. Bihlmeyer, *Die apostolischen Väter*, I. Teil (Tübingen 1924) 114-20.

Other modern translations of note are the following:

Bosio, G., *I Padri apostolici* 2 (Corona Patrum Salesiana, ser. graeca 14, Turin 1942) 163-201.

Krüger, G., in E. Hennecke's *Neutestamentliche Apokryphen* (2nd ed., Tübingen 1924) 537-40.

Lake, K., *The Apostolic Fathers* 1 (Loeb Classical Library, London 1912) 279-301.

Lelong, A., *Les Pères apostoliques* 3 (Textes et documents 12, 2nd ed., Paris 1927) 108-28.

Lightfoot, J. B., *The Apostolic Fathers* (ed. by J. R. Harmer, London 1898) 175-81.

Zeller, F., *Die apostolischen Väter* (Bibliothek der Kirchenväter 35, Munich 1918) 157-70.

THE EPISTLE\<S\> OF SAINT POLYCARP
BISHOP OF SMYRNA AND HOLY MARTYR
TO THE PHILIPPIANS

The First Epistle (Covering Note)

[**13.**] Both you and Ignatius write that when someone is leaving for Syria,[1] he should take your letter along with him. To this I will attend as soon as I find a convenient opportunity—either myself or the person whom I shall send to represent you as well as me. 2 The epistles of Ignatius [2]— those addressed by him to us and any others in our possession —we are sending you herewith in compliance with your request. They are attached to this note. You will be able to derive great profit from them, for they deal with faith, patient endurance, and, in general, with matters that bear upon spiritual growth [3] in Our Lord. As for Ignatius himself and those who are with him, let us know whatever reliable information you may obtain.[4]

The Second Epistle

Polycarp and his assistants, the presbyters,[1] to the Church of God [2] which resides as a stranger at Philippi: may mercy and peace from Almighty God and Jesus Christ our Savior be yours in abundance.[3]

6 *

1. In Our Lord Jesus Christ [4] I share the great joy [5] you experienced in welcoming the images of the True Love [6] and, as was proper for you, speeding on their way the men locked in fetters that are fit for saints—those diadems of the true elect of God and Our Lord! [7] 2 I also congratulate you on the fact that your firmly rooted faith,[8] celebrated ever since the earliest days,[9] persists till now and still brings forth fruit to the honor [10] of Our Lord Jesus Christ, who patiently went to meet His death for our sins [11]—*He whom God raised by ending the throes of death. 3 You never saw Him, and yet believe in Him with sublime and inexpressible joy*—a joy which many desire to experience.[12] You are assured that *you have been saved by a gratuitous gift, not by our actions* [13]—no, but by the will of God through Jesus Christ.

2. *Therefore gird your loins and serve God in fear* [14] and in truth: leave untouched the idle prattle [15] and the error of the masses; *believe in Him who raised Our Lord Jesus Christ from the dead, and gave Him glory* [16] and a throne at His right. *To Him all things in heaven and on earth were subjected;* [17] *Him every breathing creature* worships; [18] He is to come as *the Judge of the living and the dead;* [19] His Blood God will avenge upon those that disobey Him. 2 Now, *He who has raised Him from the dead will raise us also,*[20] provided we do His will, make His commandments our rule of life, and love what He loves; [21] if we abstain from every kind of wrongdoing, avarice, love of money, slander, and false testimony; if we *do not repay wrong with wrong, abuse with abuse,*[22] blow with blow, curse with curse, 3 but, on the contrary, bear in mind what the Lord taught when He said: *Do not judge, that you may not be judged; forgive, and you* *will be forgiven; show mercy, that you may have mercy shown you; the measure you use in measuring will be used in measuring out your share;* [23] and, *Blessed are the humble souls and those that are persecuted for conscience' sake, for theirs is the kingdom of God.* [24]

3. It is not at my own instance, [25] brethren, that I am sending you this written instruction on the practice of holy living; I do so because you first invited me. 2 Surely, neither am I, nor is anybody else like me, able to keep pace with the wisdom of blessed and glorious Paul. [26] Present among you—face to face with the generation then living—he accurately and authoritatively [27] expounded to you the word of truth, and, again, when he was absent, wrote to you letters a careful study of which will enable you to grow strong [28] in the faith delivered to you— 3 a faith *which is the mother of us all,* [29] while hope is her companion, and the love of God and Christ and the neighbor is paramount. [30] When a man is engrossed in these, [31] he has fulfilled the commandment which insures justification. He who possesses love is entirely out of the reach of sin.

4. *The beginning of all evils is the love of money.* [32] Realizing, then, that *we brought nothing into the world and cannot take anything out of it either,* [33] *let us put on the armor of a holy life,* [34] and first train ourselves to make the Lord's commandment our rule of life; [35] 2 next, [36] instruct your wives in the faith delivered to them, as well as in love and chastity: they must be attached to their husbands with perfect fidelity, love all others as well with perfect self-control, and impart to their children an education based on the fear of God. 3 Your widows must be discreet in keeping the faith plighted to the Lord; [37] they must pray unceasingly for the community, and refrain absolutely from calumny, gossip, false testimony, love of money, and, in fact, evil of any kind. They must feel that they are God's altar, that He inspects everything for blemishes, and that nothing escapes Him—whether it is a thought or a sentiment or *anything kept hidden in the heart.*[38]

5. Being assured, therefore, that *God is not mocked,*[39] we are obliged to live in a manner befitting His commandment and glory. 2 Deacons,[40] likewise, must be blameless when judged by His rule of rectitude. They are God's and Christ's servants, and not men's: they must not be slanderous, not double-tongued, not attached to money, temperate in all things, tender-hearted, zealous—thus realizing in their conduct the Lord's ideal,[41] who became the Servant of all. If we win His approval in the present world, we shall also win the world to come: He has promised us to raise us from the dead. If we behave as worthy citizens of His kingdom, we shall also share in His royalty [42]—that is, provided we persevere in faith. 3 Furthermore, young men must be absolutely above reproach; [43] in particular, they must have regard for chastity, and refrain from every evil. It is, indeed, a noble thing to cut oneself off from the lusts that are rampant in the world. *Lust* of any kind *makes war upon the spirit,*[44] and *neither fornicators nor the effeminate nor sodomites will inherit the kingdom of God,*[45] nor those who do the unbecoming. Therefore it is a duty to refrain from all these things, and obey the presbyters and deacons [46] as God and Christ. Young women must keep their conscience pure and undefiled.[47]

6. Furthermore: the presbyters must be kind-hearted, merciful toward all, trying to reclaim what has gone astray,[48] visiting any that are sick, not neglecting widow, orphan, or the poor. On the contrary, *they must always have an eye to good behavior in the sight of God and men.*[49] They must refrain entirely from anger, partiality, unjust judgment, have nothing at all to do with love of money, and be neither quick to believe evil of anyone nor hasty in judging. They should realize that we all are debtors in the matter of sin. 2 If, accordingly, we pray the Lord to forgive us, we, too, are obliged to forgive. We all are in the full view of the Lord and God. *All must stand at the judgment seat of Christ, and each must give an account of himself.*[50] 3 *Let us*, then, *serve Him in awe and deepest reverence.*[51] This is what He Himself, the Apostles, who preached the Gospel to us,[52] and the Prophets, who announced in advance the coming of Our Lord, have commanded us. Ambitious of noble deeds, let us keep aloof from seducers, false brethren, and such as bear the name of the Lord but for a mask. Such people lead empty-headed folk astray.

7. Indeed, *whoever does not acknowledge Jesus Christ to have come in human flesh* [53] *is Antichrist;* [54] whoever does not admit the testimony of the Cross *is sprung from the Devil;* [55] whoever wrests the Lord's Gospel [56] to suit his own lusts and denies both resurrection and judgment—such a one is the first-born of Satan.[57] 2 Therefore let us leave untouched the senseless speculations [58] of the masses and the false doctrines, and turn to the teaching delivered to us in the beginning; let us *be temperate and ready for our prayers*,[59] persevere in fasting, and fervently implore the All-seeing God *not to expose us to temptation*,[60] since the Lord has said: *The spirit is willing, but the flesh is weak.*[61]

8. Unceasingly, then, let us cling to *our Hope* [62] and the Pledge of our justification, that is, Christ Jesus, who *in His*

own *Body took the weight of our sins up to the Cross; who
did no wrong; nor was treachery found on His lips.*[63] On the
contrary, for our sakes—that we might live in Him—He
endured everything. 2 Therefore let us become imitators [64]
of ⟨His⟩ patient endurance and glorify Him whenever we
suffer for the sake of His name. This is the example He has
set us in His own Person, and this is what we have learnt to
believe.

9. I therefore exhort you all to carry out *the lesson in
holiness* [65] and practice patient endurance to the limit—an
endurance of which you have had an object lesson not only
in those blessed persons, Ignatius, Zosimus, and Rufus,[66] but
also in members of your own community as well as in Paul
himself and the other Apostles. 2 Be persuaded that all these
men *did not run their race in vain,*[67] but in faith and holiness,
and that they are now in the place due to them [68] with the
Lord whose sufferings they shared. Indeed, they did not *love
this present world,*[69] but Him who died for us and was raised
to life by God [70] for our sake.

10. These, then, are the things in which you must stand
firm and follow the Lord's example: *be steadfast and immov-
able in the faith; love the brotherhood; cherish one another;* [71] be united in the truth; with the meekness of the
Lord [72] give precedence to one another; despise no one. 2
When able to do a work of charity, do not put it off; [73] *for
almsgiving delivers from death.*[74] One and all, submit to
each other's rights; *your life among the Gentiles must be
beyond reproach; thus by your good example* [75] you will win
praise for yourselves, and the Lord will not be blasphemed on
your account. 3 *But perdition awaits him through whom the*

name of the Lord is blasphemed.[76] Therefore train all to self-control, which you yourselves are practicing.[77]

11. I am exceedingly sorry for Valens,[78] once your presbyter, because he so little appreciates the office conferred on him. I admonish you, therefore: shun avarice, and be pure and honest. *Shun evil of any kind.*[79] 2 When a man is not able to practice self-control in these matters, how can he urge it on another?[80] If a man does not shun avarice, he will be defiled by idolatry[81] and reckoned among the heathen, who *do not know the judgment of the Lord. Or do we not know that the saints will pass judgment on the world?*[82] So Paul teaches. 3 For my part, I have not observed or heard of anything of the kind among you in whose midst the blessed Paul labored, and who are mentioned in the beginning of his epistle.[83] Of you, indeed, *he boasts in* all *the churches,*[84]— such, that is, as had alone by that time come to know God, when we had not as yet learnt to know Him. 4 I am, then, exceedingly sorry for that man and his wife. *May the Lord grant them sincere repentance.*[85] And you, too, therefore, must be considerate in this matter: *do not treat such persons as enemies,*[86] but reclaim them as diseased and straying members,[87] so that you may preserve the whole of your community intact. In fact, by acting thus, you promote your personal spiritual growth.[88]

12. I am confident that you are well-trained in the Scriptures[89] and nothing escapes your attention—a privilege not granted to me. So I only say what has been said in the following texts: *Let no resentment lead you into sin; and do not let the sun go down on your resentment.*[90] Happy the man who remembers this; and this, I trust, is true of you. 2 May God and the Father of Our Lord Jesus Christ, and the eternal High Priest Himself,[91] the Son of God, Jesus Christ, further your growth in faith and truth and in meekness that is perfect and without a vestige of resentment, as well as in patient endurance and long-suffering and perseverance and purity. May He also grant perfect fellowship with His saints [92] to you, and along with you, to us, and indeed to all who are under heaven and destined to believe in Our Lord Jesus Christ and His Father, who has raised Him from the dead.[93] 3 Pray for all the saints.[94] Pray also for kings and magistrates and rulers,[95] and for such as persecute and hate you,[96] as well as for the enemies of the Cross.[97] Thus all will come to see how well you are doing,[98] and you will be perfect in Him.[99]

14. I am sending you this letter through the kindness of Crescens,[100] whom I lately recommended to you and now recommend again. He has shown himself to be a man of irreproachable character during his stay with us, as, I am sure, he also will during his stay in your midst. I herewith commend to your kind attention his sister, as soon as she comes to you. Farewell in the Lord Jesus Christ in grace [101] —you and all your people. Amen.

THE MARTYRDOM OF
SAINT POLYCARP

INTRODUCTION

The *Martyrdom of Polycarp* [1] is the story, in the form of a letter, of the death which the bishop of Smyrna suffered at the hands of the Roman authorities in Asia for the defense of the Christian faith. It is an account of eyewitnesses, composed in the name of the Church of Smyrna by a certain Marcion,[2] committed to paper by one Evarestus, and, though sent to the Christians at Philomelium in Phrygia, intended from the outset for world-wide circulation. In asking for a detailed description of the glorious event, the Philomelians may be said to have atoned for the indiscreet zeal of one of their number if the surmise is correct that the Phrygian Quintus was a member of the Philomelian community and had by his conduct started the persecution of the Christians at Smyrna.[3] At all events, the Smyrnaeans complied with the request and thus inaugurated a branch of Christian literature [4] which grew to considerable importance in the early centuries and survives, in one form or another, to this day.

The inscription states the name of the Church responsible for this account, and that of the addressees, the Church at Philomelium and "all the communities of the holy and Catholic Church, residing in any place." [5] It closes with a greeting modelled on that of the Epistle of St. Jude. The writer begins by pointing out what might be called his leitmotif, a feature in Polycarp's martyrdom of which he never loses sight: its resemblance to the Passion of Christ.[6] It was, he says, of the type of martyrdom narrated in the Gospel. He then discourses on the extraordinary heroism of the martyrs and accounts for it by the invisible presence of Jesus Christ in their hour of torture. Particularly noteworthy was the conduct of a certain Germanicus, which so enraged the pagans that they demanded the execution of Polycarp. The rest of the letter is devoted to the story of the death of this "most wonderful" man. Since the program of "the hunting sports" was closed for that day, he was condemned to be burnt alive, instead of being thrown before the wild beasts. The description of Polycarp on the pyre and his prayer to God the Father are profoundly pathetic. But the fire failed to touch Polycarp, and he was finally stabbed to death. There follows an account of the struggle for the remains of the martyr: the Christians and, instigated by the Devil, the Jews and the pagans wished to secure them. The proconsul put an end to this "contentiousness" by declaring the body public property and having it burnt. The Christians then reverently gathered what was left of him and interred it in a decent place, in the hope of returning to it on the anniversary of his death.

We could wish we knew more than we actually do about Polycarp's career. Even so, however, we are in one important detail better informed about him than about Ignatius of Antioch. There is no positive attestation of Ignatius's martyrdom; it is merely a certain inference from the way Polycarp speaks of him in his letter to the Philippians about twenty years later. Regarding Polycarp, on the other hand, we here have not only an authentic statement of the fact, but also an elaborate description of the manner, of his martyrdom. Besides, some notices preserved by Irenaeus and Eusebius,[7] and, above all, his letter to the Philippians and the Ignatian epistles addressed to him and to the Church of Smyrna, make us feel that his martrydom was, as it were, the natural climax of a long life spent in the service of his King. "Keep faith with me to the death," St. John was told to write to the angel of the Church in Smyrna, "and I will crown you with life." About the same time or a little later Ignatius wrote to Polycarp: "As God's athlete, be sober; the stake is immortality and eternal life."

We do not know when or by whom Polycarp was appointed bishop of Smyrna.[8] That he was rather young at the time of his appointment seems certain. It has been conjectured that he was "the angel of Smyrna" mentioned in Apoc. 2. 8-11. Somewhere in the last years of Trajan's reign —let us say between the years 110 and 115—he had the great pleasure of meeting at Smyrna Ignatius of Antioch on the latter's journey to Rome. The two men were of one mind both in the defense of the faith and in their ardent desire to prove their devotion to Christ, or, as they said, their "discipleship," by dying for Him. A noteworthy result of this meeting was Polycarp's interest in the Ignatian correspondence, a fact of the greatest importance in settling the controversy over the genuineness of the Ignatian epistles.[9] We may take for granted that Polycarp acceded to Ignatius's wish conveyed to him from Troas and Philippi, and sent a delegation to Antioch, unless he went there himself, with a congratulatory letter to the Syrian community on the restoration of peace. We now lose sight of Polycarp until we hear that in or about the year 154 he went to Rome to confer with Pope Anicetus about the Paschal controversy. Anicetus permitted him to continue to celebrate the feast on the day on which he had been accustomed to do so.[10]

The *Martyrdom* is a noble monument erected by a grateful flock to its supreme shepherd. It harmoniously rounds out the picture, both of the man and of the churchman, that is gained from such other ancient writings as deal with him. Here the man rises to the heroic stature of a true athlete of Christ, and the churchman's career [11] is summed up in enviable tributes from friend and foe. " Of the elect," says the Christan author of the *Martyrdom*, " the most wonderful Polycarp is certainly one—an apostolic and prophetic teacher in our times "; and the pagans, clamoring for his death, are forced to say that " he is the teacher of Asia, the father of the Christians, the destroyer of our gods."

Judged by other specimens of the so-called *Acta Martyrum*, the Smyrnaean account is remarkably free from legendary matter. The appearance of a dove is probably a later addition. The incident of the fire being " cool " to him is matched by a similar fact told in the *Book of Daniel*.

The feast of St. Polycarp is kept by the Western Church on January 26. The name " Polycarp " means " fruitful; rich in fruit."

The two last chapters, 21 and 22, are chronological appendixes. The first of these (21) contains important details for fixing the date of Polycarp's martyrdom. The doxology closely resembles that of Clement of Rome's letter to the Corinthians.[12]

The second appendix (22. 1) appears neither in the Moscow manuscript nor in the Latin version. It, too, ends with a doxology. Its date and authorship are unknown.

The third appendix (22. 2 and 3) gives the story of the transmission of the *Martyrdom*. It falls into two parts. A certain Socrates (or Isocrates) made a copy of the letter from a transcript made by one Gaius, a contemporary of Irenaeus.

The scribe who calls himself Pionius is not the martyr Pionius who died in 250, but the author of a *Life of Polycarp* written in the second half of the 4th century. This life has little historical value.[13]

The *Martyrdom* has come down to us in five Greek manuscripts, of which that preserved in Moscow is appraised as the most trustworthy. Large extracts of the *Martyrdom* also survive in the *Ecclesiastical History* of Eusebius. Besides, ancient translations into at least four languages—Latin, Armenian, Syriac, and Coptic—show how well-suited the *Martyrdom* was to the spiritual needs of Christian readers in different parts of the world.

*   *   *

The text used for this translation is that of F. X. Funk, revised by K. Bihlmeyer, *Die apostolischen Väter*, 1. Teil (Tübingen 1924) 120-32.

The following modern translations may also be noted:

Bosio, G., *I Padri apostolici* 2 (Corona Patrum Salesiana, *ser. graeca* 14, Turin 1942) 203-47.

Lake, K., *The Apostolic Fathers* 2 (Loeb Classical Library, London 1913) 307-45.

Lelong, A., *Les Pères apostoliques* 3 (Textes et documents 12, 2nd ed., Paris 1927) 128-61.

Lightfoot, J. B., *The Apostolic Fathers* (ed. by J. R. Harmer, London 1898) 201-11.

Rauschen, G., *Frühchristliche Apologeten und Märtyrerakten* 2 (Bibliothek der Kirchenväter 14, Munich 1913) 297-308.

THE MARTYRDOM OF SAINT POLYCARP
BISHOP OF SMYRNA

The Church of God which resides as a stranger at Smyrna,[1] to the Church of God residing at Philomelium,[2] and to all the communities of the holy and Catholic Church, residing in any place: *may mercy, peace, and love* of God the Father and Our Lord Jesus Christ *be* yours *in abundance!* [3]

1. We are sending you, brethren, a written account of the martyrs and, in particular, of blessed Polycarp, whose witness to the faith as it were sealed the persecution and put an end to it.[4] By almost every step that led up to it the Lord intended to exhibit to us anew the type of martyrdom narrated in the Gospel. 2 For instance, just as the Lord had done, he waited to be betrayed,[5] that we, too, might follow his example, *not with an eye to ourselves alone, but also to our neighbors.*[6] It is certainly a mark of true and steadfast love, not only to desire one's own salvation, but that of all the brethren as well.

2. To begin with, blessed and heroic are all the martyrdoms that have taken place according to the will of God; for, of course, we must be reverent enough to attribute to God the right to dispose of everything. 2 And indeed, is there anyone who would not admire their heroism, their patient endurance, and their love of the Master? Some of them were cut up by scourging until the anatomy of the body could be seen down to the veins and arteries within; and still they remained steadfast, so that even the bystanders would take pity on them and weep aloud. Some, again, proved themselves so heroic that not one of them uttered cry or moan, and thus they made it clear to all of us that in that hour of their torture the most noble martyrs of Christ were no longer in the flesh, or rather that the Lord stood beside them and conversed with them.[7] 3 And so, their minds fixed on the grace of Christ, they despised the world's torments and in the space of a single hour purchased eternal life.[8] To them the fire of their inhuman torturers was cold, for what they envisaged was escape from the eternal and unquenchable fire. With their mind's eyes they gazed upon the good things reserved for those who persevere—*things which neither ear has heard nor eye seen nor human heart conceived;*[9] but to them—no longer men, but already angels—a glimpse of these things was granted by the Lord. 4 In like manner those condemned to the wild beasts underwent frightful torments: they were bedded on sharp shells and subjected to various other kinds of punishment, in the hope that the excutioner[10] might, if possible, induce them to deny the faith by the prolonged torture.

3. Numerous, at any rate, were the stratagems which the Devil employed against them; but, thanks be to God, he did not prevail against any of them.[11] The most noble Germanicus strengthened their natural timidity by the patient endurance he exhibited. He also gloriously wrestled with the beast: when the proconsul[12] wished to pursuade him and urged him to have pity on his youth, he forcibly dragged the beast toward him,[13] desiring to get away the more quickly from the utter depravity of those people! 2 At this moment the whole mob, astonished at the heroism of the God-loving and God-fearing race of the Christians, shouted: "Away with the atheists! [14] Let Polycarp be searched for!"

4. One, however, Quintus by name, a Phrygian lately arrived from Phrygia, lost heart at the sight of the beasts. But he was one that had intruded himself and had pressed others to come forward of their own accord. The proconsul earnestly entreated this man and persuaded him to take the oath and offer incense. For this reason, then, brethren, we do not commend those who volunteer to come forward, since this is not the teaching of the Gospel.[15]

5. The most wonderful Polycarp, on the other hand, was not at all disturbed when the news reached him, and, in fact, his impulse was to tarry in the city. But the majority were in favor of his withdrawal; and so he withdrew to a farm not far from the city, where he stayed with a few friends.[16] Day and night he did nothing but pray for all and for the Churches throughout the world, as was his custom.[17] 2 And it was in prayer, three days before his arrest, that he had a vision: he saw his pillow consumed by fire; and, turning to his companions, he declared: "I must be burnt alive."

6. While the search for him continued, he had no sooner removed to another farm when his pursuers came upon the scene.[18] Since they did not find him, they arrested two young slaves, one of whom confessed under torture. 2 It was really impossible for him to escape detection. Those who were ready to betray him were of his own household; and besides, the chief of police, who providentially bore the same name as Herod, was in a hurry to bring him into the arena. In this way he was to fulfill his own destiny by entering into partnership with Christ, while his betrayers were to meet with the same punishment as Judas.

7. Taking, then, the slave with them, mounted policemen set out on Friday at about suppertime, armed in their usual way,[19] *as though they were in* hot *pursuit of a robber.*[20] Closing in upon him late in the day, they found him hidden in a small room under the roof. Even there escape to another place was still possible; but he decided against it, saying: " *God's will be done!* " [21] 2 So when he heard of their arrival, he came down and conversed with them. The onlookers were wondering at his age and his composure, and that there was so much ado about arresting a man so old. Then, late as it was, he at once ordered food and drink to be served them as much as they wished, and begged them to allow him an hour for undisturbed prayer. 3 They granted his request; and there he stood,[22] rapt in prayer, so overflowing with the grace of God that for two hours he was unable to stop speaking! Those that heard him were struck with admiration, and many were sorry they had come to fetch so old a man of God.

8. When he had at last ended his prayer, in which he remembered all that had met him at any time—both small and great, both known and unknown to fame, and the whole world-wide Catholic Church [23]—the moment of departure arrived, and, seating him on an ass,[24] they led him into the city. It was a great Sabbath. 2 He was met by Herod, the chief of police, and his father Nicetas. They had him transferred to their carriage and, seated at his side, tried to win him over.

" Really," they said, " what harm is there in saying ' Lord

Caesar,' [25] and offering incense "—and what goes with it—
" and thus being saved? "

At first he did not answer them; but when they persisted,
he said: " I am not going to do what you counsel me."

3 So they failed to win him over, and with dire threats
made him get down so hurriedly that in leaving the carriage
he bruised his shin. But without turning round, as though
he had suffered no injury, he walked briskly as he was led
to the arena. The uproar in the arena was so tremendous
that no one could even be heard.

9. As Polycarp entered the arena, a voice was heard from
heaven: *Be strong*, Polycarp, *and act manfully.*[26] Nobody
saw the speaker, but those of our people who were present
heard the voice. When he was finally led up to the tribunal,
there was a terrific uproar among the people on hearing that
Polycarp had been arrested.

2 So when he had been led up, the proconsul questioned
him whether he was Polycarp, and, when he admitted the
fact, tried to persuade him to deny the faith.

He said to him, " Respect your age," and all the rest they
were accustomed to say; " swear by the Fortune of Caesar; [27]
change your mind; say, ' Away with the atheists! ' "

But Polycarp looked with a stern mien at the whole rabble
of lawless heathen in the arena; he then groaned and, looking
up to heaven, said, with a wave of his hand at them: " Away
with the atheists! "

3 When the proconsul insisted and said: " Take the oath
and I will set you free; revile Christ," Polycarp replied: " For
six and eighty years I have been serving Him, and He has
done no wrong to me; how, then, dare I blaspheme my King
who has saved me! " [28]

10. But he again insisted and said: "Swear by the Fortune of Caesar."

He answered: "If you flatter yourself that I shall swear by the Fortune of Caesar, as you suggest, and if you pretend not to know me, let me frankly tell you: I am a Christian! [29] If you wish to learn the teaching of Christianity, fix a day and let me explain."

2 "Talk to the crowd," the procounsul next said.[30]

"You," replied Polycarp, "I indeed consider entitled to an explanation; for we have been trained to render honor, in so far as it does not harm us, to magistrates and authorities appointed by God; [31] but as to that crowd, I do not think it proper to make an appeal to them."

11. "Well," said the procounsul, "I have wild beasts, and shall have you thrown before them if you do not change your mind."

"Call for them," he replied; "to us a change from better to worse is impossible; but it is noble to change from what is evil to what is good." [32]

2 Again he said to him: "If you make little of the beasts, I shall have you consumed by fire unless you change your mind."

"The fire which you threaten," replied Polycarp, "is one that burns for a little while, and after a short time goes out. You evidently do not know the fire of the judgment to come and the eternal punishment, which awaits the wicked. But why do you delay? Go ahead; do what you want."

12. As he said this and more besides, he was animated with courage and joy, and his countenance was suffused with beauty. As a result, he did not collapse from fright at what was being said to him; the proconsul, on the other hand, was astounded, and sent his herald to announce three times in the centre of the arena: " Polycarp has confessed to being a Christian." 2 Upon this announcement of the herald, the whole multitude of heathens and of Jews [33] living at Smyrna shouted with uncontrolled anger and at the top of their voices: " This is the teacher of Asia, the father of the Christians, the destroyer of our gods! He teaches many not to sacrifice and not to worship! " Amid this noisy demonstration, they called upon Philip, the minister of public worship in Asia,[34] to let loose a lion upon Polycarp. But he replied he had no authority to do so, since he had already closed the hunting sports.[35] 3 Then they decided with one accord to demand that he should burn Polycarp alive. Of course, the vision that had appeared to him in connection with the pillow—when he saw it on fire during his prayer and then turned to his trusted friends with the prophetic remark: " I must be burnt alive "—had to be fulfilled! [36]

13. Then the thing was done more quickly than can be told, the crowds being in so great a hurry to gather logs and firewood from the shops and baths! And the Jews, too, as is their custom,[37] were particularly zealous in lending a hand. 2 When the pyre was prepared, he laid aside all his clothes, unfastened the loin cloth, and prepared also to take off his shoes. He had not been in the habit of doing this, because the faithful always vied with each other to see which of them would be the first to touch his body. Even before his martyrdom, he had always been honored for holiness of life. 3 Without delay the material prepared for the pyre was piled up round him; but when they intended to nail him as well, he said: " Leave me just as I am. He who enables me to endure the fire will also enable me to remain on the pyre unbudging, without the security afforded by your nails."

14. So they did not nail him, but just fastened him. And there he was, with his hands put behind him, and fastened, like a ram towering above a large flock, ready for sacrifice, a holocaust prepared and acceptable to God! And he looked up to heaven and said:

> "O Lord God, O Almighty,[38] Father of Thy beloved and blessed Son Jesus Christ, through whom we have received the knowledge of you— *God of angels and hosts and all creation* [39]—and of the whole race of saints who live under your eyes! 2 I bless Thee, because Thou hast seen fit to bestow upon me this day and this hour,[40] that I may share, among the number of the martyrs, the cup [41] of Thy Anointed and *rise to* eternal *life* [42] both in soul and in body, in virtue of the immortality of the Holy Spirit. May I be accepted among them in Thy sight today as a rich and pleasing sacrifice,[43] such as Thou, the true God that cannot utter a falsehood, hast prearranged, revealed in advance, and now consummated. 3 And therefore I praise Thee for everything; I bless Thee; I glorify Thee through the eternal and heavenly High Priest Jesus Christ, Thy beloved Son, through whom be glory to Thee together with Him and the Holy Spirit, both now and for the ages yet to come. Amen." [44]

15. When he had wafted up the *Amen* and finished the prayer, the men attending to the fire lit it; and when a mighty flame shot up, we, who were privileged to see it, saw a wonderful thing; and we have been spared to tell the tale to the rest. 2 The fire produced the likeness of a vaulted chamber, like a ship's sail bellying to the breeze, and surrounded the martyr's body as with a wall; and he was in the centre of it, not as burning flesh, but as bread that is baking, or as gold and silver refined in a furnace! In fact, we even caught an aroma such as the scent of incense or of some other precious spice.

16. At length, seeing that his body could not be consumed by fire, those impious people ordered an executioner to approach him and run a dagger into him. This done, there issued [a dove and] [45] a great quantity of blood, with the result that the fire was quenched and the whole crowd was struck by the difference between unbelievers and elect. 2 And of the elect the most wonderful Polycarp was certainly one—an apostolic and prophetic teacher in our times, and a bishop of the Catholic Church at Smyrna. [46] In fact, every word his lips have uttered has been, or will yet be, fulfilled.

17. But the jealous and malicious rival, the adversary of the race of saints, had witnessed the splendor of his martyrdom, had seen that his life was blameless from the beginning, and now saw him adorned with the crown of immortality and carrying off an incontestable prize. And so he busied himself preventing even his poor body from being laid hold of by us. Many, of course, were eager to do so and have a share in the possession of his holy remains. [47] 2 He therefore instigated Nicetas, Herod's father and Alce's brother, [48] to plead with the magistrate not to deliver up his body; " or else," he said, " they will abandon the Crucified and worship this man in good earnest." This he said at the urgent representations of the Jews, who were again on the alert when we intended to take him out of the fire. They did not realize that we shall never bring ourselves either to abandon Christ, who suffered for the salvation of all those that are saved in the whole world

—*the Innocent for sinners!* [49]—or to worship any other. 3 Him we worship as being the Son of God, the martyrs we love as being disciples and imitators of the Lord; and deservedly so, because of their unsurpassable devotion to their King and Teacher. May it be our good fortune, too, to be their companions and fellow disciples!

18. When the centurion noticed the contentiousness of the Jews, he declared the body public property [50] and, according to their custom, burnt it. 2 And thus it came about that we afterwards took up his bones, more precious than costly stones and more excellent than gold, and interred them in a decent place. 3 There the Lord will permit us, as far as possible, to assemble in rapturous joy and celebrate his martyrdom—his birthday [51]—both in order to commemorate the heroes that have gone before, and to train and prepare the heroes yet to come.

19. Such is the story of blessed Polycarp. Although he suffered martyrdom at Smyrna with eleven others from Philadelphia,[52] he alone is universally remembered by preference, so much so that even the heathen speak of him in every place. Not only was he a celebrated teacher, but also an outstanding martyr, whose martyrdom all desire to imitate because it was in accord with the Gospel of Christ. 2 By his patient endurance he overcame the unjust magistrate, and thus won the incorruptible crown; and now, exulting with the Apostles and all the saints, he glorifies God and the Father Almighty, and blesses Our Lord Jesus Christ, the Savior of our souls, the Captain of our bodies, and Shepherd of the world-wide Catholic Church.[53]

20. You asked, it is true, for a more detailed account of the events, but for the present we are giving you only a summary report through the good offices of our brother Marcion.[54] Take note, then, of the contents and forward the letter to the brethren farther on. They too, should glorify the Lord, who makes His choice from among His servants.

2 To Him who is able, by His bountiful grace, to bring us all into His eternal kingdom through His Son Jesus Christ, the Only-begotten, be glory, honor, might, and majesty forever. Greetings to all the saints. Those who are with us and especially Evarestus, who committed this letter to paper, with his whole family, wish to be remembered to you.

21. The day of blessed Polycarp's martyrdom is the second of the first half of the month of Xanthicus, the seventh before the kalends of March.[55] It was a great Sabbath; [56] the time was two in the afternoon. He was arrested by Herod, when Philip of Tralles was high priest, and Statius Quadratus proconsul, during the unending reign [57] of Our Lord Jesus Christ. To Him belongs the glory, honor, majesty, and an eternal throne from generation to generation. Amen.

22. We say farewell to you, brethren. Make the teaching of Jesus Christ, as expressed in the Gospel, your rule of life. Together with Him be glory to God—the Father and the Holy Spirit—for the salvation of the holy elect. It was thus [58] that the blessed Polycarp suffered martyrdom. May we be privileged to follow in his footsteps and arrive in the kingdom of Jesus Christ.

2 A transcript of this letter was made by Gaius [59] from a manuscript in the possession of Irenaeus. He was a contemporary of Irenaeus, who in turn was a disciple of Polycarp. And I, Socrates, copied it out in Corinth from the duplicates of Gaius. Grace be with you all!

3 And I, Pionius,[60] in my turn, copied it out from the aforesaid manuscript, after I had discovered it through a revelation made to me by blessed Polycarp, as I shall explain in the sequel. I gathered the leaves when they were already almost worn out by age. May the Lord Jesus Christ gather me,[61] too, together with His elect into His heavenly kingdom. To Him belongs the glory with the Father and the Holy Spirit forever and ever. Amen.

Another Epilogue from the Moscow Manuscript

A transcript of this account was made by Gaius from the writings of Irenaeus. He was also a contemporary of Irenaeus, who in turn was a disciple of Saint Polycarp. 2 This Irenaeus, by the way, was at the time of the martyrdom of Bishop Polycarp at Rome, where he taught a great many persons. Many most beautiful and altogether orthodox writings of his are still in circulation, in which he mentions Polycarp as having been his teacher.[62] He also wrote a solid refutation of every heresy and, besides, handed down the ecclesiastical and Catholic rule of faith, just as he had received it from the saint. 3 Among other things he narrates [63] that Marcion, the founder of the so-called Marcionites, one day met Saint Polycarp and said: "Do you know me, Polycarp?" "Yes, yes," he said to Marcion; "I know very well the first-born of Satan." 4 The following fact, likewise, is recorded in the writings of Irenaeus: on the day and at the hour when Polycarp suffered martyrdom at Smyrna, Irenaeus happened to be in the city of Rome and heard a voice which sounded like a trumpet, saying: "Polycarp has suffered martyrdom."

5 From these writings of Irenaeus, then, as has been stated

above, Gaius made a transcript; and from the duplicates of Gaius Isocrates made a copy of it at Corinth. And I, Pionius, in turn, made a copy from the duplicates of Isocrates, after discovering it through a revelation made by Saint Polycarp. I gathered the leaves when they were already almost worn out by age. May the Lord Jesus Christ gather me, too, together with His elect into His heavenly kingdom. To Him belongs the glory with the Father and the Son and the Holy Spirit forever and ever. Amen.

THE FRAGMENTS OF PAPIAS

INTRODUCTION

Papias, bishop of Hierapolis in Phrygia, Asia Minor, is in many respects an interesting, if not irritating, figure in early Church history. Little known to us because of scantiness of data, he was yet highly esteemed, much talked about, and amply quoted in the first centuries.

The date of Papias's birth is unknown, but it is safe to say that he was born before the year 80.[1] Eusebius relates that he was " a hearer of John, a friend of Polycarp, a man of the primitive age." [2] The John just mentioned is undoubtedly the Apostle, and Papias may well have acted as his amanuensis.[3] If we may judge of him by the few fragments that are extant, we must picture him to ourselves as a man with an alert mind, a strong desire for knowledge not expressly conveyed by the Gospels, a pronounced flair for the curious, and no capacity for great thoughts. We know nothing of his career or character as a bishop. Equally unknown are the time, the place, and the manner of his death.

Papias is best remembered by the student of primitive Christianity as the author of five books, entitled *Exegesis of the Lord's Gospel*.[4] Of the value or contents of this work we can form no adequate idea. But the fact that it contained " interpretations " seems to indicate that its purpose was to illustrate the words of the Gospels by a sort of running commentary based upon such explanations as had come to his knowledge " from the presbyters," that is, disciples of the

Lord. His interpretations, he tells us, were interwoven with sundry oral traditions obtained from responsible persons. One extract from his *Exegesis*, usually printed as Fr. 2, has won him a permanent place in the history of the New Testament Canon. His remarks on the Gospel of St. Matthew and on what "the presbyter" had to say about that of St. Mark, are precious. Unfortunately, he has also the distinction of being the first expounder, in our extant literature, of chiliasm or millenarianism.[5] It is mainly on this ground that Eusebius, a sturdy opponent of chiliastic speculations, characterizes him as "a man of very mediocre intelligence."[6] Fr. 1 graphically illustrates the dreams of the defenders of this strange error by describing a miraculous vintage in the millennium. In Fr. 3 the gruesome account of the end of Judas the traitor shows to what extent Papias, in spite of his passion for "the truth," was ready to admit into his "interpretations" grotesque legendary matter. By way of palliation it should be borne in mind that the authenticity of some of the excerpts has been seriously questioned.

On the whole, therefore, his Fragments do not make pleasant reading. Just the same, we must be grateful to him for the few things in his extracts which are real contributions to our knowledge of the Christian mind in the century following the death of the Apostles.

It may be well to approach the interpretation of Fr. 2 by examining verse 4 first. It tells us three things: first, the names of some of those persons who informed Papias about "the sayings and doings of the Lord"; secondly, the channel by which he obtained this information; thirdly, the reason why he considered oral information superior to written records: "I took for granted that book knowledge would not help me so much as a living or still surviving voice."

The reason just given is an answer to the question why Papias, in his quest of "the truth," was not content with either the Gospels or the written records left by other writers. Which these were we have no means of knowing. He was, of course, acquainted with the whole New Testament, even if we cannot trace this acquaintance in every detail. But he shared the Greek feeling about books in general.[7] They have their say, but, in case of doubt, leave the reader in the lurch; they make statements, but answer no questions. He therefore looked for "a living voice" and found it in utterances made orally by competent men. Such were the Apostles or "any other disciples of the Lord." But at the time of his inquiry, or the date of composition, the Apostles were dead (with the exception of John), and so was the greater number of the Lord's immediate disciples; consequently, he "carefully gathered" their utterances through the medium of men that had been "closely associated" with them. Those utterances were the "living voice" or, in the case of "Aristion and the presbyter John," the still "surviving voice."

It is now important to realize that Papias calls his informants "presbyters." In the New Testament and in early Christian literature, the term "presbyter" is somewhat vague in its connotations. By itself it means "an elderly person"; later it came to designate a person who, by reason of his age, possessed rank and influence in his community. It is so used by the Pharisees who accused Our Lord's disciples of "going against the tradition of the Elders" (Matt. 15. 2). On the lips of the early Christians it designated a man of influence, considered qualified to do important Church work, as in Acts 15. 2 ff. and in 16. 4. It has perhaps an even wider meaning in Acts 11. 30, where it seems to include the Apostles. Another connotation attaching to the term is that of "a man of the older generation." It follows, then, that we are justified in identifying Papias's " presbyters " as *disciples of the Lord regardless of whether they were also Apostles or not*. After all, a man's competence as a witness to what Jesus did or said is sufficiently guaranteed by his having been a disciple of the Lord. Now, Papias inquired of persons "closely associated" with these "presbyters," not what the intermediaries themselves knew or thought about the sayings and doings of the Lord, but what they had heard from "the presbyters." The statements of the presbyters in general came to the knowledge of Papias through intermediaries; those of Aristion and " the presbyter John " reached him in two ways; first, through the medium of their followers; secondly, directly, by word of mouth. *This is the reason why John is mentioned twice and Aristion is mentioned by name.*

Papias's condensed report of his manner of obtaining information is tantalizing (like some other of his statements), and its wording is not very lucid. But although he fails to name his intermediaries, we may suspect who some of them were. Papias was a friend of Polycarp, the bishop of Smyrna, who, like Papias, was a disciple of the Apostle John. Could he not tell Papias what he had heard from John? Ignatius of Antioch was brought up under the eyes of three illustrious Apostles, Saints Peter, Barnabas, and Paul, and, of course, of many other disciples of the Lord: could he not pass on to Polycarp, when he visited Smyrna, and through him to Papias, what he had learned about Christ while still at Antioch? We do not know of any personal meeting between Ignatius and Papias; but it is not absurd to suppose that Papias made a point of meeting this great light of the Asian Church on his trip from Smyrna to Troas, which was not at any extraordinarily great distance from Hierapolis even for those days. The Evangelist Philip, one of the seven deacons of the Church of Jerusalem, was certainly "closely associated" with the Apostles, if not also a disciple of the Lord: could he not during his stay at Hierapolis [8] communicate to Papias such information as Papias may have asked for? Whether Papias ever met any of the Twelve Apostles, besides John, we do not know; but surely, after the destruction of Jerusalem, we should suppose that many men and women went westward to preach the Gospel in the Province of Asia. Ephesus, the capital of Asia, at any rate, was not only the key point for the valleys of the Cayster, the Meander, the Hermus, and the Caicus, but also a veritable beehive of Christian missionary activity. Some of the cities in this territory were made famous by the letters of Ignatius: Magnesia, Tralles, Philadelphia, Troas; others are known to us from the Epistles of St. Paul: Colossae, Laodicea, Hierapolis. It would be a wonder if a man of Papias's inquisitive mind had shut himself up in Hierapolis, instead of availing himself of his many opportunities of meeting men acquainted with the disciples of the Lord! He certainly travelled to Ephesus to meet and be the hearer of St. John. Verse 3 of this passage suggests that he also met some who delighted in talking too much; but it was not to these that he turned for reliable information. His great purpose was to meet men qualified "to teach the truth." After declaring his readiness (in verse 3) to set down, along with his interpretations, all the information about the Gospels which he had "carefully gathered from the presbyters," he states the reason why he relied on those men exclusively: the object of his search was not "the longest accounts" or "the commandments of others," but "the truth" and information about "the commandments of the Lord."

He then proceeds in verse 4 to explain by what channel he had obtained the statements of " the presbyters." Its opening words are rendered by some scholars: " And so, too, when anyone, etc.," under the impression that he describes a second group of informants, distinct from the presbyters in verse 3. That the words may bear this sense cannot be questioned; but, if this is the sense intended, there arises the question *whether there were enough Apostles and immediate disciples of the Lord at Papias's time and in his surroundings* to make a separate group. The same scholars suppose that information from the first group was obtained by word of mouth,[9] while that of the second was received from persons " closely associated with the presbyters." It seems more reasonable, therefore, if not imperative, to assign to δέ in verse 4 its usual adversative meaning, as though Papias wished to say: " No, I did *not* listen to men given to much talking, etc., *but* only to men qualified to testify to what the presbyters had said."

After saying in verse 3 that, in gathering material for his work, he relied on " the presbyters " for authentic information, he might have gone on to tell who the presbyters were, but he chose to give first the reason (οὐ γάρ) why he had selected these men exclusively. Then, in verse 4, he names some of the presbyters referred to in verse 3, and characterizes all of them as " disciples of the Lord." But, since at the time of inquiring or at least of writing, these men were no longer among the living, he had to state by what method he obtained their information: he consulted their friends and followers. Only two of the presbyters were consulted both directly and indirectly, Aristion and " the presbyter John." [10] It is fortunate for us that Papias identified this John as " the presbyter," for had he omitted to do so, we should be puzzled to know whom he meant. The sense of the whole clause is: "the presbyter John *whom I have just mentioned* with the Apostles." This, surely, is a reasonable way of removing that stumbling block of so many interpreters. It is, however, also possible, if not in fact probable, that ὁ πρεσβύτερος in this context means, not "the presbyter," as Eusebius explains, but, simply, "the Old Man John."[11] Any reader of St. John's second and third Epistles knew at once whom Papias meant. The expression was a sort of affectionate nickname for the aged and dearly loved Apostle.[12]

Regarding verse 15, it is needful to remember that John's statement is an answer to some persons in his entourage who had belittled, or at least deplored, the relative brevity of the Gospel according to St. Mark. We wonder who these persons were. But we shall not go wrong if we include among them Papias, the very man who wrote this extract. Papias, in a sense, was not satisfied with any of the Gospels that tell of "the deeds and sayings of the Lord." Was not this the reason for his search for more complete information among the "presbyters"? Naturally to a man of his inquisitive mind the second Gospel was least satisfactory in this respect. John takes occasion to tell the critics that, although Mark did not write with that completeness which might have been desirable, yet his Gospel has one advantage peculiar to itself: it is from start to finish a faithful summary of what he has heard from St. Peter—one of those very "presbyters" mentioned in 2. 4!—and should therefore commend itself to Papias and other critics. The proper interpretation of this extract hinges exclusively on the much-disputed words οὐ μέντοι τάξει, which are generally rendered "though not in order," although scholars are puzzled to know just what order (chronological and any other) can possibly be meant. The puzzle vanishes into thin air if we assign to τάξει a meaning often expressed in the Koine and even in Modern Greek: 'verbatim, with full detail, without any gaps in the narrative.' In addition to this acceptation of τάξις, it is instructive to examine the extract in the light of contemporary literature.[13] For the rest, I may refer the reader to a somewhat extensive exposition of the fragment, published elsewhere.[14]

It is difficult for us to gauge the genius of this Apostolic Father. His mind was capable of lodging two extremes. Possessed of a real passion for " the truth " about the words and deeds of Our Lord, he deserves our admiration. He had not himself seen or heard Christ, but he felt that His message must be preserved. It was largely preserved in the Gospels; yet how much there was that never found its way into the inspired accounts! Being a disciple of St. John, he had no doubt frequent opportunities to be made aware of this fact (John 21.25). He therefore turned to well-authenticated traditions handed down by " the disciples of the Lord," and since the number of these men was rapidly decreasing, he appealed to their immediate followers. In Papias's opinion, then, tradition was a rule of faith as well as the New Testament, that is, a lawful way of knowing " the commandments given by the Lord to be believed and stemming directly from the Truth." And yet, our admiration for Papias is tinged with sadness, for he evidently swerved from his original purpose and permitted accounts of " a rather mythical nature " to creep into his writings. As a result, Fr. 2 stands out as practically the sole monument to his greatness—such as it is. Later ages were more discriminating in sifting the chaff from the wheat. His chiliastic dreams, in particular, were vigorously opposed by the best minds in Christendom.

The text used for the present translation is that of F. X. Funk, revised by K. Bihlmeyer, *Die apostolischen Väter*, 1. Teil (Tübingen 1924) 133-40. Bihlmeyer limits his collection to extracts from, and references to, Papias's lost work.

The following modern translations may also be mentioned:

Bosio, G., *I Padri apostolici* 2 (Corona Patrum Salesiana, ser graeca 14, Turin 1942) 249-85.

Hennecke, E.,–Ficker, G., in E. Hennecke, *Neutestamentliche Apokryphen* (2nd ed., Tübingen 1924) 129 f.

Lightfoot, J. B., *The Apostolic Fathers* (ed. by J. R. Harmer, London 1898) 525-35.

PAPIAS

Fr. 1

[Irenaeus, *Adv. haer.* 5. 33. 3-4 (§ 4 in Greek: Eusebius, *Hist. eccl.* 3. 39. 1)]

When,[1] too, creation, once made new and liberated, will produce an abundance of food of every kind from the dew of heaven and the fertility of the earth. This is in accord with what presbyters[2] who saw John, the Lord's disciple, remember having heard from him, namely, what the Lord taught concerning those times when He said:

2 "A time is coming when vineyards spring up,[3] each having ten thousand vines, and each vine ten thousand branches, and each branch ten thousand shoots; and on every shoot will be ten thousand clusters, and in every cluster ten thousand grapes, and every grape, when pressed, will yield twenty-five measures of wine.[4] 3 And when anyone of the saints takes hold of one of their clusters, another cluster will cry out: 'I am better. Take me; use me to bless the Lord.' In like manner a grain of wheat will grow ten thousand heads, and every head will contain ten thousand grains, and every grain will yield ten pounds of clear, pure flour; but the other fruit trees, too, as well as seeds and herbs, will bear in proportions suited to each kind; and all animals, feeding on these products of the earth, will become peaceable and friendly to each other, and be completely subject to man."

4 To this state of things Papias, too,—a man of the primitive age, a hearer of John and companion of Polycarp—bears written testimony in the fourth of his books; actually, there are five books composed by him.[5] And then he adds:

5 "These things are believable to believers." And when Judas, the traitor, refused to believe and asked, "How, then, will such growths be brought about by the Lord?" the Lord, he says, replied: "Those will see who will then be living."

Fr. 2

[Eusebius, *Hist. eccl.* 3. 39]

Of Papias, five books in all are in circulation. They bear the title *Exegesis of the Lord's Gospel.*[6] Irenaeus, too, makes mention of them, suggesting that they were the only works written by him. He says as follows: "To this state of things, etc." 2 Thus far Irenaeus. For himself, however, Papias indicates in the preface to his treatises that he was in no way a hearer or eyewitness of the holy Apostles, but had received the matters concerning the faith from their acquaintances. He points this out by the language he uses:

3 "I shall not hesitate to set down for you, along with my interpretations, all the information I have ever carefully gathered from the presbyters.[7] I carefully committed it to memory and vouch for its truth. In fact, unlike most people, I did not care for men who gave the longest accounts,[8] but for men whose teachings were true; nor yet for men who reported the commandments of others, but for such as related those given by the Lord to be believed and stemming directly from the Truth.[9] 4 But when someone turned up who had been closely associated with the presbyters, it was the words of the presbyters that I would ascertain: 'What did Andrew

say? What Peter? What Philip? What Thomas or James? What John or Matthew or any other of the Lord's disciples?' [10] I also ascertained [11] what Aristion and the presbyter John, disciples of the Lord, had to say. I simply took for granted that book knowledge [12] would not help me so much as a living or still surviving voice."

5 Here, by the way, it is worth while to call attention to his twice listing the name of John. The first of the two men he classes with Peter, James, Matthew, and the rest of the Apostles, plainly indicating that he means the Evangelist; then, by breaking the narrative to make room for others, he places the second John [13] in a group outside the number of the Apostles, in which he puts him after Aristion and expressly calls him a presbyter. 6 Incidentally, therefore, this device proves the truth of the story of those who have maintained that there were two persons in Asia who bore the same name, and that there are two tombs in Ephesus, [14] each of which is to this day said to be John's. It is necessary to note this, for it is likely that the second of the two men, unless one should prefer the first, has seen the apocalyptic vision which goes by the name of John. 7 Furthermore, the same Papias of whom we are now speaking, confesses having received the words of the Apostles from persons closely associated with them, but adds that he had been a personal hearer of Aristion and the presbyter John. At any rate, he often mentions them by name, and in his writings quotes their traditions. Let this statement of ours not be wasted on the reader.

8 It is worth while, however, to add to Papias's sayings already quoted, other statements of his, in which he recounts some other events of a strange character, purporting to have reached him by tradition. 9 For example: it has been shown earlier in the narrative that Philip the missionary [15] lived in

Hierapolis with his daughters; but it now remains to be told that Papias, who was their contemporary, relates that he had received a marvellous tale from Philip's daughters, namely, the rising of a dead man in his own time, and again another marvellous event in connection with Justus surnamed Barsabas—how he drank a deadly poison and, by the grace of the Lord, suffered no untoward consequences. 10 That after the Ascension of the Savior the holy Apostles proposed this Justus together with Matthias and prayed for the choice by lot of the one who was to fill up their number in place of the traitor Judas, is related as follows in the Acts: *They proposed two men, Joseph, called Barsabas and surnamed Justus, and Matthias; and they offered the following prayer.*[16] 11 The same writer published other accounts purporting to have reached him by an unwritten tradition, as well as some strange parables and teachings of the Savior, and certain other things of a somewhat mythical character. 12 Among these he says that there will be a millennium[17] after the resurrection of the dead, when the kingdom of Christ will be established on this earth in material form. I believe that he assumed these things by twisting the Apostolic interpretations without duly considering that the language employed therein was figurative and implied a hidden meaning. 13 He certainly appears to have been a man of very meagre intelligence, as anyone would say that judged him by his own words. For all that, he is also partly responsible for the fact that ever so many ecclesiastical writers after him, on the plea of the man's antiquity, held the same opinion as himself, as, for example, Irenaeus and whoever else has expressed like views. 14 In his work he also hands down the aforesaid Aristion's explanations of the Lord's words and the traditions of the presbyter John, to which we refer those interested in research. For the moment, however, it must suffice to add to his previously quoted sayings a tradition which he relates regarding Mark, the author of the Gospel, in the following words:

15 " This, too, the presbyter [18] said: When Mark became Peter's interpreter, he wrote down, though by no means verbatim,[19] as much as he accurately remembered of the words and works of the Lord; for he had neither heard the Lord nor been in His company; but he subsequently joined Peter, as I said. Now, Peter did not intend to give a complete exposition of the Lord's ministry, but delivered his instructions to meet the needs of the moment. It follows, then, that Mark was guilty of no blunder if he wrote, simply to the best of his recollections, an incomplete account. For of one matter he took forethought—not to omit anything he had heard or to falsify the account in any detail."

This account, then, is the result of Papias's inquiries about Mark. 16 Concerning Matthew he has made the following statement:

" Matthew, at any rate, used the Hebrew language [20] in his exposition of the Gospel, and each one translated it as best he could."

17 The same writer has availed himself of testimonies from the *First Epistle of John* and from that of Peter. He has also published another story about a woman who had been accused before the Lord of many transgressions,[21] a story which the *Gospel according to the Hebrews* contains. Let this bare minimum be borne in mind by us, in addition to the extracts given.

Fr. 3

[Apollinaris of Laodicea, text reconstructed from various sources:
A. Hilgenfeld, " Papias von Hierapolis," *Zeitschr. f. wiss. Theol.*
18 (1875) 262-65]

From Apollinaris.[22] Judas did not die by the halter, but,
after being taken down, lived on before choking to death.
The *Acts of the Apostles* makes this plain: *After he had
fallen head foremost, his belly burst open and his bowels
gushed out.* Papias, John's disciple, relates this incident more
clearly when he says as follows in the fourth book of his
Exegesis of the Lord's Gospel:

2 " Judas's earthly career [23] was a striking example of im-
piety. His body bloated to such an extent that, even where a
wagon passes with ease, he was not able to pass; no, not even
his bloated head by itself could do so. His eyelids, for example, swelled to such dimensions, they say, that neither
could he himself see the light at all, nor could his eyes be
detected even by a physician's optical instrument: to such
depths had they sunk below the outer surface. His private
part was larger and presented a more loathsome sight than
has ever been witnessed; and through it there oozed from
every part of the body a stream of pus and worms to his
shame, even as he relieved nature. 3 After suffering an
agony of pain and punishment, he finally went, as they express it, to his own place; [24] and owing to the stench the
ground has been deserted and uninhabited till now; in fact,
even to the present day nobody can pass that place without
holding his nose. So abundant was the discharge from his
body and so far over the ground did it spread."

Fr. 4

[Andrew of Caesarea, *In Apoc.* c. 34, *serm.* 12: PG 106. 325]

Papias says verbatim as follows: "To some of them"—evidently, of the angels who had formerly been holy—"He assigned also the duty of presiding over the orderly arrangement of the earth, and enjoined them to preside well." And next he says: "And it happened that in the end their charge came to nothing." [25]

Fr. 5

[Andrew of Caesarea, *Praef. in Apoc.*: PG 106. 217 B]

Regarding, however, the divine inspiration of the book (the *Apocalypse* of John), we think it a waste of time to spin out the discussion any further, since those blessed men, Gregory the Theologian, I mean, and Cyril,[26] and in addition Papias, Irenaeus, Methodius, and Hippolytus—all of them men of the older generation—bear additional testimony to its trustworthiness.

Fr. 6

[Anastasius of Sinai, *Anagog. contempl. in Hexaëm.* 1: J. B. Pitra, *Anal. sacra* 2 (1884) 160]

We take occasion from statements made by the excellent Papias of Hierapolis, the disciple of (the Lord's) bosom friend,[27] by Clement, by Pantaenus the Alexandrian priest, and by the most learned Ammonius [28]—those ancient and preconciliar exegetes,[29] who understood the whole of the Hexaëmeron as an allegory referring to Christ and the Church.

Fr. 7

[Anastasius of Sinai, *Anagog. contempl. in Hexaëm.* 7: PG 89.961 D]

The older of the ecclesiastical exegetes, therefore—I mean, of course, Philo the philosopher and contemporary of the Apostles, and the famous Papias of Hierapolis, the disciple of John the Evangelist . . . and their associates, interpreted the story of Paradise allegorically with reference to the Church of Christ.[30]

Fr. 8

[Maximus Confessor, *Schol. in Dionys. Areop. De caelesti hierarchia* 2: PG 4. 48 D]

Those who practice Godlike guilelessness [31] were called by them "children," as also Papias shows in the first book of his *Exegesis of the Lord's Gospel*, as well as Clement in his *Pedagogue*.[32]

Fr. 9

[Maximus Confessor, *Schol. in Dionys. Areop. De ecclesiastica hierarchia* 7: PG 4. 176 C]

This he says, vaguely referring, I think, to Papias, who was then bishop of Asia and flourished at the same time with the divine Evangelist John. This Papias spoke, in the fourth book of his *the Lord's Gospel*, of the pleasures derived from the enjoyment of foods in the Risen Life, . . . and Irenaeus of Lyons says the same thing in the fifth book of his *Against Heresies* and cites the afore-mentioned Papias as witness to his statements.[33]

Fr. 10

[Stephen Gobarus, cited by Photius, *Biblioth. cod.* 232: PG 103.
1104 A]

Nevertheless, Stephen approves neither of Papias of Hierapolis, bishop and martyr, nor of Irenaeus, the holy bishop of
Lyons, in the passages where they say that " the kingdom of
heaven " means the enjoyment of certain material foods.[34]

Fr. 11

[Philip of Side, *Hist. Christ.*: C. de Boor, *Texte und Untersuchungen*
5. 2 (1888) 170]

Papias, bishop of Hierapolis, a disciple of John the theologian [35] and friend of Polycarp, wrote *The Lord's Gospel*
in five books. There he gave a list of Apostles and, after
enumerating Peter and John, Philip and Thomas and Matthew, recorded as " disciples of the Lord " Aristion and
another John, whom he also called " presbyter." [36] As a
result, some believe that ⟨this⟩ John is the author of the two
short *Catholic Epistles*, which circulate under the name of
John, their reason being that the men of the primitive age
accept the *First Epistle* only. Some have also erroneously
believed the *Apocalypse* to be this man's work. Papias, too,
is in error about the Millennium, and so is, in consequence,
Irenaeus. 2 Papias says in the second book that John the
Evangelist and his brother James were slain by the Jews.[37]
The aforesaid Papias related, alleging as his source of information the daughters of Philip, that Barsabas, the same Justus
that passed the scrutiny,[38] was forced by the unbelievers to
drink snake poison, but was in the name of Christ preserved
unharmed. He relates still other marvellous events, in par-

ticular the rising of Manaemus's mother from the dead.[39] Regarding those who were raised from the dead by Christ, he says that they survived till Hadrian's time.

Fr. 12

[Georgius Hamartolus, *Chronicon* (cod. Coisl. 305): H. Nolte, *Theol. Quartalschr.* 44 (1862) 466 f.]

After Domitian, Nerva was emperor for one year. He recalled John from the island [40] and left him free to settle in Ephesus. He was then the only survivor of the twelve disciples, and, after composing the Gospel named after him, received the honor of martyrdom. 2 For Papias,[41] bishop of Hierapolis, who had seen John with his own eyes, says in the second book of *The Lord's Gospel* that he was slain by Jews. Thus, together with his brother, he evidently made good Christ's prediction concerning them, as well as their own confession and assent regarding this matter. For when the Lord had said to them, *Can you drink the cup which I have to drink?* they eagerly assented and agreed to it, and He continued: *You will drink the cup which I have to drink, and be baptized with the baptism with which I have to be baptized.*[42] And this is very plausible, since it is impossible for God to utter a falsehood. 3 The learned Origen,[43] too, vouches for the truth of this account in his interpretation of the Gospel according to Matthew, intimating that he had this information from the successors of the Apostles. And furthermore, the well-informed Eusebius says in his *Ecclesiastical History*: [44] "Thomas was allotted Parthia, while John received Asia as his share, among whose people he spent and ended his life at Ephesus."

9 *

Fr. 13

[Vatican Codex Alexandrinus 14: J. B. Pitra, *Anal. sacra* 2 (1884) 160]

Here begins the discussion of the Gospel according to John.

John's Gospel was made public and given to the Churches by John while he was still in the flesh. An inhabitant of Hierapolis by the name of Papias, John's beloved disciple, has stated as much in the exoteric,[45] that is, the last, portions of his five books. 2 [He made a correct copy of the Gospel at the dictation of John. Of course, the heretic Marcion, who had been censured by John on the ground of different doctrine, was rejected by him.[46] He had delivered to him writings or epistles from the brethren who lived in the Pontus.]

THE EPISTLE TO DIOGNETUS

INTRODUCTION

The *Epistle to Diognetus* is an apology for Christianity, presented by an unknown writer to a pagan of high social or political rank. It purports to be a response to a real or assumed request for information concerning the Christian religion. It may have been designed to gratify the wishes of the high addressee exclusively, or to serve as an open letter to an imaginary inquirer. That it was destined for a wider circle may perhaps be inferred from the apparent freedom with which the writer uses the plural as well as the singular number of the second personal pronoun. There were three puzzles in the mind of Diognetus: what sort of cult is Christianity to enable its adherents to spurn both the pagan gods and the superstition of the Jews? What is the secret of their affectionate love for one another?[1] Why did the new religion come into existence at so late a date in the history of the world (1)?

The writer proceeds to answer the first question by unrestrainedly ridiculing the current idol-worship: the pagan gods, he says in substance, are no better than the pots and pans in daily use (2). He next castigates the fussiness of the Jews in the matter of foods, their superstition regarding the Sabbath, their boasting about their circumcision, and their assumed air of importance in observing fast days and new moons. The Jews, it is true, worship the one true God; but in their manner of worshiping Him they resemble the pagans

(3 and 4). Chapters 5 and 6 draw an extraordinarily attractive picture of the daily life of the Christians, the secret source of which is the divine origin of the Christian religion (7–8. 6). The writer then answers the question why this " new blood and spirit " has made its appearance in the world only recently (8. 7–9). The ultimate solution of the riddle of Christianity is to be found in God's unfathomable love for mankind. A thorough knowledge of God the Father will put the inquirer in possession of the happiness which every Christian enjoys in being an imitator of God (10). Chapters 11 and 12 unfold, warmly and somewhat extensively, " the mysteries of the Father."

Not all the chapters are of equal merit or of equal interest to the modern reader. The crudities of idolatry and their somewhat blunt refutation do not attract us. We are more interested in the way the writer takes Judaism to task, partly because its claims were a burning question even in New Testament times, and especially because it is here that this Epistle invites comparison with that of Barnabas.[2] The Jewish religion was a real danger to the nascent Church till deep into the second century. The Jews, the writer says, are right in upholding monotheism, but utterly mistaken in their belief that God " needs " sacrifices; their ritual is arbitrary and derogatory to God. It is noteworthy that he describes the Jewish cult in the present tense. Long after the destruction of Jerusalem in the year 70, the orthodox Jew regarded the whole system as still obligatory.

The writer's portrayal of Christian life in Chapters 5 and 6 is of great beauty. Christians are citizens and aliens at the same time. Unostentatious in their civic relations, they yet draw upon themselves the admiration of the whole world. " In the world, yet not of the world " is their motto. They are the soul of the world. The author is not fond of quoting the Scriptures, for, after all, what does " the Scripture " mean to a pagan? Nonetheless, his picture of Christian life reads like a commentary on certain portions of the Gospels and the Epistles of St. Paul. Christian otherworldliness has its root in the divine origin of Christianity. This is, of course, a telling blow at paganism and its man-begotten deities. " It was really the Lord of all, the Creator of all, the invisible God Himself " that has enshrined in the hearts of men " the truth and the holy and incomprehensible Word." Here the writer launches into a warm eulogy of Christ, the Only-begotten Son of God. The Savior of mankind was sent " as God," and " as Man to men." His mission " was an act of gracious clemency, as when a king sends his son who is himself a king." And as He loved men, so men love Him. Diognetus himself is witness to the fact that they gladly lay down their lives for Him. They are " imitators of God." He was sent now, and not before, because the human race needed time to realize its sinfulness and utter helplessness. To possess oneself of the blessings of Christianity one must have knowledge and love of God.

Here Chapter 10 ends, and the manuscript shows a gap. Naturally, then, the question arises whether Chapters 11 and 12 belong to the original Epistle. " The evidence," we are assured, " has satisfied almost all scholars that the last two chapters are no part of the letter, but a fragment of a later work." [3] This all but unanimous verdict is not wholly convincing, or, at best, states only a half-truth. Differences in style [4] are not necessarily decisive in a question of genuineness. We may perhaps be helped in forming our judgment by a reference to Aristotle, who held that a perfect composition requires " a beginning, a middle, and an end." [5]

Now, if this Epistle ends at 10, it does have a beginning and
a middle, but it has no " end." It is a tree without a crown.
If we follow the writer's endeavor to furnish a *complete*
answer to the inquirer and make Christianity wholly acceptable to him, we must admit that his letter demanded some
such epilogue as Chapters 11 and 12 provide. After depicting
the truly wonderful life of the Christians in the midst of
pagan surroundings, he would have failed in his exposition
had he not gone on to inform the inquirer that of this very
life the Church is the natural home. As a Christian, he knew
that Christ had organized His disciples into an ἐκκλησία,
that is, a definite body of men brought together for the
purpose of legislating for it and managing its affairs, as any
ἐκκλησία would do in any Greek city. He also knew that St.
Paul had defined the Church as the Body of Christ,[6] though,
in speaking to a pagan, he could hardly use this terminology
without puzzling him. To the early Christians the Church
was a very concrete reality, whose function was to produce
that life in her members which proved so striking an object
lesson to the pagans. Furthermore, since the earlier chapters
extol the objective revelation of God in Christ, was it not
natural to reveal also its subjective, its mystical, side? The
letter fairly revels in showing that a Christian's knowledge
and love of God tend to make of him a " paradise of delight."
The term μυστήριον is one of the key notes of this Epistle.
Mysticism has always flourished in the Church, and of her
ample mystical literature this letter is the first extra-canonical
attempt to show its necessity. The Church can no more
dispense with mysticism than a tree can with foliage.

It is, of course, legitimate to wonder how the gap came into
the manuscript at the end of Chapter 10.[7] But one can offer
no more than conjectures. It may be that the original docu-

ment ended here, and that the author, after realizing his mistake, added the closing chapters, or, again, if the epilogue was part of the Epistle, it was lost and later, when discovered, put in its present place. It is also possible that another writer noticed the incompleteness of the plea made by the author and added what he thought was needed to round out the subject. At any rate, the authorship of Chapters 11 and 12 is uncertain. From the nature of the case, however, it should be clear that the body of the Epistle, stripped of the two Chapters, is a torso. In Ch. 11, by the way, we are told that the writer was a disciple of Apostles. The doxology at the end of 12 is another indication that the real " end " of the letter is there, and not at the close of 10.

Another knotty problem is the authorship of the rest of the Epistle (1-10). There is no clue to be obtained from external attestation, for nowhere in all Christian literature is any reference made to it, distinguished as it is by great beauty of style [8] and admired for its testimony to the true religion. Naturally, a mass of conjectures has been advanced to supply the lack of external evidence. As possible authors of the Epistle have been suggested: Clement of Rome, Apollos, Quadratus, Justin Martyr, Marcion, Apelles the Marcionite, Aristides the apologist. Each candidate for the honor has had his advocate; and there is no agreement.[9] A few years ago it was shown that there is much to be said in favor of attributing the epistle to Theophilus, bishop of Antioch, the author of three books *Ad Autolycum*.[10] But by far the most careful analysis of the internal evidence ever undertaken to unravel the puzzle, is that made by P. Andriessen in favor of his thesis that the *Epistle to Diognetus* is the supposedly lost *Apology* of Quadratus.[11] By means of circumstantial evidence the writer is at pains to show that Quadratus, presumably a

missionary bishop who had come to Athens, presented this
document to the emperor Hadrian, who visited the city in
125 and was initiated in the Eleusinian mystery cults.[12]
"Diognetus," then, is but one of the many names by which
Hadrian was known to his contemporaries, by which, too, it
seems, Marcus Aurelius refers to him when naming the
persons to whom he was indebted for his education.[13]

It is, of course, too early to pronounce on the merits of
this enticing theory; but as one follows its author through the
mass of details, one can hardly resist the feeling that his
conclusions may well be the true solution of this intricate
problem.

The doctrinal content of the Epistle is not very ample. In
addressing a pagan, the author was wise in restricting himself
to certain broad features of Christianity and avoiding topics
of a more recondite nature.[14] The Holy Spirit is not mentioned, unless the expression "the grace of the Church" is
a veiled reference to Him. There is no attack made on
current heresies. If "Diognetus" was none other than the
emperor Hadrian, he must of course be told that Christians
abhor the gross idolatry of paganism; he must also realize
that Christians cannot be identified with the much-hated
Jews, who gave him so much concern at the Eastern frontier;
he must be reminded that his Christian subjects are, by the
testimony of the pagans themselves, quiet and law-abiding
citizens, that they are no "atheists"[15] and therefore no
danger to the State; he must know that the Christian religion
is of divine origin, that God the Father, in His own good
time, took pity on the human race and, from sheer love of
men, sent His own Son to relieve them of the burden of sin.
Above all, since Hadrian was a votary of the Greek mystery
cults and craved mystical experience, he must know that

the greatest μυστήριον, vouchsafed by God to man, is Christianity.[16]

We do not know what effect this Epistle had on " Diognetus."[17] For ourselves its lessons are obvious. The warmth of tone in discoursing on certain fundamental truths of our religion is truly astonishing. How much the author has to say in this short letter about the love of God for man, the Logos, the Incarnation, the atonement, the sinfulness of the pre-Christian world, which yet elicited, not God's anger, but His goodness, kindness, graciousness! And with what detail he tries to impress the pagan with Christ's ἐκκλησία, a term chosen because of its appeal to an emperor or the head of a state! As we weigh the expression " the grace of the Church," we are almost reminded of Heb. 4. 16, where St. Paul speaks of " the throne of grace ": for as God's throne was a throne of grace because Christ, the " auctor salutis " (Heb. 2. 10), is seated at the right hand of God, so " the Church is enriched and grace is multiplied by Him," because to her guardianship He has entrusted the means of salvation. Furthermore, the Savior came late, but come He did, and now invites all men (including " Diognetus," 12.7) to become " a garden of delight" and taste to the full its blessings. No child's play is a truly Christian life with its ever-present prospect of punishment and even death; yet how much there is in this " paradise " to compensate a Christian for the sacrifice of worldly comforts and advantages!

The survival of the *Epistle to Diognetus* in one solitary manuscript of the thirteenth or fourteenth century has been termed "one of the most romantic episodes in the history of literature."[18] In the sixteenth century we find it in possession of the celebrated humanist Reuchlin. Late in the eighteenth century is was placed in the municipal library of Strassburg, only to be destroyed by fire in 1870 during the shelling of that city. Fortunately, centuries before this accident occurred, transcripts had been made by competent scholars, one in 1580 by the humanist M. B. Haus for Martin Crusius in Tübingen, another in 1586 by H. Estienne (Stephanus), the famous scholar-editor, which he first published in 1592. In the manuscript it appeared side by side with certain works ascribed to Justin Martyr, and the first editor published it as a writing by Justin. This ascription persisted till late in the nineteenth century. In almost startling contrast to the great interest and study devoted to the Epistle by scholars since the time of Estienne stands the fact that it is never quoted or even mentioned by any writer of antiquity.

The text used for this translation is that of F. X. Funk, revised by K. Bihlmeyer, *Die apostolischen Väter*, 1 Teil (Tübingen 1924) 141-49.

Other modern translations of worth are contained in the following works:

Bosio, G., *I Padri apostolici* 2 (Corona Patrum Salesiana, ser. graeca 14, Turin 1942) 287-333.

Geffcken, J., in E. Hennecke's *Neutestamentliche Apokryphen* (2nd ed., Tübingen 1924) 619-23; omits Chapters 11 and 12.

Lake, K., *The Apostolic Fathers* 2 (Loeb Classical Library, London 1913) 348-79.

Lightfoot, J. B., *The Apostolic Fathers* (ed. by J. R. Harmer, London 1898) 501-11.

Radford, L. B., *The Epistle to Diognetus* (Society for Promoting Christian Knowledge, London 1908).

Rauschen, G., in *Frühchristliche Apologeten* 1 (Bibliothek der Kirchenväter 12, Munich 1913) 157-73.

THE EPISTLE TO DIOGNETUS

Your Excellency:

I see, Diognetus,[1] that you are very much in earnest about investigating the religion of the Christians and make very exact and careful inquiries concerning them. Who is the God in whom they trust—you wonder—and what kind of cult is theirs, because one and all, they disdain the world and despise death? They neither recognize the gods believed in by the Greeks nor practice the superstition of the Jews![2] And what is the secret of the strong affection they have for one another? And why, you wonder, has this new blood and spirit[3] come into the world we live in now, and not before? I certainly welcome this eagerness of yours and beg two gifts of God, who bestows upon us speech as well as hearing: may I so speak that you will derive the greatest possible benefit from hearing, and may you so hear that the speaker will have no regrets!

2. Well, then, purge yourself of all the prejudices clinging to you[4] and put away your old, habitual fallacies. Make as it were a fresh start and become *a new man,*[5] since you may yet become a hearer also of what by your own admission is a new message. Use not only your eyes, but also your judgment, to see of what stuff and nature those beings are whom you call and consider to be gods. 2 This is stone, like the pavement under the feet; that one, metal, no better than the utensils forged for our use; this one, wood, and perhaps rotten wood by now; that one, silver, which needs a watchman to keep it from being stolen; ⁶ another, iron, subject to corrosion by rust; still another, earthenware, no better to look at than anything fashioned for the most ignoble service. Is it not so? 3 Are they not all of perishable material? Have they not been forged by iron and fire? On this one, a stonecutter has plied his craft, on that, a coppersmith, on a third, a silversmith, and on a fourth, a potter. Is it not so? And before they were shaped by the skill of these men to represent those several objects, did not every craftsman see in every one of them— and, in fact, does see in them even now—an object of different shape? And might not utensils of the same material be made to resemble objects like these, if they happened to be handled by the same craftsmen? 4 And conversely, might not these objects, now worshipped by you, be made by human hands into utensils resembling other utensils? Are they not all deaf and blind and lifeless and senseless and motionless? Are they not all rotting away, not all doomed to perish? 5 These things you call gods; these you serve; these you worship; and in the end you become like them! ⁷ 6 And here is the reason why you hate the Christians—they do not believe these objects to be gods. 7 You, of course, are firmly convinced you are glorifying them; yet do you not show all the more contempt for them? Do you not much rather make perfect laughingstocks of them if you leave unguarded the gods you worship, when they are made of stone or clay, while you lock up for the night those made of silver or gold, and post guards beside them in the day, to prevent their being stolen? 8 And as for the honors you imagine you pay them—well, if they are aware of them, you are actually punishing them; and if they lack sensation, you are showing them up by worshipping them with blood and victims' fat! 9 Just let one of you submit to such treatment; let one of you permit such things to happen to him! No, there is no human being that would voluntarily submit to such a punishment; for a human being feels and reasons. A stone, of course, submits; for it has no feeling. Therefore, you really disprove its sensibility, do you not? [8] 10 And so I might go on and on showing that Christians are not enslaved to gods like these. But if anyone should think even the little I have said to be inadequate, I consider it superfluous to say more.

3. Next I suppose you most desire to hear about the difference between their worship and that of the Jews. 2 Well, the Jews hold aloof from the worship just described, and in so far they are right in claiming to honor one God and Lord of the universe; but in so far as they offer Him this worship in a manner resembling the one just explained, they are altogether mistaken. 3 The Greeks, it is plain, make offerings to things insensible and deaf, and, by doing so, give proof of want of intelligence; the Jews, if they but realized [9] that they are making offerings to God exactly as if He needed them, might rightly consider this an act of folly rather than religion. 4 Surely, He *who made heaven and earth and all that is in them* [10] and supplies us with all we need, cannot Himself need any of the things He Himself provides to those who fancy they are giving them. 5 At any rate, people who believe they are performing sacrifices to Him by means of blood and victims' fat and whole burnt offerings, and honoring Him by such tokens of respect, do not seem to me to differ in the least [11] from people who display the same reverence toward insensible objects. Both fancy they are making real offerings, the latter to objects unable to appreciate the honor, the former to Him who stands in need of nothing! [12]

4. Furthermore, there is that fussiness of theirs in the matter of foods, their superstition [13] about the Sabbath, their bragging about their circumcision, and the show they make of the fast days and new moons.[14] These things are ridiculous and undeserving of consideration, and I do not suppose you wish me to instruct you about them. 2 In fact, is it not obviously wrong to accept some of the things created by God for the use of men as created for a useful purpose, and reject others as useless and superfluous? 3 And is it not impious to misrepresent God as forbidding an act of kindness on the Sabbath? [15] 4 And is it not ridiculous to vaunt the mutilation of the flesh as a mark of election,[16] as though men were in a singular manner beloved by God on its account? 5 Again, they closely watch the stars and the moon to regulate the scrupulous observance of months and days,[17] and by a distinction between the seasons which is due to God's arrangement, set aside some for festivals, others for times of sorrow— merely to suit their own inclinations! Who can consider this a proof of religion, and not, rather, of lack of understanding? 6 Now, then, I think you have learned enough to realize that the Christians are right in holding aloof from the thoughtless aberrations common to both groups, and, in particular, from the boastful officiousness of the Jews. But as regards the mystery of their own religion,[18] do not expect to be able to learn it from human lips.[19]

5. Christians are not distinguished from the rest of mankind by either country, speech, or customs; 2 the fact is, they nowhere settle in cities of their own; they use no peculiar language; they cultivate no eccentric mode of life. 3 Certainly, this creed of theirs is no discovery due to some fancy or speculation of inquisitive men; [20] nor do they, as some do,

champion a doctrine of human origin. 4 Yet while they dwell
in both Greek and non-Greek cities, as each one's lot was
cast, and conform to the customs of the country in dress,
food, and mode of life in general, the whole tenor of their
way of living stamps it as worthy of admiration [21] and ad-
mittedly extraordinary. 5 They reside in their respective
countries, but only as aliens.[22] They take part in everything
as citizens and put up with everything as foreigners. Every
foreign land is their home, and every home a foreign land.
6 They marry like all others and beget children; but they do
not expose their offspring.[23] 7 Their board they spread for
all, but not their bed. 8 They find themselves *in the flesh*,
but do not live *according to the flesh*.[24] 9 They spend their
days on earth, but hold citizenship in heaven. 10 They obey
the established laws, but in their private lives they rise above
the laws. 11 They love all men, but are persecuted by all.
12 They are unknown,[25] yet are condemned; they are put to
death, but it is life that they receive. 13 *They are poor, and
enrich many*; [26] destitute of everything, they abound in everything. 14 They are dishonored, and in their dishonor find
their glory. They are calumniated, and are vindicated. 15
They are reviled, and they bless; [27] they are insulted and
render honor. 16 Doing good, they are penalized as evildoers;
when penalized, they rejoice because they are quickened
into life. 17 The Jews make war on them as foreigners; [28] the
Greeks persecute them; and those who hate them are at a loss
to explain their hatred.

6. In a word: what the soul is in the body, that the
Christians are in the world.[29] 2 The soul is spread through
all the members of the body, and the Christians throughout
the cities of the world. 3 The soul dwells in the body, but

10 •

is not part and parcel of the body; so Christians dwell in the world, but are not part and parcel of the world.[30] 4 Itself invisible, the soul is kept shut up in the visible body; so Christians are known as such in the world, but their religion remains invisible.[31] 5 The flesh, though suffering no wrong from the soul, yet hates and makes war on it,[32] because it is hindered from indulging its passions; so, too, the world, though suffering no wrong from Christians, hates them because they oppose its pleasures. 6 The soul loves the flesh [33] that hates it, and its members; so, too, Christians love those that hate them. 7 The soul is locked up in the body, yet is the very thing that holds the body together; so, too, Christians are shut up in the world as in a prison, yet it is precisely they that hold the world together.[34] 8 Immortal, the soul is lodged in a mortal tenement; so, too, Christians, though residing as strangers among corruptible things, look forward to the incorruptibility that awaits them in heaven.[35] 9 The soul, when stinting itself in food and drink, fares the better for it; so, too, Christians, when penalized, show a daily increase in numbers on that account.[36] 10 Such is the important post to which God has assigned them, and they are not at liberty to desert it.

7. And no wonder.[37] It was not an earthly invention, as I have said, that was committed to their keeping; it was not a product of a mortal brain that they consider worth safeguarding so anxiously; nor have they been entrusted with the dispensing of merely human mysteries. 2 Quite the contrary! It was really the Lord of all, the Creator of all, the invisible God Himself, who, of His own free will, from heaven, lodged among men the truth and the holy incomprehensible Word,[38] and firmly established it in their hearts. Nor did He do this, as one might conjecture, by sending to men some subordinate,[39] whether angel, or principality, or one of those in charge of earthly things, or one entrusted with the administration of heavenly things. No, He sent the Designer and Architect of the universe in person [40]—Him by whom He created the heavens, by whom [41] He enclosed the sea within its proper bounds, whose inscrutable counsels [42] all the elements of nature faithfully carry out, from whom ⟨the sun⟩ has received the schedule of the daily courses it is to keep, whom the moon obeys as He bids her give light at night, whom the stars obey in following the course of the moon, from whom all things have received their order, their bounds, and their due place in the universe—the heavens and the things in the heavens, the earth and the things in the earth, the sea and the things in the sea, the fire, the air, the underworld, the things in the heights above, the things in the deep below, the things in the intermediate space.[43] Such was He whom He sent to them! 3 And did He do so, as a human brain might conceive, to tyrannize, to frighten, and to terrorize? 4 Certainly not! [44] On the contrary, His mission was an act of gracious clemency, as when a king sends his son who is himself a king! He sent Him as God. He sent Him ⟨as Man⟩ to men. The wish to save, to persuade, and not to coerce, inspired His mission. Coercion is incompatible with God. 5 His mission was an invitation, not a vindictive measure; an act of love, not an act of justice. 6 Some day, of course, He will send Him as a Judge and—who will then endure His coming! [45] . . . 7 ⟨Do you not see⟩ how they are thrown before the wild beasts to make them disown the Lord, and they refuse to be overcome? 8 Do you not see that the more of them are penalized, the more their numbers grow?

9 Such things do not point to a human agency. Here is the power of God, here the proofs of His abiding presence!

8. In fact, before He [46] came, what man at all understood what God is? 2 Or do you accept the nonsense trumped up by those pretentious philosophers, some of whom maintained that God was fire [47]—the very thing for which they are headed they call God!—while others said He was water, still others some other of the elements created by God? 3 And yet, if any one of these doctrines is acceptable, then every one of the rest of the creatures might just as well be proved to be God! 4 No, this is nothing but jugglery and imposture dished up by quacks. 5 No man has either seen or made known God; [48] but He has revealed Himself. 6 And He did reveal Himself by faith, through which alone it has been vouchsafed us to see God. 7 For God, the Lord and Creator of the universe, who made all things and assigned to each its proper place, not only proved Himself man's friend, but long-suffering as well. 8 But He always was and is and will be such—kind and good and unimpassioned and true; in fact, He alone is good. [49] 9 And after conceiving a great and unutterable purpose, He communicated it to His Son alone. 10 Now, as long as He kept His own wise counsel to Himself and guarded it as a secret, He was seemingly wholly unconcerned about us; [50] 11 but once He revealed it through His beloved Son and made known what had been prepared from the beginning, He granted us all things at once. He made us partake of His benefits, and see and comprehend things which none of us could ever have expected.

9. After, then, He had already planned everything in His own counsels in union with the Son, He yet permitted us, all through the intervening time, [51] to be carried away, just as we chose, by unruly passions—victims of *unbridled desires!* Not that He took at all delight in our transgressions; no, He merely exercised patience. Nor did He approve of that former era of wickedness, but, on the contrary, was all the time shaping the present era of holiness. It was His intention that we, after our own conduct in the past had proved us unworthy of life, should now be rendered worthy by the goodness of God, and that, after we had demonstrated our inability, as far as in us lay, *to enter the kingdom of God,*[52] should be enabled to do so by the power of God. 2 And when the cup of our iniquities was filled, and it had become perfectly clear that their wages—the punishment of death—had to be expected, then the season arrived during which [53] God had determined to reveal henceforth His goodness and power. O the surpassing kindness and love of God for man! [54] No, He did not hate us, or discard us, or remember our wrongs; He exercised forbearance and long-suffering! In mercy, of His own accord, He lifted the burden of our sins! [55] Of His own accord *He gave up His own Son* [56] as a ransom for us—the Saint for sinners, the Guiltless for the guilty, *the Innocent for the wicked,*[57] the Incorruptible for the corruptible, the Immortal for the mortal! 3 Indeed, what else could have covered our sins but His holiness? [58] 4 In whom could we, the lawless and impious, be sanctified but in the Son of God alone? 5 O sweetest exchange! O unfathomable accomplishment! O unexpected blessings—the sinfulness of many is buried in One who is holy, the holiness of One sanctifies the many who are sinners! 6 In the previous time He had demonstrated our nature's inability to win life, and now He revealed the Savior who is powerful to save even what is powerless; and on both grounds He wished us to have faith in His loving-kindness, to consider Him Nurse,

Father, Teacher, Counsellor, Physician, Mind, Light, Honor, Glory, Strength, Life, and—not to be solicitous about clothing and food! [59]

10. If this is the faith which you, too, desire, then you should, first of all, acquire a thorough knowledge of the Father. 2 The fact is, God loved men, and it was for their sake that He made the world; at their service He placed everything on earth; to them He gave reason and intelligence; them alone He endowed with the ability to look up to Him; them He formed after His own image; to them *He sent His Only-begotten Son;* [60] to them He promised the kingdom in heaven, and this He will give to those that love Him. 3 And when you have acquired this knowledge, with what joy do you think you will be filled! Or how intensely will you love Him who first loved you so! 4 And once you love Him, you will be an imitator of His kindness. [61] And you must not be surprised that man can become an imitator of God. He can, since He so wills. 5 Certainly, to be happy does not mean to tyrannize over one's neighbors, or to wish to have an advantage over the weaker ones, or to be rich and therefore able to use force against one's inferiors. It is not in such matters that one can imitate God; no, such matters are foreign to His majesty. 6 On the other hand, he who takes his neighbor's burden upon himself, [62] who is willing to benefit his inferior in a matter in which he is his superior, who provides the needy with what he himself has received from God and thus becomes the god of the recipients—he, I say, is an imitator of God! 7 Then [63] you will realize, while your lot is on earth, that God lives in heaven; then you will in good earnest discourse on the mysteries of God; then you will love and admire those who submit to punishment for their

refusal to deny God; then you will condemn the deceitfulness
of the world and its error once you understand the real life
in heaven, once you despise the apparent death here below,
once you fear the real death reserved for those who are
condemned to the eternal fire, which will forever [64] torment
those delivered up to it. 8 Then you will admire and pronounce happy those who, for conscience' sake, endure the
fire that lasts but for a while—once you grasp the nature of
that other fire.

* * * * *

11. There is nothing strange in my discourse, nor is my
argument contrary to reason.[65] No, after becoming a disciple
of Apostles, I am now becoming a teacher of the Gentiles.
What has been handed down I deliver exactly to such as
become disciples of the Truth. 2 Really, can anyone that has
been correctly taught and has fallen in love with the Logos,
fail to strive to learn exactly what has been plainly shown by
the Logos to disciples to whom the Logos appeared in person
and made revelations in plain language? He was not understood by unbelievers, but gave a detailed explanation to disciples, and these, reckoned by Him as trustworthy, came to
know the mysteries of the Father. 3 For this reason He sent
the Logos to appear in the world, who, discredited by His
people, was preached by Apostles, and believed by Gentile
nations. 4 He was [66] in the beginning, appeared new and
was found to be old, and is ever born anew in the hearts of
the saints. 5 He is the Eternal One, ⟨who⟩ today is accounted
a Son; by Him the Church is enriched, and grace,[67] ever
unfolding in the saints, is multiplied—the grace which grants
understanding,[68] reveals mysteries, announces seasons, glories
in believers, gives freely to seekers—such as do not break their

plighted troth [69] or transgress the bounds fixed by the fathers.[70] 6 And then fear of the Lord becomes a theme of song,[71] prophetic inspiration is recognized, the trustworthiness of the Gospels is firmly established, Apostolic tradition is observed, and the grace of the Church is exultant. 7 And if you do not grieve this grace,[72] you will appreciate what the Logos communicates through whomsoever He chooses and whenever He pleases. 8 After all, urged by love for the revelations made to us, we but share with you whatever, in obedience to the command of the Logos, we felt prompted to speak out with difficulty.

12. If you [73] read this and listen attentively, you will find out what blessings God bestows on those who love Him as they should. Since they become *a paradise of delight*,[74] they rear in themselves a fruitful tree in fullest bloom, and are adorned with a variety of fruit; 2 for in this garden *a tree of knowledge and a tree of life have been planted.*[75] But mark, it is not the tree of knowledge that is fatal; no, it is disobedience that is fatal. 3 In fact, there is deep significance in the Scripture text which states that in the beginning God planted ⟨*a tree of knowledge and*⟩ *a tree of life in the midst of paradise*, indicating that knowledge is the avenue to life. Because the first men did not make use of it with singleness of heart, they found themselves stripped by the deceit of the serpent. 4 Neither is there life without knowledge, nor is knowledge safe without true life. For this reason we find the two trees planted close to each other. 5 The Apostle saw the significance of this, and so he blames knowledge when applied to life without regard to the real force of the commandment, and says: *Knowledge makes conceited; it is love that builds up.*[76] 6 Certain it is that he who thinks he knows anything without a knowledge that is true and attested by life as genuine, has not yet learnt to know. He is deceived by the serpent, simply because he does not love life. But he who, guided by fear, has attained to full knowledge and goes in quest of life, can plant in hope and look for a harvest.[77]

7 As for you,[78] let knowledge be your heart, and your life the full realization of the true word. 8 When this is the tree you cultivate, and this the fruit you pluck, you will always harvest the blessings desirable in the sight of God—blessings which no serpent can touch, no deceit defile by its contact. Then Eve is not seduced; on the contrary, a virgin can be trusted. 9 Then, too, salvation is pointed out,[79] apostles are instructed, the Lord's Passover comes along, wax tapers are assembled and arranged in order, and the Logos delights to teach the saints—He who glorifies the Father. To Him be the glory for evermore. Amen.

NOTES

THE DIDACHE

INTRODUCTION

[1] The publication of the *Didache* precipitated a sensation among scholars such as has seldom been paralleled. In 1886 M. B. Riddle wrote in the Introductory Note of his translation (cf. ANF 7. 372 f.): 'At the close of 1883 he (Bryennios) published in Constantinople the text of the *Teaching*, with prolegomena and notes. A copy of the volume was received in Germany in January, 1884; was translated into German, and published Feb. 3, 1884; translated from German into English, and published in America, Feb. 28, 1884; Archdeacon Farrar published (*Contemporary Review*) a version from the Greek in May, 1884. Before the close of the year the literature on the subject, exclusive of newspaper articles, covered fifty titles . . . in Western Europe and America.'

Since then there has been a vast output of text editions, translations, monographs, and smaller studies of the *Didache*. Bibliographies may be found in the standard histories of early Christian literature (Bardenhewer, Altaner-Ferrua, etc.); cf. also H. Leclercq, 'Didaché,' *Dict. d'archéol. chrét. et de lit.* 4. 1 (1920) 794-98. In an incisive study, 'Die Lehre der zwölf Apostel, eine Schrift des ersten Jahrhunderts' (*Zeitschr. f. kath. Theol.* 10 [1886] 629-76), K. München shows convincingly that 'there is nothing in the contents of the *Didache* to compel us to date it beyond the year 100, or even the year 70.' The intricacies of the problem which must be met by those who date it in the second and third centuries, can best be seen by a study of a series of articles that appeared in the *Journal of Theological Studies* from vol. 13 (1912) on for many years, and in the *Downside Review* 55 (1937).

[2] 'The fact that the *Didache* does not yet know the presbyterate as a third office, intermediary between the episcopate and the diaconate, is an infallible proof of its great antiquity' (A. Ehrhard, *Urkirche und Frühkatholizismus* [Bonn 1935] 93). 'We believe . . . that it (the *Didache*) certainly belongs to the last decades of the first

century. . . . It testifies to thoughts and institutions that are unquestionably primitive' (P. Batiffol, *Primitive Catholicism* [trans. by H. L. Brianceau from the 5th ed. of *L'Eglise naissante*, New York 1911] 105).

[3] See München's essay referred to in n. 1. E. J. Goodspeed, 'The Didache, Barnabas, and the Doctrina,' *Anglic. Theol. Rev.* 27 (1945) 228-47, comes to the conclusion, based on a study of the parallel portions in *Doctrina, Didache,* and Barnabas, that 'the Greek document of which *Doctrina* is a translation is the basic "Two Ways" underlying all six—Didache, Barnabas, Church Ordinances, Summary of Doctrine, Fides Nicaena, and Life of Schnudi; and, through the Didache, influencing also the Didascalia and the Apostolic Constitutions.' Goodspeed's article was written in criticism of F. E. Vokes's *The Riddle of the Didache.* See n. 10.

[4] J. B. Lightfoot, *The Apostolic Fathers* (ed. by J. R. Harmer, London 1898) 215 f., may be quoted as representing the opinion prevailing among scholars for decades: 'The work is obviously of very early date. . . . Indications point to the first or the beginning of the second century as the date of the work in its present form.' The primitive character of the Didachist's vocabulary is pointed out by K. München, *op. cit.* 648. T. Klauser, *op. cit.* 2, terms the document *pervetusta.* I am greatly indebted to Klauser (*ibid.*) and to O. Bardenhewer, *Geschichte der altkirchlichen Literatur* I (2nd ed., Freiburg i. Br. 1913) 93 f., for the summaries that follow.

[5] Cf. Klauser, *ibid.*

[6] Following the example of H. Lietzmann, *Messe und Herrenmahl* (Arbeiten z. Kirchengesch. 8, Bonn 1926) 231 ff., Klauser proposes the following rearrangement of Chapters 9 and 10 as necessary for their understanding: 9. 1-9. 4; 10. 6; 10. 1-10. 5; 10. 7; 9. 5; and this in spite of the fact that the Didachist shows a good sense of order everywhere else in the treatise!

[7] *Ep. ad Traian.* 96. 7.

[8] Note that the Greek word for 'confession of sins' in Mark 1. 5 is ἐξομολογεῖσθαι, while the same writer uses μετανοεῖν (1. 15) to express 'conversion,' not 'confession.' We have the same terminology in the *Didache.*

[9] 'He who has trained his eye by a study of *the later liturgies,*' says H. Lietzmann, *op. cit.* 236, 'will not for a moment doubt where these sentences (10. 6) belong: after the blessing of the elements and before Holy Communion; therefore *before* the prayer in 10. 1-5,

and *before* the direction given in 9. 5.' Naturally, since 'confession' (see n. 8 on μετανοεῖν!) precedes Holy Communion, it follows that 10. 6 belongs before 10. 1!

¹⁰ H. Connolly's main argument for relegating the *Didache* to the third century is that 'it would have satisfied any Montanist as authority for the distinct teachings and practices of his sect.' Accordingly, he says, a Montanist of the third century 'intended,' by writing the *Didache*, 'to provide that authority' ('The Didache and Montanism,' *Downside Rev.* 55 [1937] 339). But is it at all likely that a Montanist of the third century, merely 'to provide authority' for two teachings dear to Montanists (fasting, and providing prophets with money), would go to the trouble of composing an entire treatise on *early* Church life? This does not, of course, preclude the possibility of the *Didache* as we know it being a Montanist 'edition' of the original. Cf. also B. T. D. Smith's review (*Jour. of Theol. Stud.* 40 [1939] 287 f.) of the ardent espousal of Connolly's theory by F. E. Vokes, *The Riddle of the Didache, Fact or Fiction, Heresy or Catholicism?* (London, 1938). See the reference to Goodspeed's article above, in n. 3.

¹¹ Cf. F. X. Funk, *Patres apostolici* 1 (Tübingen 1901) 20 f.; H. L. Strack–P. Billerbeck, *Kommentar zum Neuen Testament aus Talmud und Midrasch* 4. 1 (Munich 1928) 236.

¹² See F. L. Cirlot, *The Early Eucharist* (London 1939) 30.

¹³ *Ibid.*; italics are Cirlot's.

¹⁴ For the Jewish heritage in the Christian liturgy, see C. W. Dugmore, *The Influence of the Synagogue upon the Divine Office* (Oxford 1944). E. Peterson thinks that the prayers in Chapters 9 and 10 are parts of a Christological hymn used by Christians of Jewish extraction in Palestine, which was later incorporated into the Eucharistic liturgy. See his article, 'Didache cap. 9 e 10,' *Ephem. liturg.* 58 (1944) 3-13.

¹⁵ Cf. J. P. Christopher, *St. Augustine: The First Catechetical Instruction*, (ACW2 (1946) 3 and 7. For the Church's method of catechizing educated persons, see the *Ep. to Diognetus*.

TEXT

¹ This shorter title was no doubt the label attached to the outside of the scroll; the fuller follows in the next sentence. 'Of the Lord': based on words of the Lord and on 'the Lord's ways' (11. 8). The

instruction is represented as being vouched for, and passed on, 'by the Twelve Apostles'; but the use of the Greek preposition rendered 'by' does not specify in what sense the Apostles are considerd responsible for the contents. J. A. Robinson, 'The Didache,' *Jour. of Theol. Stud.* 35 (1934) 224, offers the attractive suggestion that, in composing this 'remarkable title,' the author was thinking of the last words in St. Matthew's Gospel (28. 18-20).

[2] The metaphor of 'Two Ways' for two modes of living was familiar to Greeks (Hercules!) and Jews (Matt. 7. 13 f.). Cf. A. Harnack, *Die Apostellehre und die jüdischen beiden Wege* (Leipzig 1886). References to Greek literature are given by R. Knopf, *Die Lehre der zwölf Apostel. Die zwei Klemensbriefe* (Handb. z. Neuen Test., Ergänzungsb: Die apostolischen Väter 1, Tübingen 1920) 4. Cf. also Sr. M. J. Suelzer's observations in ACW 4 (1947) 191 n. 68.

[3] Matt. 22. 37, 39; Deut. 6. 5; Lev. 19. 18.

[4] For the Golden Rule (here in negative form), see Matt. 7. 12. Cf. L. J. Philippidis, *Die "Goldene Regel," religionsgeschichtlich untersucht* (Leipzig 1929).

[5] Matt. 5. 44, 46 f.; Luke 6. 27 f., 32 f. 'Fast for your persecutors': prayer is made more effective by fasting. Knopf compares Hermas, *Sim.* 5. 3. 7: 'Fast, and reckon the price of the foods which you would have eaten, and give it to a widow or an orphan or to someone in need.' See Robinson, *art. cit.* 231; R. H. Connolly, 'Canon Streeter on the Didache,' *Jour. of Theol. Stud.* 38 (1937) 270 f.

[6] Either: 'you will have no enemy' (your conduct will win them over; 1 Peter 2. 15), or, better, be perfect (see 1. 4) and 'have no enemy'; treat no one as an enemy.

[7] 'And bodily' is used in the codex found by Bryennios; but an older witness, the first of two papyrus fragments dating from the fourth century, does not have the expression.

[8] 1 Peter 2. 11.

[9] Matt. 5. 39, 48.

[10] *Ibid.* 40.

[11] Luke 6. 30.

[12] 'You cannot do it': either, 'you are powerless anyway,' since a poor Christian was not likely to obtain redress from a wealthy pagan (Funk); or: since you are striving for perfection, 'you cannot bring yourself to insist on redress.'

[13] Luke 6. 30; Matt. 5. 42. In the following the sense of ἰδίων is not clear; either, as in the text, 'His own,' or, the Father wants His

gifts, 'though possessed by individuals,' to be shared. Cf. Robinson, *art. cit.* 232-36.

[14] Here are echoes of Matt. 5. 25 f.; see also Matt. 18. 34. This section likewise shows a marked affinity with Hermas, *Mand.* 2. 4-6; hence the perennial chronological question: who is dependent on whom? Cf. Klauser, *op. cit.* 11.

[15] This saying is not found in the Bible; but see Eccli. 12. 1. The precept in Luke 6. 30 is here not annulled, but modified. Cf. Augustine, *Enarr. in Ps.* 102. 12: 'Desudet eleemosyna in manu tua, donec invenias iustum, cui eam tradas.' See also Barnabas 1. 4.

[16] 'A further,' not 'a (or, the) second commandment.' For the following, cf. Matt. 19. 18; Exod. 20. 13-15, 17; Barnabas 19. 4. The practice of magic was widespread in antiquity. Cf. Acts 8. 9 ff.; 13. 6-8.

[17] Matt. 5. 33; 15. 19; 19. 18.

[18] Cf. Prov. 21. 6. For sins of the tongue, see James 3. 5 ff.

[19] 'Covetous, or hypocritical': greed and hypocrisy are often branded in the early Christian writers. See Barnabas n. 187. Cf. A. Vögtle, *Die Tugend- und Lasterkataloge im Neuen Testament* (Neutest. Abh. 16, Münster i. W. 1936).

[20] The *Didache* seems to distinguish three groups: one should be corrected, another needs our prayer, a third should be loved even with the sacrifice of one's own life. Still, if 'no man' is to be hated, then *all* men are to be loved, though this love will manifest itself in different ways according to circumstances: 'love one group by correcting its faults, another by praying for it, still another by sacrificing your life for it.' If this is the Didachist's meaning, the phrase 'as a proof of your love' belongs in sense to all three groups.

[21] The proper address for one *reborn* by baptism. Note the impressive and affectionate use of the singular number.

[22] The word ζηλωτής is sometimes used in a good sense (1 Cor. 14. 12; Gal. 1. 14; Titus 2. 14); another possible meaning is 'jealous.' There were, however, 'fanatics' among the Jews that were ready to resort to violence in their opposition to the Romans. See the commentaries on Luke 6. 15, where Simon is called 'the Zealot.' On the presence of Ch. 3 in the *Didache*, see R. H. Connolly, 'The *Didache* in Relation to the Epistle of Barnabas,' *Jour. of Theol. Stud.* 33 (1932) 241 f.

[23] One who divined future events by observing the flight of birds. 'Enchanter': charmer. 'Expiator': a professional diviner and an

expert on purificatory ceremonies. For particulars, see W. L. Knox, 'Περικαθαίρων (Didache III, 4),' Jour. of Theol. Stud. 40 (1939) 146-9; F. Cumont, Les religions orientales (4th ed., Paris 1929) 151-79.

[24] One given to groundless self-conceit and empty pride, vices that tempt one to make a show in the world and, as a means to it, to commit theft, fraud, robbery, embezzlement, etc.

[25] The grumbling here condemned is querulous discontent with divine Providence. An αὐθάδης is self-willed, headstrong, arrogant, making light of authority, 'not afraid to bring in new and blasphemous ways of thought' (2 Peter 2. 10 [Knox]).

[26] Ps. 36. 11; Matt. 5. 4.

[27] A description of a 'quiet' man (one quietly attending to his own affairs) is given in 1 Thess. 4. 11. The quotation that follows is from Isa. 66. 2.

[28] Giving up former associations with 'the mighty' and keeping company with 'the holy and lowly' is often a severe trial to converts. Cf. Rom. 12. 16; James 2. 2, 3. An ἐνέργημα ('casualty') is an action or effect brought about by some external force or agency, esp. demons, in the sense in which we speak of 'blows of adversity,' 'strokes of fortune,' the 'knocks' of life.

[29] Heb. 13. 7. 'His lordship': God's greatness and majesty. 'There is the Lord': cf. Matt. 18. 20. 'The saints': as the Israelites were 'the holy ones' because God had selected them from the other nations and set them apart to serve Him (cf. Ps. 51. 11), so a Christian is 'holy' or 'a saint' for the same reason (cf. 1 Peter 2. 9). The word has, of course, also a more restricted sense. In 10. 6, the context requires the wider sense (without excluding the narrower). See Intro. 10.

[30] Deut. 1. 16, 17; Prov. 31. 9.

[31] An obscure saying, which also occurs in Barnabas 19. 5. Coming after the expression, 'be just in your judgment,' the sense may be: and once you have reached a decision, 'do not doubt' whether the rebuke should be administered or not. See Barnabas n. 179.

[32] The interpretation depends on whether the comma is after σου or before διά; hence 1) if you have means 'at your disposal' or 'by the labor of your hands'; 2) pay a ransom 'by (the right use of) your hands' (that is, by almsgiving). Cf. Tob. 4. 11; 12. 9; Luke 11. 41.

[33] Cf. Acts 2. 44; 4. 32; Rom. 15. 27.

[34] For these and similar special injunctions to members of the household, see T. Klauser's note on this passage; also E. G. Selwyn, *The First Epistle of St. Peter* (London 1947), who discusses (471-80) the Jewish and Gentile use of ethical codes and the primitive Christian code or codes in the N. T. For the New Testament, compare Eph. 5. 22-6. 9; Col. 3. 18-4. 1; 1 Peter 2. 18-3. 7. See also K. Weidinger, *Die Haustafeln. Ein Stück urchristlicher Paränese* (Unters. z. Neuen Test. 14, Leipzig 1928) 56-58.

[35] 'Come' and 'call' are eschatological terms. They are also key words in the treatises on salvific grace.

[36] Even the life of a slave is ennobled by the habit of seeing God in his masters. See Eph. 6. 5; also Rom. 13. 1 ff.

[37] See Barnabas n. 184.

[38] Cf. Deut. 4. 2; 13. 1 (12. 32).

[39] 'In church': when the congregation meets. See 14. 1. The author means public confession, whether individual or general, with or without sacramental absolution. See K. Prümm, *Christentum als Neuheitserlebnis* (Freiburg i. Br. 1939) 399; B. Poschmann, *Paenitentia secunda* (Epiphaneia 1, Bonn 1940) 88-92.

[40] Cf. Matt. 15. 19; Mark 7. 21 f.; Rom. 1. 29 f.; Gal. 5. 20. For a study of such lists of virtues and vices, see A. Vögtle, *op. cit.*

[41] Cf. Rom. 12. 9.

[42] Cf. Ps. 4. 3; Isa. 1. 23.

[43] Cf. Wisd. 5. 12. 'Destroyers of God's image': procurers of abortion (the old Latin translation has *abortuantes*). For the passage, cf. F. J. Dölger, 'Das Lebensrecht des ungeborenen Kindes und die Fruchtabtreibung in der Bewertung der heidnischen und christlichen Antike,' *Antike u. Christentum* 4 (1934) 23 f. See Barnabas n. 190.

[44] Cf. Matt. 24. 4.

[45] 'The Lord's yoke': this is not a reference to Matt. 11. 29 f. 'In its entirety': including commandments and counsels; others understand the words of those practices 'quae ascetae subire consueverunt, praecipue de abstinentia carnali' (Klauser, following Harnack). Cf. Matt. 19. 21.

[46] Many converts from Judaism were slow to realize that the new religion had abrogated the law concerning 'common and unclean food' (Mark 7. 19; Acts 10. 15). To them the proclamation of perfect freedom (1 Cor. 10. 23) was a *sermo durus*. Even the Apostles assembled in council (A. D. 49 or 50) demanded of pagan converts abstention from sacrificial meat, from blood, and from what

is strangled (Acts 15. 29). When the *Apocalypse* was written, these regulations were found to be unpractical and went out of force (Apoc. 2. 14, 20); but both the *Apocalypse* and the *Didache* insist on avoidance of sacrificial meat (no doubt, for the reason given in 1 Cor. 10. 20), and the latter still counsels abstaining from the two other kinds of food, for those 'who can stand it.' If we knew for certain when this passage was penned (see Intro. 4 ff.), we might know whether Montanist asceticism could, or could not, be held responsible for the counsel here given. 'Dead gods': cf. Ps. 113 B. 4; Isa. 40. 18 ff.; 1 Cor. 8. 4 and 10. 20.

[47] Apparently the author now addresses the pagans who have just been baptized. But this is not certain, since the tract beginning with Ch. 7 may be a later addition to the introductory tract addressed to catechumens. Note the use of the plural number in 'Baptize.' Were all Christians permitted to take upon themselves the work of 'explaining' all the points mentioned earlier, or was it reserved to certain officials in the Church? Ignatius of Antioch (*Smyrn.* 8. 2) says: 'It is not permitted without authorization from the bishop either to baptize or to hold an agape.' But the plural use of 'you' here should not be overstressed.

'After first explaining': the Didachist does not consider infant baptism. For the baptismal formula, see Matt. 28. 19; Justin, *Apol.* 1. 61. A shorter formula (Acts 8. 16) is indicated in 9. 5.

[48] Lit., 'in living water'; therefore, not in pools or cisterns, but in fountains, streams, and the like. Tertullian (*De bapt.* 4) states that this requirement was not essential. On this passage, cf. T. Klauser, 'Taufet in lebendigem Wasser!' *Pisciculi, Stud. F. J. Dölger* (Münster i. W. 1939) 157-64.

[49] The author envisages the possibility of lack of water sufficient for immersion; in such a case baptism was to be conferred by infusion.

[50] See also Justin, *Apol.* 1. 61. 2; Tertullian, *De bapt.* 20. 1.

[51] 'The hypocrites': the Pharisees or, perhaps, the Jews in general. See Barnabas n. 187. The converts here addressed evidently lived in Jewish surroundings. For the Jewish practice of fasting, see H. Strack—P. Billerbeck, *op. cit.* 2 (1924) 241-44; 4. 1 (1928) 77-114. 'Wednesdays and Fridays': the very days preferred in our modern practice. The same days are mentioned as fast days by Tertullian (*De ieiun.* 2) and Clement of Alexandria (*Strom.* 7. 12. 75. 2). Cf. J. Schümmer, *Die altchristliche Fastenpraxis* (Liturgiegesch. Quellen u. Forsch. 27, Münster i. W. 1933) 95-99.

[52] Matt. 6. 5; 6. 9-13. 'The Gospel': either that of St. Matthew or all four Gospels taken as a unit. Some writers wonder why the Didachist finds it necessary to quote the Lord's Prayer in full. But where or when were pagans to learn this prayer if not in their first instruction? The beautiful doxology at the end is not found in all manuscripts of the Gospels. Note also the omission of the words 'the kingdom.' See F. H. Chase, *The Lord's Prayer in the Early Church* (Texts and Stud. 1. 3, Cambridge 1891).

[53] The Jews were accustomed to recite certain prayers twice a day, morning and evening, corresponding to our Lauds and Vespers. Regarding the Christian practice of prayer at the third, sixth, and ninth hours, cf. Tertullian, *De or.* 25; *De ieiun.* 10; Clement of Alexandria, *Strom.* 7. 7. 40. 3. See A. Baumstark, *Vom geschichtlichen Werden der Liturgie* (Freiburg i. Br. 1923) 13 ff.

[54] Chapters 9 and 10 are a unit; see Intro. 7 ff. Some think that they describe the *agape*, the ancient Christian love feast (see Ignatius, *Smyrn.* 8. 2: ACW 1 [1946] 93 and 142 n. 30); cf., e. g., R. H. Connolly, 'Agape and Eucharist in the Didache,' *Downside Rev.* 55 (1937) 477-89. Others hold that there can be question of the celebration of the Eucharist only; cf., e. g., H. Lietzmann, *op. cit.* A summary of the views of scholars on this much-disputed section is given by A. Arnold, *Der Ursprung des christlichen Abendmahls im Lichte der neuesten liturgiegeschichtlichen Forschung* (Freiburg i. Br. 1937) 23-29. Cf. also M. Dibelius, 'Die Mahlgebete der Didache,' *Zeitschr. f. d. neutest. Wissenschaft* 37 (1938) 32-41; R. D. Middleton, 'The Eucharistic Prayers of the Didache,' *Jour. of Theol. Stud.* 36 (1935) 259-67; F. L. Cirlot, *op. cit.* 30 ff.

The word εὐχαριστία by itself is ambiguous. In the New Testament it means 1) thankfulness; 2) a giving of thanks, esp. for God's blessings. In the present passage note the article: ' *the* peculiar (well-known, customary) thanksgiving'; and since the context shows that the writer thinks of the Christian Eucharist, the rendering 'regarding the Eucharist' is justified. Furthermore, the Eucharist is called θυσία in 14. 1-3; see also Ignatius, *Ephes.* 13. 1; *Philad.* 4. 1; *Smyrn.* 7. 1; 8. 1.

The Eucharistic prayers are here set off as dialogue. Note the recurrence of the doxology, 'To Thee be the glory for evermore'; also the animated versicles and responses in 10. 6. There is no indication of the clerical rank of the λειτουργός or minister who leads the congregation in this exchange of prayer. Most noteworthy is the use of the plural in 'We give Thee thanks,' which survives in the Ordinary of the Mass today, and generally in the Liturgy, and exemplifies St. Peter's characterization of the entire Church as 'a holy priesthood' (1 Peter 2. 5). Cf. K. Prümm, *op. cit.* 325.

⁵⁵ The expression may have been modelled on 'The Root of David.' There is, perhaps, an allusion to Ps. 79. 15. The 'Vine' has been interpreted as a symbol of Christ (see John 15. 1), or of Israel (the Church), or of the Blood of Christ in the Eucharist, or of life. For patristic parallels, cf. J. Quasten, *Monumenta eucharistica et liturgica vetustissima* (Flor. Patr. 7, Bonn. 1935) 10 n. 6.

⁵⁶ Cf. Acts 3. 13 and 26; Clement of Rome 59. 2. In Matt. 12. 18 the rendering 'Servant' (not 'Son') seems imperative.

⁵⁷ 'The breaking of the bread': this expression came in course of time to designate the celebration of Mass and Holy Communion; but caution is needed in interpreting certain texts in the New Testament; as Luke 24. 35; Acts 2. 42, 46; 20. 7, 11; 27. 35; 1 Cor. 10. 16.

⁵⁸ There are numerous references in the New Testament to 'life and knowledge' as Christ's unique gift to mankind; e. g., Luke 1. 77; 2 Cor. 4. 6; John 3. 15; 5. 26; 6. 68 f. The *life*-giving principle of the Church is the Eucharist.

⁵⁹ 'One mass': St. Cyprian beautifully develops this idea to illustrate the unity of Christ and the Church; cf. *Ep.* 63. 13; 69. 5. Since the Didachist speaks of the bread as having been first scattered over the hills (or mountains), many scholars infer that these Eucharistic prayers originated in Palestine. See Intro. 4.

⁶⁰ The idea of Israel being 'scattered' and then 'gathered' was familiar to the Jews: Deut. 28. 25; Jer. 34. 17; Judith 5. 23; Ps. 146. 2. Cf. Ps. 105. 47: 'Congrega nos de nationibus.' 'Thy kingdom': the Greek admits of two interpretations; 1) may Thy Church be gathered 'into Thy kingdom,' and 2) may Thy Church 'become Thy kingdom' (Matt. 24. 31). See also n. 52. 'From the ends of the earth': the Apostolic Fathers frequently refer to the universality of Christ's kingdom or the Church; cf. Clement of Rome 42; 60. 4; *Didache* 10.5; Ignatius, *Smyrn.* 1. 2; 8. 2; *Ephes.* 3. 2; Barnabas 5. 7; 7. 5 ('the new people'); *Mart. Pol.* inscr.; 5. 1; *Ep. ad Diogn.* 6. 2.

⁶¹ Matt. 7. 6. In liturgical language τὸ ἅγιον came to mean Holy Communion; in the Old Testament it was used for sacrificial meat: Lev. 22. 14.

⁶² 'Enshrined' (cf. John 1. 14): this may mean 1) that God dwells

in us, which is literally true in Holy Communion; or 2) that through Holy Communion God is glorified in us (John 13. 31). 'The name of God': God's nature, power, and majesty; a common Biblical use.

[63] Cf. Wisd. 1. 14; Eccli. 18. 1; Apoc. 4. 11. 'Because Thou art mighty': cf. 'propter magnam gloriam tuam' in the *Gloria*. In the following, observe the use of two different verbs ('given' and 'vouchsafed' or 'graciously given') to designate the order of nature (ordinary food) and the order of grace (the Eucharist).

[64] 'Remember': cf. '*Memento*, Domine, famulorum tuorum,' occurring in the Roman Missal. 'Thy Church' recalls '*my* Church' in Matt. 16. 18. 'Deliver': cf. '*Libera* nos, Domine, ab omnibus malis.'

[65] Cf. Matt. 24. 31.

[66] 'Grace': For Χάρις as a name for Christ, cf. F. J. Dölger, *Sol Salutis. Gebet und Gesang im christlichen Altertum* (Liturgiegesch. Forsch. 4-5, 2nd ed., Münster i. W. 1925) 206-9.

Owing to Christ's warning (Matt. 24. 42) and to a misunderstanding of St. Paul's teaching (1 Thess. 4. 15), there was a widespread impression among the early Christians that the end of the world and the glorious coming of Christ were near at hand. The end of the world was prayed for (Apoc. 22. 17, 20).

[67] Matt. 21. 9 and 15; also 22. 42-45.

[68] 1 Cor. 16. 22. The Aramaic *maran atha* = 'the Lord has come'; if written *marana tha*, the meaning is 'Lord, come.' The latter form seems preferable here, since this wish for the Lord's *parousia*—His coming—is also expressed at the close of the Apocalypse (22. 20). Cf. J. Sickenberger, *Die Briefe des heiligen Paulus an die Korinther und Römer* (Die hl. Schrift des Neuen Test. 6, 4th ed., Bonn 1932) 88.

[69] Because of their charismatic endowments prophets were not bound by either the tenor or the length of the foregoing thanksgiving.

[70] The Didache knows three classes of men engaged in teaching Christian doctrine: 1) *doctors*—men distinguished for their gift of imparting doctrine; 2) *apostles*—itinerant preachers of the Gospel; we should say 'missionaries'; 3) *prophets*—resident or itinerant Christians, who are endowed with charisms and instruct, comfort, encourage, rebuke, stimulate, their hearers. Cf. 1 Cor. 14. 1 ff.; Eph. 3. 5. Cf. Klauser's note, and his reference to A. v. Harnack, *Mission und Ausbreitung des Christentums* 1 (4th ed., Leipzig 1924) 332-77.

[71] Cf. Matt. 7. 15 ff.; 10. 5 ff.; Luke 9. 1-6; 10. 4 ff.

[72] 'One day': an apostle must keep going from place to place; the work begun by him could be carried on by another. Eusebius, *Hist. eccl.* 3. 37, speaks of the fruitful activity of these wandering evangelists. St. Francis Xavier was an 'apostle' of the kind here described. Hospitality, a necessary and highly valued virtue in antiquity, was often abused. Cf. D. W. Riddle, 'Early Christian Hospitality,' *Jour. of Bibl. Lit.* 57 (1938) 141-54. 'A false prophet': one who utters falsehood under the plea of divine inspiration, or, as here, one who abuses the privileges accorded a true prophet.

[73] Compare the instructions which Christ gave to His disciples for their first missionary tour: Matt. 10. 9 ff.; Mark 6. 8 ff.; Luke 9. 3.

[74] 'In ecstasy': lit., 'in the Spirit,' under the special influence of the Holy Spirit.' Cf. 1 Cor. 12. 3; 14. 2; Apoc. 1. 10; etc. 'Do not test him': that is, by watching his behavior. This sort of testing, when needed, was prescribed by Our Lord: Matt. 7. 20. 'Entertain no doubts': the prophet is supposed to have already been tested; to doubt in such a case would be a sin against the Holy Spirit. Cf. Matt. 12. 31; also Mark 3. 28 f.

[75] 'The Lord's way': poverty, humility, self-sacrifice in the service of others. See Phil. 2. 21: 'Quae sua sunt quaerunt, non quae sunt Iesu Christi.'

[76] Possibly for the holding of an agape. Cf. K. Völker, *Mysterium und Agape. Die gemeinsamen Mahlzeiten in der alten Kirche* (Gotha 1927).

[77] Compare Matt. 23. 3; Ignatius, *Ephes.* 15. 1, 2.

[78] Many commentators (cf. Klauser, note) think that the reference is to some unusual or reprehensible marriage relationship lived in by the prophet, who thus symbolized 'in an earthly manner' the Church, that is, her spiritual nuptials with Christ; in 'the Prophets of old' there may be an allusion to the Prophet Osee (1. 2 ff.) and his 'wife of fornications.' There is a passage in Irenaeus that shows affinity with the present text: *Adv. haer.* 4. 24. 12.

[79] Cf. Matt. 10. 8: 'Gratis accepistis, gratis date.'

[80] Ps. 117. 26; Matt. 21. 9. 'Coming,' as a travelling preacher would, 'in the name of the Lord,' that is, to teach Christian doctrine, or, simply, on the ground that he is 'a Christian' (Matt. 10. 40 ff.).

[81] The Greek expression seems to be modelled on Jonas 4. 11, where mention is made of men that do not know the difference between right and wrong ('that do not have right and left understanding').

⁸² Cf. 2 Thess. 3. 10; Acts 18. 3.

⁸³ 'A Christmonger' (so Bigg), 'a trader in Christ': religion is not to be turned into a source of lucre; 1 Tim. 6. 5; but note Knox's rendering: 'Religion, they think, will provide them with a *living*.' Compare St. Paul's self-defense in 1 Cor. 9. 3 ff.

⁸⁴ Matt. 10. 10; 1 Tim. 5. 18; cf. also 1 Cor. 9. 13.

⁸⁵ The Jews had been commanded to do the same for their priests: cf. Exod. 22. 29 f.; Num. 15. 19 ff.; Deut. 18. 3 f.; 2 Esdr. 10. 37. So, too, the ancient Romans offered to their gods and priests their *primitiae*—the first grain, the first beans, the first grapes, etc.; cf. G. Wissowa, *Religion und Kultus der Römer* (2nd ed., Munich 1912) 409 f. The *Didache* is silent about tithes, unless the remark in 13. 7 be so interpreted. It is important to note that the 'prophets' are likened to the Jewish high priests; they were, therefore, *officials* of one kind or another. Were they also 'priests' in the Christian sense? See below, 15. 1, and n. 93.

⁸⁶ Lit., 'On the Lord's day of the Lord': a somewhat pleonastic expression, to present the idea that the Sunday is very specially set aside to honor the Lord. The term 'the Lord's Day' for 'Sunday' is also found in the *Apocalypse* (1. 10). Ignatius, *Magn.* 9. 1, states that Christians 'no longer observe the Sabbath, but regulate their calendar by the Lord's Day.' In the second century Melito of Sardes (Eusebius, *Hist. eccl.* 4. 26) wrote a treatise on *The Lord's Day*. For the history of the Sunday observance from its New Testament beginnings, see H. Dumaine, "Dimanche," *Dict. d'archéol. chrét. et de lit.*, 4. 1 (1920) 858 ff.

Since the *Didache* is not a manual for the use of bishops and deacons, but addressed to the 'people,' it follows that the two imperatives 'break' and 'offer' express the subordinate thought of the sentence, while the leading thought is contained in the participle, 'assemble to break break.' This use of the participle is not unusual in Greek.

⁸⁷ 'To break bread and offer thanks': a reference to Chapters 9 and 10; hence, 'to celebrate the Eucharist.' 'First confess your sins': this reminds us of the *Confiteor* at the foot of the altar before Mass begins. Note here, as in 4. 14, the technical term for 'confession,' not to be confused with the exhortation 'to be converted' in 10. 6. See Intro. n. 8.

⁸⁸ Cf. Matt. 5. 23 f.

⁸⁹ Since in the *Didache* Κύριος uniformly means Christ (Inscr.;

6.2; 8.2; 9.5; 10.5; 12.1), we have here an Old Testament prophecy (Mal. 1.11, 14) ascribed to Our Lord.

⁹⁰ 'Accordingly': a significant οὖν. The preceding chapter mentioned Mass, Holy Communion, and confession as part of the regular Sunday service, and *therefore* it was necessary for each community to have its bishops and deacons. The contemporary Clement of Rome (44.4) says that it was the duty of 'presbyters' to 'offer the gifts of the people.' Each community had to have men in its midst qualified to exercise such functions.

⁹¹ 'Elect': it was the privilege of 'the people' to elect candidates for these offices. The custom of electing ecclesiastical superiors was continued till deep into the Middle Ages. That these men also needed ordination by the proper authorities (cf. 1 Tim. 4.14; 5.22; 2 Tim. 1.6) the Didachist does not say; nor does he explain the manner of offering the Eucharist (9.5), or the manner of conducting the Sunday services (14.1). His purpose is not to instruct bishops, but pagan converts. See A. Ehrhard, *Urkirche und Frühkatholizismus* (Bonn 1935) 91 ff.

'Bishops and deacons': this terse expression raises many vexing problems. Compare its use in Phil. 1.1 and see Polycarp n. 46. Note the plural number in 'bishops.' If the writer meant bishops in the later technical sense, he probably had in mind several occasions or several communities (Funk). But since the terminology of Church officials was still in a flux at that early date, the plural 'bishops' was perhaps meant to mean 'a bishop and his presbyters.' Also the term 'deacon' is far from clear-cut, since in the New Testament (Rom. 15.8; Mark 9.35; etc.) even Christ, the High Priest, is called διάκονος; again, Apostles and other eminent men are grouped together as διάκονοι in 1 Cor. 3.5; Col. 1.7; 4.7; 1 Thess. 3.2; 1 Tim. 4.6; etc. The fact that the *Didache* makes no mention of 'presbyters,' although Clement of Rome speaks of them frequently, must have some bearing on its date of composition. See Intro. n. 2.

⁹² See St. Paul's list of qualities demanded of bishops: 1 Tim. 3.2 ff.; Titus 1.7 ff.

⁹³ The *Didache* distinguishes two classes of Church officials: 1) bishops and deacons; 2) prophets and teachers. The first group owed its power or jurisdiction as leaders of the Church (τετιμημένοι) to their appointment by the Apostles or their successors (see 1 Tim. 4.14; 5.22; and the letters of Ignatius); the second, to their charisms (τὸ Πνεῦμα). Both groups served the spiritual needs of the people

($\dot{v}\mu\hat{\iota}v$). The verb λειτουργέω and its derivatives occur fifteen times in
the New Testament; in six passages they denote a 'priestly' function
(Luke 1. 23; Rom. 15. 16; Heb. 8. 2; 8. 6; 9. 21; 10. 11). Since *all*
these men were active in 'building up the Body of Christ' (Eph.
4. 11, 12; Acts 13. 2; 1 Cor. 12. 28), it has been argued that the
persons called 'prophets and teachers' had priestly power, that is,
were in reality 'presbyters.' Note, moreover, that in 13. 3 the
'prophets' are compared to the Jewish high *priests*. Finally, in 10. 7
the 'prophets' are mentioned as enjoying certain privileges in the
celebration of the Eucharist. Here, as elsewhere, the *Didache* leaves
much unsaid.

[94] The fact that the prophets and teachers were, apparently, more
highly honored than the bishops and deacons is generally adduced as
one of the reasons for ascribing to the *Didache* a very early date of
composition. Bishops and deacons, the Didachist says, must not be
slighted: they do the same work as prophets and teachers.

[95] On the duty of administering and accepting correction, see
Clement of Rome 56.

[96] This section continues the exhortations of Ch. 14. The Greek
here may mean, 'nor should he hear from you,' and is generally so
rendered. But after telling the converts that, when anyone offends
his neighbor, 'no one should speak with him,' it is a very jejune
advice to add that the offender 'should not hear from you.' We gain
a better meaning if we take the Greek verb in the passive sense, 'to
be spoken of.' The translation in the text agrees with the admonition
of Ignatius, *Smyrn.* 7. 2: 'Avoid associating with such people and
do not even speak about them.' Cf. Ps. 15. 4: 'Nec pronuntiabo
nomina eorum labiis meis.'

[97] See n. 52. The expression 'as you have it in the Gospel' seems
to indicate the existence of a written Gospel.

[98] The Lord comes soon and suddenly. See Matt. 24. 42, 44;
25. 13; Luke 12. 35; Eph. 6. 14; 1 Peter 1. 13.

[99] 'In great numbers' (Funk), or 'often' (Knopf). Compare
Ignatius, *Ephes.* 20. 2; 13. 1; *Pol.* 4. 2.

[100] Cf. Barnabas 4. 9.

[101] The severest trials are to come just before the end of the world:
Matt. 10. 22; 24. 5 ff.; Mark 13. 13; Clement 35. 4.

[102] Cf. Matt. 24. 10 ff.; 7. 15; 2 Peter 3. 3.

[103] The author speaks of the Antichrist ('claiming to be the Son
of God'); cf. Apoc. 12. 9; 2 John 7; Matt. 24. 24; 2 Thess. 2. 4, 9;
Apoc. 13. 2, 13, 14; 19. 20. See Barnabas 4. 3.

[104] 'The fiery test': 1 Peter 4. 12. The quotation following is from Matt. 24. 10, 13. 'The Accursed': probably a designation of Christ, who will then be cursed by the reprobates. Others interpret the word of Antichrist, referring to Apoc. 22. 3. See Barnabas n. 87.

[105] Matt. 24. 30. It will then be shown or 'proved' that Christ had preached the truth, and that in announcing the end of the world He had spoken the truth; these 'signs' will establish the fact that Christ is 'the Truth' (John 14. 6).

[106] Others explain the expression as 'a sign spread out in heaven,' that is, Christ appearing on the Cross with outstretched arms, the joy of the redeemed, the terror of the damned. Still others derive the word from πέτομαι: 'a being caught up, a flying up, to heaven.' Cf. 1 Thess. 4. 17. For 'the sounding of the trumpet,' see Matt. 24. 31.

[107] Cf. Zach. 14. 5; 1 Thess. 3. 13; Matt. 24. 30; 26. 64.

THE EPISTLE OF BARNABAS

Introduction

[1] Compare the summaries given by F. X. Funk, *Patres apostolici* 1 (2nd ed., Tübingen 1901) xx-xxxii; K. Bihlmeyer, *Die apostolischen Väter*, 1. Teil (Tübingen 1924) xx-xxiv; T. Klauser, *Doctrina duodecim apostolorum. Barnabae epistula* (Flor. Patr. 1, Bonn 1940) 5-13. The date of composition is ably discussed by M. d'Herbigny, 'La date de l'épître de Barnabé,' *Rech. de science rel.* 1 (1910) 417-43, 540-66. This writer bases his conclusions mainly on Daniel's apocalyptic statement quoted in Barnabas 4. 5, instead of the mention of the stumbling block in 4. 3 and the reference to a restoration of the Temple in 16. 4. The most recent attempt at solving the Barnabas-puzzle is found in K. Thieme's able study, *Kirche und Synagoge* (Olten 1944). See also H. Veil, 'Barnabasbrief,' in E. Hennecke's *Neutestamentliche Apokryphen* (2nd ed., Tübingen 1924) 503; J. Muilenberg, *The Literary Relations of the Epistle of Barnabas and the Teaching of the Twelve Apostles* (Marburg 1929).

[2] E. J. Goodspeed discusses the problem of literary dependence in his article, 'The Didache, Barnabas, and the Doctrina,' *Anglic. Theol. Rev.* 27 (1945) 228-47. Cf. *Didache*, Intro. n. 3.

[3] See *Didache* n. 46.

[4] See H. J. Schoeps, *Die Tempelzerstörung des Jahres 70 in der jüdischen Religionsgeschichte* (Coniect. Neotest. 6, Uppsala 1942) 1-45.

[5] Thus Thieme, *op. cit.* 29 f.; 225. J. Lebreton, *Histoire du dogme de la Trinité* 2 (Paris 1928) 332, considers the epistle 'almost heretical.'

[6] This milder interpretation of Barnabas's view of the Old Testament institutions is in accord with the *Epistle to the Hebrews* (7. 18), where the writer characterizes the Aaronitic priesthood, though instituted by God, as 'useless,' merely because, compared with the priesthood of Christ, it lacked 'completeness,' 'finality,' absoluteness (τελείωσις).

[7] See M. Meinertz, *Einleitung in das Neue Testament* (4th ed., Paderborn 1939) 159.

[8] See T. Klauser, *op. cit.* 7-12; K. Bihlmeyer, *op. cit.* xxiii. See the introduction to the *Didache*, 13.

TEXT

[1] The salutation is unique in ancient Christian epistolography. Cf. 7. 1; 9. 7; 15. 4; 21. 9.

[2] For the difficult word δικαίωμα (cf. also 2. 1; 4. 11; 10. 2; 10. 11; 16. 9; 21. 1; 21. 5), see G. Schrenk, *Theol. Wörterb. z. N. T.* 2 (1935) 223-27.

[3] Predicated of man, πνεῦμα is that part which gives life (Luke 8. 55); or the rational part which thinks, wills, feels (Matt. 5. 3); or the spirit of man under the influence of the Holy Spirit (Rom. 8. 16). Significant uses of the term in this epistle are in 1. 5; 7. 3; 9. 7; 19. 2; 21. 9.

[4] Cf. Titus 3. 5-7. 'The Lord's fountainhead': or, 'from the Fountainhead, the Lord.' Compare τῆς καρδίας in 6. 15; 16. 7.

[5] 'Since': either 'from the time when' or 'seeing that,' 'inasmuch as' I spoke to you. 'Holiness': the Greek word means fundamentally 'what is right' in one sense or another, or 'the doing of what is right' (cf. Matt. 3. 15). Compare the same word used in 1. 6; 3. 4; 4. 12; 13. 7; 14. 7; 20. 2.

[6] 'I, too': in imitation of Jesus; John 3. 16; 10. 11. 'More than myself': cf. also 4. 6; 19. 5; *Did.* 2. 7. See below, n. 180.

[7] Titus 1. 2; 3. 7.

[8] The writer's aim is to help his readers to a genuine knowledge, an enlightened understanding, of the economy of salvation in general, and of the Old Testament in particular. His ultimate purpose is to fortify them against the great temptation (4. 3) now threatening them. See n. 13.

⁹ Titus 1. 2; 3. 7. Early Christianity was properly aware of the value of the three theological virtues: faith, hope, and love. 'The first' (lit., 'the beginning'): through hope of life men are attracted to the faith (cf. Polycarp 1. 3 and 3. 3 with nn. 12 and 30). 'The last' (lit., 'the end'): animated by this hope, they persevere in the faith.

¹⁰ 'Holiness': right living, the keeping of the commandments, justification; see n. 5. Love 'radiates (or, results in) genuine happiness': cf. Acts 2. 28 and 46; 1 Peter 1. 8. The text here is uncertain. See Polycarp 3. 1 and n. 25.

¹¹ 'The Master': a term used particularly often by Clement of Rome; cf. ACW 1 (1946) 106 n. 35. For the Biblical usage, see H. Rengstorf, *Theol. Wörterb. z. N. T.* 2 (1935) 43-48. 'The past': especially the precepts given to the Jews; 'the future': a reference to the final stumbling block (4. 3).

¹² 'Not as a teacher': so again in 4. 6, 9. Why this disclaimer of authority? See the Intro. 29, 34. Is Barnabas perhaps thinking of Matt. 23. 8 ff., where the Apostles are admonished not to call themselves Rabbis or teachers? Or was he conscious that he did not qualify as a 'prophet' or a 'teacher,' but merely as an 'apostle' (*Did.* 11. 3 and 13. 2 with nn. 70 and 93), who, after visiting the Church here addressed wished to keep in communication with it by means of this letter?

¹³ Eph. 5. 16. 'The Agent': that is, of evil; 'the evil power-at-work'; cf. Eph. 2. 2; 6. 12; 2 Thess. 2. 9, 11. Further references to the Devil are found below: 2. 10; 4. 10; 9. 4; 12. 9; 18. 1; 20. 1. In Apoc. 12. 9 no fewer than five titles for the Devil are piled up in one sentence. See nn. 36 and 187. The readers possess faith already; if they listen to Barnabas, they will also acquire 'wisdom, understanding, insight, and knowledge' (see 21. 5). The use of synonyms for the sake of fullness is a known rhetorical device. This is the first hint in Christian literature of St. Anselm's maxim: 'Credo ut intellegam' (St. Augustine: 'Crede ut intellegas').

¹⁴ Barnabas uses the term both in the strict and in the wider sense ('inspired writer or spokesman').

¹⁵ Isa. 1. 11-13. 'My court': the courts of the tabernacle and of the temple. 'New moon': the Jewish festival held at the time of the new moon. See *Ad Diogn.* 4. 1 and n. 14.

¹⁶ It was generally held that, in Barnabas's opinion, the ceremonial Law was, from the start, not meant to be taken literally, but to

convey an exclusively spiritual lesson. Some scholars, however, dissent. See n. 121 and Intro. 33. The expression 'He has superseded (invalidated)' seems to imply that it had been valid for some time. See K. Thieme, *Kirche und Synagoge* (Olten 1944) 30, 225. Barnabas's main contention, that the relation between the Old Testament and the New is that of 'promise' and 'fulfillment' or of 'type' and 'reality,' is of course correct. See Jer. 31. 31 ff., Matt. 5. 17.

¹⁷ 'The New Law': a law of love; John 13. 34; 1 John 2. 7. In the writer's opinion, the ceremonial law was a *yoke forced* upon the Jews by a bad angel. See n. 121. According to Origen, *Comm. in Ex. hom.* 4. 6, the Mosaic Law was intended as a disciplinary measure, a means of punishment and correction. The Law of Christ is a law of freedom (James 1. 25). The Christian 'oblation' is not a 'man-made one,' because both the Offerer and the Gift offered are divine. Cf. 1 Cor. 5. 7; Heb. 9. 11 ff.

¹⁸ Jer. 7. 22 f.

¹⁹ Zach. 8. 17; 7. 10.

²⁰ 'As *they* did': the Jews. 'Going astray': in Barnabas's time the Jews, and perhaps some Judaizing Christians, hoped that the rebuilding of the temple would lead to a revival of the Jewish religion. Cf. Acts 15. 5; Gal. 2. 12. See n. 29.

²¹ Cf. Ps. 50. 19. The latter part of the quotation is not found in the Bible; but cf. Irenaeus, *Adv. haer.* 4. 29. 3.

²² Cf. Isa. 58. 4 f.

²³ *Ibid.* 6-10. 'Your light': the night of calamity will be followed by a dawn of prosperity; 'your healing' (the reading ἰάματα seems preferable to ἱμάτια): the Jewish commonwealth, now ravaged by social and other evils, will be speedily restored to health. E. J. Kissane (*The Book of Isaiah* 2 [Dublin 1941] 233) remarks that the Hebrew word rendered 'healing' literally means 'the new flesh' which 'sprouts' and gradually covers the old wound. 'Holiness': the nation will, on its pilgrimage through life, like the Jews wandering through the desert, enjoy God's special protection. Cf. Exod. 13. 21; 14. 19. The word here rendered 'violence' may mean no more than 'pointing the finger of scorn'; for this contemptuous gesture, cf. Prov. 6. 13.

²⁴ 'In (or, through) His Beloved': an affectionate reference to Our Lord. Cf. Eph. 1. 6; see also my remarks on Ignatius, *Magn.* inscr.: ACW 1. 125 n. 1; *ibid.* 58. 'Unadulterated': a faith based on the genuine sense, not merely on the letter, of the Law.

²⁵ 'The present situation': the present age, the trend of the times, the Zeitgeist, with special reference to the great temptation (4. 3); hence almost 'the present crisis.' Somewhere in the early years of Hadrian's reign, the Jewish hopes for the restoration of the temple had, it seems, owing to the emperor's conciliatory policy, reached a climax. See K. Thieme, op. cit. 13 f., 221 f.

²⁶ The rebuilding of the temple was a stumbling block, a severe temptation, to many Jewish-Christians; it was 'final' because the Antichrist (cf. Did. 16. 4 f.) was predicted to precede the end of the world. Another rendering of the Greek noun would be 'the Archseducer.' The quotation is not found in the apocryphal Book of Henoch as it has come down to us, but the author may have had in mind certain sections of this work, 89. 61-64 and 90. 17.

²⁷ Cf. Dan. 7. 24.

²⁸ Ibid. 7. 7. Daniel's apocalyptic statement has been the subject of much debate. It is doubtful whether any certain information regarding the date of this epistle can be drawn from the quotation. For the most recent discussion of a possible allusion to the reign of certain Roman emperors, see K. Thieme, op. cit. 226-28. See above, n. 1.

²⁹ 'Now': at this juncture; in the present crisis. See nn. 25 and 26. 'Certain people': evidently, Christians of Jewish descent who were wavering in their adherence to Christianity. 'Ours also': it is ours in the sense in which a type is merged in the reality (the Synagogue being a type of the Church); not in the sense that a type is still valid after the reality has appeared. Cf. Heb. 10. 1 and Matt. 5. 17. See n. 121.

³⁰ The expression εἰς τέλος is puzzling. Some render 'completely,' 'forever,' 'once for all'; but the Jews did not forfeit the covenant forever (Rom. 11. 25; Matt. 23. 39; Luke 13. 35; Apoc. 7. 1-8). If Barnabas is here thinking of the final conversion of the Jews, the phrase may be rendered 'in the end,' 'finally,' or, better, 'till the end,' 'up to the end.' See nn. 146 and 150. However, the somewhat drastic rendering 'forever' or 'once for all' would be in keeping with the writer's generally sweeping assertions in speaking of the Jews.

³¹ A conflation of Exod. 31. 18 and 34. 28.

³² Cf. ibid. 32. 7; Deut. 9. 12.

³³ 'Sealed in our heart': see F. J. Dölger, Sphragis (Stud. z. Gesch. u. Kult. d. Altert., Paderborn 1911) 108.

³⁴ For this expression, see Ignatius, *Ephes.* 8. 1, and my remarks ACW 1. 122 n. 25. This sentence, like some others in this letter, is a grammatical puzzle. See n. 162.

³⁵ For this and the following, see *Did.* 16. 1-3.

³⁶ A designation for the Devil, which explains itself when we note that his helpers—'the angels of Satan'—rule the Way of Darkness (18. 1); for the passage and similar instances in the ancient Christian documents, cf. F. J. Dölger, *Die Sonne der Gerechtigkeit und der Schwarze* (Liturgiegesch. Quellen und Forsch. 14, Münster i. W. 1916) 49 ff. See nn. 13 and 187.

³⁷ It is 'idle,' futile, worthless, 'nonsense,' to look forward to a restoration of the Jewish religion. For the Greek word rendered 'idle' in the Apostolic Fathers (27 instances), see below, Polycarp 2. 1; 7. 2, with n. 15. 'The Wicked Way': see Ch. 20.

³⁸ Is Barnabas perhaps warning his readers against the hermit life then beginning in Egypt? (Thieme, *op. cit.* 229). The Fathers frequently recommend regular attendance at Church meetings as an effective means of stifling heretical or schismatical tendencies. See Clement of Rome 34. 7; Ignatius, *Ephes.* 5. 3; *Magn.* 7; *Pol.* 6. 1.

³⁹ Isa. 5. 21. Instead of hoping for the building of the temple of stone, let the readers try to be 'a finished (spiritual) temple.' See 16. 1 ff. For the idea, see Ignatius, *Ephes.* 9. 1 f. The next quotation is from Isa. 33. 18.

⁴⁰ Cf. 1 Peter 1. 17; Rom. 2. 11; Gal. 2. 6.

⁴¹ 'Called': the members of the Church; Rom. 1. 6 f.

⁴² Matt. 20. 16; 22. 14.

⁴³ Cf. Heb. 12. 24; 1 Peter 1. 2. See n. 97.

⁴⁴ Isa. 53. 5, 7; Clement of Rome 16. 7.

⁴⁵ 'The past': here probably the expiatory death of Christ.' The future': the Judgment to come.

⁴⁶ Prov. 1. 17. 'The Way of Darkness': here, especially, the Jewish ceremonial Law regarded as binding for all time.

⁴⁷ Gen. 1. 26. Barnabas offers three considerations to show the need or appropriateness (*convenientia*) of the Incarnation; 1) 5. 5-7: by His own death and His resurrection Jesus destroyed the power of death; 2) 5. 8-10: men confidently approach Him whose unveiled sight would be unbearable to them; 3) 5. 12-6. 7: Jesus fulfilled what the Prophets had foretold about His sufferings. In Gen. 1. 26 the plural 'we' is a reference to the Blessed Trinity; see M. A. van den Oudenrijn, "Genesis I 26 und Grundsätzliches zur trinitarischen Auslegung," *Divus Thomas* 15 (1937) 145-56.

12 ⁸

⁴⁸ 'The gift': that is, of prophesying. In the New Testament the word generally rendered 'grace' sometimes means an 'office' or 'ability' bestowed on a person by the *grace* of God for the salvation of others (cf. Eph. 4. 7; 1 Peter 4. 10). See also G. P. Wetter, *Charis* (Leipzig 1913) 94.

⁴⁹ Cf. 1 Tim. 3. 16. 'It was ordained': the verb δεῖ often indicates 'necessity' arising from a decree or ordinance of God.

⁵⁰ Cf. 2 Tim. 1. 10. 'Establish the truth of the resurrection': the Jews either denied the possibility of a resurrection (as did the Sadducees), or else had no certainty of it (1 Cor. 15. 20 ff.).

⁵¹ An exaggeration, of course; but see Matt. 9. 10-13 (the last verse is here quoted); Origen, *C. Cels.* 1. 62; also Jerome, *Adv. Pel.* 3. 2, who quotes the present passage, but ascribes it to Ignatius. Barnabas is thinking of Matthew, the tax collector, Peter (Luke 5. 8), Paul-Saul (1 Cor. 15. 9; 1 Tim. 1. 15), Judas, etc. 'Revealed Himself as the Son of God': by the miracles which accompanied the calling of the Apostles (Luke 5. 8; John 1. 46; 2. 11; compare also 2 Peter 1. 16-18); but note that the particle τότε need not cover the same moment as ὅτε, and may mean 'later.' Besides, the power to make 'saints' out of 'sinners' is by itself a sufficient proof of Christ's divinity.

⁵² A commonplace with the Fathers; e. g. Theophilus, *Ad Autol.* 1. 5; Minucius Felix, *Oct.* 32. 5 f.; Cyril of Jerusalem, *Cat.* 10. 7; 12. 13; etc.

⁵³ Cf. Luke 11. 47 ff.

⁵⁴ Cf. Zach. 13. 7; Matt. 26. 31.

⁵⁵ Cf. Ps. 21. 21; 118. 120; 21. 17.

⁵⁶ Cf. Isa. 50. 6 f.

⁵⁷ 'The command': that is, to die for our sins. See Luke 24. 26.

⁵⁸ Isa. 50. 8 f. 'The Servant': Christ. Cf. Matt. 12. 18; Acts 3. 13; *Did.* 9. 2, 3; Clement of Rome 59. 2, 3, 4 ('Son' or 'Servant'); *Mart. Pol.* 14. 1; 20. 2; *Ad Diogn.* 8. 9, 11.

⁵⁹ The meaning of the Greek word is not quite clear. The allusion may be to Matt. 21. 44 (omitted in some MSS); but the formation of the word (τρίβω) seems to indicate that Barnabas thought of Christ as 'a strong stone' specially fit to be 'polished' for ornamental purposes. This agrees well with what follows.

⁶⁰ Cf. Isa. 28. 16.

⁶¹ Cf. *ibid.*

⁶² Cf. Isa. 50. 7.

[63] Cf. Ps. 117. 22; Matt. 21. 42.

[64] Cf. Ps. 117. 23 f.; 1 Peter 2. 6.

[65] See above, n. 34.

[66] Ps. 21. 17; 117. 12; 21. 19.

[67] Cf. 1 Tim. 3. 16.

[68] Isa. 3. 9 f.; Wisd. 2. 12.

[69] Cf. Exod. 33. 1, 3; Lev. 20. 24.

[70] 'Passible': that is, receptive of, or suffering, a change; here, 'capable of being moulded into a human being.' There is a double allusion to Christ: His 'suffering' to be made out of earth into the Second Adam, and His 'suffering' physical pain and death to redeem the first Adam.

[71] Cf. Eph. 4. 22-24. See Ignatius, *Magn.* 5. 2: 'The believers, animated by love, bear the stamp of God the Father through Jesus Christ.' Cf. J. F. Dölger, *Sphragis*, 113. f.

[72] Gen. 1. 26, 28. 'Our fair creation': Adam and Eve—a really fine appreciation of God's handiwork in the human compound (cf. Gen. 1. 10, 12; etc.). See n. 195.

[73] This verse is not found in Scripture, but may be a reminiscence of Matt. 19. 30 (20. 16) and, perhaps, even of Eph. 1. 10: 'omnia *instaurare* in Christo.'

[74] Cf. Gal. 6. 15.

[75] Cf. Ezech. 11. 19; 36. 26. 'Dwell in us': cf. Eph. 3. 17.

[76] See n. 39. The genitive καρδίας is epexegetic.

[77] Cf. Ps. 41. 3.

[78] Cf. *ibid.* 21. 23; 107. 4. 'We, then': that is, the Church.

[79] 'Milk and honey': 'faith' and the Word, that is, the written word of the Gospels and the teaching of them (κήρυγμα) by the Church.

[80] In the final rebirth (Matt. 19. 28; Luke 22. 30), when the elect are 'perfect heirs of the covenant' (see 6. 19), they will have power (ἄρχειν) and authority (ἐξουσία) over all inanimate creation, which Adam possessed in the state of original justice (Gen. 1. 28; 2 Peter 3. 13). Compare the description of the 'Messianic peace' in Isa. 11. 6 ff.; Rom. 8. 19 ff.; Papias, Fr. 1.

[81] 2 Tim. 4. 1.

[82] Cf. Matt. 27. 34, 48.

[83] Lev. 23. 29. 'The vessel of His spirit': His body. The fast prescribed to the Jews was a type of the sufferings of Christ.

[84] This quotation is not found in the Bible; it was probably known

to the writer from Jewish rituals. Cf. F. X. Funk, *Patres apostolici* I (2nd ed., Tübingen 1901) 58 f.

⁸⁵ 'To me': Christ is speaking. 'The new people': the Christians. Cf. Luke 1. 17.

⁸⁶ Cf. Ps. 68. 22; Matt. 27. 34, 48.

⁸⁷ Cf. Lev. 16. 7 ff. 'Accursed'': Lev. 16. 8, 10. Compare the strange expression κατάθεμα in the *Didache*, 16. 5 and n. 104.

⁸⁸ Source unknown. Cf. Justin, *Dial.* 40. 3; Tertullian, *C. Marc.* 3. 7.

⁸⁹ 'Wreathed': prefiguring the crown of thorns. 'That Day': the *parousia*; 1 Cor. 3. 13; 1 Thess. 5. 4. 'The scarlet robe': Apoc. 1. 13; also Matt. 27. 28 and Wisd. 5. 3, 5.

⁹⁰ 'They shall be struck (or, terrified)': that is, when to their own horror the infidel Jews then 'see' with their own eyes that the glorified Christ is the very one whom *they* had pierced (John 19. 37; Apo. 1. 7). The actual piercing was done by the Romans, but it was done as part of the crucifixion, for which the Jews were responsible.

⁹¹ Cf. Matt. 11. 12 and Luke 16. 16.

⁹² What follows is an amplification of Num. 19. In characterizing the old men in this uncomplimentary way, Barnabas is probably thinking of the 'sinners' whom they typified: Matt. 26. 45. 'Sanctified': St. Paul mentions the ceremony of sprinkling with hyssop and the ashes of a heifer to show the effects of Christ's sacrifice: Heb. 9. 13, 19.

⁹³ 'He speaks': that is, the Lord. 'Gone are the men': this is probably the meaning of the Greek, a sort of pious ejaculation after the mention of these cruel men. See n. 92. Their 'glory' consisted in offering a heifer as a type of Christ. Barnabas seems to say: Let us forget about these pitiful figures and their pitiful sacrifice, and turn to the Apostles (Funk). The supposition of a corrupt text (Lightfoot, Lake) or of a marginal gloss (Bosio) does not seem necessary.

⁹⁴ See Matt. 19. 28. 'To represent': a μαρτύριον in the wider sense is a thing or person that puts one in mind of another thing or person, as when one represents another. While Jesus was alive, the Apostles were to limit their activity to 'the lost sheep of the house of Israel' (Matt. 10. 5 f.; Acts 26. 7).

⁹⁵ 'Great in the sight of God': Barnabas was not anti-Semitic in the modern sense. His abhorrence of the Jews was not racial. The Synagogue was to him a divinely established type of Christianity;

but, of course, he abhorred a return to it after it had been invalidated by Christ. Cf. Thieme, *op. cit.* 231.

[96] The Cross, and a reminiscence of 'the life-giving tree' (Apoc. 2. 7; Gal. 3. 13; cf. also Ps. 95. 10). See Justin, *Dial.* 73. 4; also recall the lines by Venantius Fortunatus in *Vexilla regis prodeunt*:

> *Regnavit a ligno Deus;*

and the lines in the same author's *Pange lingua gloriosi*:

> *Crux* fidelis, inter omnes
> *arbor* una nobilis.

[97] Cf. Heb. 9. 19; John 19. 29. The sprinkling of the people 'with water and scarlet wool and hyssop' was a type of the cleansing of the soul from sin through the Passion and death of Christ. 'In His kingdom': in His Church here on earth. 'Foul and evil times': times defiled by sins committed after baptism. The Christian who sins 'is to be saved' and cleansed from sin 'by the foulness of the hyssop': by the Passion of Christ, which is the antitype of the hyssop dipped in lustral water that had been made foul or muddy by the ashes of a heifer (Funk). Perhaps, too, hyssop was pulverized and mixed with the water. The Christian who relapses into sin after baptism is said to be 'ailing in regard to the flesh,' that is, 'ailing through the frailty of the flesh or human nature.' The word rendered 'flesh' is often used in the New Testament for 'frail human nature' (cf. Gal. 5. 19). In framing this sentence Barnabas may have remembered 1 Peter 3. 21, where all three important words ('save,' 'body' or 'flesh,' and 'foulness') occur; but there St. Peter says that Christian baptism is *not* a cleansing of *bodily* or outward defilement, while Barnabas indicates that the Passion of Christ *does* cleanse anyone ailing through the frailty of human nature. His statement is, therefore, a reference to confession after baptism.

[98] 'Obscure to them': to the Jews, blinded by their misinterpretation of the purpose of the ceremonial Law. 'They did not understand': that is, so *listen* as to understand. Cf. Mark 4. 12.

[99] Ps. 17. 45. The New Latin Psalter reads: '*ad primum auditum obedivit mihi.*'

[100] Cf. Isa. 33. 13.
[101] Cf. Jer. 4. 4.
[102] Cf. *ibid.* 7. 2.
[103] Cf. Ps. 33. 13, and Exod. 15. 26.
[104] Cf. Isa. 1. 2. 'To serve as evidence': not found in the original.

This 'evidence' is for or against one, according as one does, or does not, listen to the voice of the Lord. The following quotations are also from Isaias: 1. 10 and 40. 3.

[105] This view is peculiar to the writer. His tendency is to over-allegorize. However, his saying, 'He did not speak,' may be only a drastic way of saying, 'He did not speak exclusively.' See Intro. 33. 'A bad angel': see Hermas, Mand. 6. 2. 1 (ἄγγελοι τῆς πονηρίας); Lactantius Inst. 2. 15. 8 (depravati angeli). This statement, if taken literally, could not have been made by any of the Apostles. Possibly, 'a bad angel' may mean no more than 'an evil suggestion,' as we speak of 'a good angel' when we mean 'a good suggestion,' See n. 121.

[106] Cf. Jer. 4. 3 f. and Deut. 10. 16. It will not do to sow 'good seed' (Matt. 13. 24)—the seed of Christian doctrine—in ground overrun with thorns (cf. Mark 4. 19). The idea of spiritual circumcision was not unknown to the Old Testament; cf. Jer. 4. 4; Deut. 10. 16; Lev. 26. 41. See Acts 7. 51; Rom. 2. 25 ff.

[107] Cf. Jer. 9. 25.

[108] 'As a seal': that is, a seal of the covenant with God. Rom. 4. 11. On circumcision as a seal, cf. F. J. Dölger's study on baptism as a seal, Sphragis 51-54.

[109] Cf. Dölger, op. cit. 52 f.

[109a] 'Children of love': the phrase is Hebraic in character; cf. similar expressions in Luke 16. 8; John 12. 36; 1 Thess. 5. 5; 2 Thess. 2. 3; etc. The idiom means that one who is a 'child' of a person or thing is considered of like nature with, and deriving his chracter from, that person or thing. Cf. 'children of joy' in 7. 1; 'children of love and peace' in 21. 9.

[110] 'In three letters': Barnabas, as Klauser remarks, forgets that the Lord did not speak to Abraham in Greek. In Greek, which uses letters to designate numbers, IH stands for 18. The same letters, transcribed (= IE), are also the initial letters of IESOUS (ΙΗΣΟΥΣ). We have here the earliest literary attestation of this abbreviation for the names of Jesus; see J. Finegan, Light from the Ancient Past (Princeton 1946) 320.

[111] Cf. Gen. 14. 14 and 17. 23-27.

[112] The Greek letter T symbolized the number 300. Other writers allegorized the number 318 in the same manner: cf., e. g., Clement of Alexandria, Strom. 6. 11. 84; Ps.-Cyprian, De Pasch. comp. 10.

[113] Cf. James 1. 21. Barnabas here ascribes his own gnosis to divine inspiration.

[114] Cf. Lev. 11 and Deut. 14.

[115] Cf. Deut. 4. 1, 5.

[116] Regarding this passage and the ancient view that fish belong to the lowest class of living beings, cf. F. J. Dölger, ΙΧΘΥΣ 2 (2nd ed. Münster i. W. 1928) 26 and 43-49.

[117] Cf. Lev. 11. 5.

[118] Cf. Aelianus, *De anim.* 1. 25; Clement of Alexandria, *Paed.* 2. 10. 83. 4; etc.

[119] The source of the quotation is unknown. 'Seducer': Klauser (50), referring to 20. 2, translates 'procurer of abortion.' Barnabas's assertion concerning the physical changes in the hyena reflects a view commonly held by the ancients: cf. Pliny, *Hist. nat.* 8. 30; Tertullian, *De pall.* 3; etc.

[120] Cf. Lev. 11. 29. For the following, cf. Aelianus, *op. cit.* 2. 55.

[121] It is difficult to understand how a Christian can deny, as Barnabas does, that the Law given to the Jews had any force at all, and was solely intended to convey to them a spiritual lesson. As O. Bardenhewer, *Geschichte der altkirchlichen Literatur* 2 (2nd ed., Freiburg i. Br. 1913) 104, states, it would appear that the author's singular point of view was never again set forth by any theologian in the Church.

[122] Ps. 1. 1.

[123] Cf. Lev. 11. 3.

[124] Barnabas seems to mean the manifold ablutions customary among the Jews. See Mark 7. 3 ff.

[125] Jer. 2. 12 f., freely quoted. Barnabas never hesitates to reword the Septuagint when it suits his purpose.

[126] Cf. Isa. 16. f.

[127] Cf. *ibid.* 45. 2 f. 'Invisible treasures': prefiguring the graces connected with baptism.

[128] Cf. *ibid.* 33. 16-18.

[129] Ps. 1. 3-6.

[130] Ezech. 20. 6? Soph. 3. 19? 'The land of Jacob': the body of Christ. 'The vessel of His spirit': see 7. 3.

[131] Cf. Ezech. 47. 1-12. 'Will live forever': perhaps an echo of John 6. 51.

[132] Cf. Acts 8. 38; Hermas, *Sim.* 9. 16. 6 f.

[133] Cf. 4 Esd. (apocryphal) 4. 33; 5. 5.

[134] Cf. Exod. 17. 8 ff. The incident related in the following is often referred to by the early Fathers as signifying the Cross and

the Divine Victim upon it: cf. Justin, *Dial.* 90. 4; 111. 1; Tertullian, *Adv. Iud.* 10; Cyprian, *De exhort. mart.* 8; etc.

135 Isa. 65. 2. 'I extended my arms': a prophecy of the Crucifixion.

136 Cf. Num. 21. 6 f.; John 3. 14 f.

137 Cf. Deut. 27. 15.

138 Cf. Num. 21. 7 f. In the original, God is speaking, not Moses.

139 Jesus = Josue, the son of Nun (= Nave); cf. Num. 13. 17.

140 Cf. Exod. 17. 14.

141 Ps. 109. 1 (Mark 12. 36).

142 Cf. Isa. 45. 1, which reads 'to Cyrus' (Κύρῳ) for 'to (my) Lord' (κυρίῳ). To the Jews, Christ the Messias was the *son* of David, but David himself calls Him 'Lord,' that is, 'God.'

143 Cf. Mark 12. 37; Matt. 22. 45.

144 'For us or for them': in reality, for both: for them, originally; for us, after their rejection. The quotation which follows is from Gen. 25. 21 f. (cf. Rom. 9. 10-12).

145 Cf. Gen. 48. 11, 9.

146 Cf. Gen. 48. 13-19. Barnabas changes the words, but gives the sense, of the original. According to him, Manasses, the older son, who represents the Chosen People, 'also shall be *blessed*,' that is, shall not lose the covenant 'forever' or 'once for all' (see 4. 7); a remnant of the race shall be saved at the end of time (Rom. 11. 25 ff.). See n. 30.

147 Cf. Gen. 17. 4; Rom. 4. 11 f.; Gal. 3. 6 ff.

148 Cf. Luke 1. 72 f.

149 Cf. Exod. 24. 18 and 31. 18. The words 'in the Spirit' are added by the writer. Perhaps he meant to indicate that, since the tablets were inscribed 'in' (or 'by') the Spirit, the commandments must be interpreted 'in a spiritual sense.'

150 Cf. Exod. 32. 7-19; Deut. 9. 12-17. The tables 'were shattered,' but the covenant was renewed: Exod. 34. 1; Deut. 9. 17. The 'loss' of the covenant was not absolute; see n. 146.

151 Cf. Heb. 3. 5; Clement of Rome 4. 12; 43. 1; 51. 3, 5; 53. 5.

152 By appearing in the flesh, Christ gave the Jews of His time an occasion to 'fill up the measure of their sins' by putting Him to death (cf. Matt. 23. 32). Since then 'the children of promise' are counted as the true descendants of Abraham.

153 Cf. Luke 1. 17, 68, 79.

154 Isa. 42. 6 f.

155 *Ibid.* 49. 6, 7.

[156] *Ibid.* 61. 1 f.; cf. Luke 4. 18 f. Here the Son is speaking. 'A year of grace': an allusion to the Jewish jubilee year (Lev. 25. 8-10), a type of the whole period of the Christian dispensation, in which men are freed from the slavery of sin and the Devil, and grace and heaven are restored.

[157] Cf. Exod. 20. 8; Deut. 5. 12. 'Clean of hand': added by the writer from Ps. 23. 4. The Sabbath was to be 'sanctified' by abstention from servile work.

[158] Cf. Jer. 17. 24 f.; Exod. 31. 13-17.

[159] Gen. 2. 2 f.

[160] 'The Lord will make an end of all things': the expression is puzzling; for, even according to Barnabas, the *real* 'end of the world' will take place at the end of the seventh millennium, just before '*another* world' begins.

The quotation following is from Ps. 89. 4; 2 Peter 3. 8 (though neither passage can be claimed in support of chiliasm). Papias (see Fr. 1) and Barnabas are the first Christian writers to advocate chiliastic ideas. They were followed by Justin, Irenaeus, Lactantius, and, at first, by St. Augustine. This opinion, fairly widespread in the first three centuries, held that before the general judgment and before the general resurrection Christ would come in visible glory to reign with the just on earth for a thousand years (a millennium). The Jews indulged similar ideas in interpreting certain Messianic texts (as Joel 3. 17 f.; Isaias 11. 6 ff.; 66. 18 ff.). Christian writers were also influenced by Apoc. 20. 4 ff. Barnabas's contribution to the development of chiliasm consists in dividing the history of the world into six (or seven) millennia and seeing these typified in the six days of the Creation, followed by the seventh day when God 'rested.' Barnabas wisely refrains from picturing the Millennium in exaggerated colors (see 15. 5). For further details, see J. Daniélou, 'La typologie millénariste de la semaine dans le christianisme primitif,' *Vig. christ.* 2 (1948) 1-16; H. Leclercq, 'Millénarisme,' *Dict. d'archéol. et de Lit.* 11. 1 (1933) 1181-95.

[161] Isa. 1. 13. Barnabas identifies 'your Sabbaths' with the Sabbaths of the present era. His seventh era *begins* when the world *ends,* and will *end* with the dawn of 'another world,'—not another millennium, but the day of eternity, 'the eighth day.' The following diagram will illustrate Barnabas' theory of days or periods:

Days: 1 | 2 | 3 | 4 | 5 | 6 the present | 7 Millennium | 8 eternity

the past

[162] For the observance of the Sunday, see *Didache* 14. 1 and n. 86. The current rendering, ' on which Jesus rose from the dead and went up to heaven,' may well be the correct one. It is generally held that Barnabas believed the Ascension to have taken place on the day of the Resurrection. This is by no means an isolated ancient view; cf. Funk, *op. cit.* 85 f. See also F. J. Dölger, *Sol Salutis* 212 f. Some writers also regard the Ascension as having occurred on the Fiftieth Day, the Pentecost. Cf. O. Casel, "Art und Sinn der ältesten christlichen Osterfeier," *Jahrb. f. Liturgiewiss.* 14 (1938) 59 f. (where further literature is indicated).

Barnabas uses the expression 'the eighth day' in two entirely different senses: 1) 'the eighth day' from the Creation, which is identical with the day of the other world, the day of eternity; and 2) 'the eighth day' which was the first day after the lapse of the preceding week (Matt. 28. 1), and therefore coincides with our Sunday. Since Jesus rose on 'the eighth day' in the second sense, we commemorate on it, by anticipation, 'the eighth day' in the first sense. There is nothing in the Greek to *compel* us to understand Barnabas to say that the Resurrection and the Ascension occurred on one and the same day.

[163] Cf. Jer. 7. 4 ff. 'Consecrating Him by the temple': that is, doing the opposite of what they should have done, namely, deriving the sacredness of the temple from Him. There is here an echo of Matt. 23. 16-22.

[164] Cf. Isa. 40. 12; 66. 1.

[165] Cf. *ibid.* 49. 17.

[166] This statement has given rise to many conjectures (see Klauser 62 f.); but ' this ' temple which is being built up ' again ' can be none other than the temple of Jerusalem. The Romans destroyed it in the year 70, and now (probably between 117 and 132) the Romans (that is, Hadrian) and their ' subjects ' (that is, the Jews) are rebuilding it. For Hadrian's conciliatory policy toward the Jews, see Thieme, *op. cit.* 22-25.

[167] Cf. Henoch 89. 56, 66 f.

[168] Lit., ' has taken place.' How does this agree with the statement that the temple is now in course of reconstruction? The use of a past tense (here ἐγένετο) for the future, when a future event is vividly represented as having actually occurred, or when assurance is expressed that it will certainly be done, was familiar to the Greeks and to the Hebrew Prophets. It certainly fits in well with Barnabas's temperament in dealing with events of Jewish history.

[169] Source unknown. Cf. Henoch 91. 13. Christ died 'when the week was coming to an end'; His death abolished the Old Law, and a new temple (the Messianic kingdom—the Church) was beginning to be built 'in splendor' (cf. Acts 2). It was built 'in the name of the Lord' (a reference to Christian baptism; see Acts 2. 38). It is likely, however, that 'the week' is a condensed expression for Daniel's 'seventy weeks of years' (Dan. 9. 2, 24-27). See Jer. 25. 12 and 29. 10.

[170] 'Before *we* believe': we, the author and his readers, whether they had been pagans or Jews before baptism. 'A nest of idolatry': one of Barnabas's strong expressions; but in the New Testament the word 'idolatry' is sometimes used in a wider sense (see, e. g. Col. 3. 5; Eph. 5. 5; also Polycarp 11. 2 and n. 81).

[171] 'In the Name': see Ignatius, *Ephes.* 2. 1 and n. 10 in my version: ACW 1. 120; also compare Acts 2. 38. 'We were made new': a terse description of the grace of baptism (Gal. 6. 15; see John 3. 3).

[172] 'His—His—He': a magnificent summation of the blessings of Christianity; cf. Clement of Rome 36 and n. 106: ACW 1. 111. 'The promised blessing': eternal salvation; 'the mouth': so that we are able to preach Christian doctrine (Eph. 6. 19); 'a renewal of spirit': a complete change of heart and mind (as in Matt. 3. 2, μετανοεῖν); 'the imperishable kingdom': the kingdom of God; the Church; heaven.

[173] To confirm what he has just said, Barnabas appeals to his and his readers' experience in entering the Church. 'The man': the human teacher, who instructs the convert; 'it is a surprise to him': after tasting the happiness of being a Christian, the convert 'is surprised' to find that he had never before realized that such blessings could be in store for him.

[174] The writer reminds us of his main purpose, to impart a deeper knowledge (*gnosis*) of the Jewish ceremonial Law ('the past'); occasionally, however, he also touched upon 'things present or yet to come.' See 4. 1, 9. The 'future' is as yet wrapt in parables, types, allegories, which permit of no precise interpretation.

[175] The author now draws heavily on the *Didache's* teaching of the Two Ways, 1. 1-6. 3. 'Two powers': the Greek word is often applied to angels or demons; cf. Eph. 6. 12; 1 Peter 3. 22; etc. 'Angels of Satan': 2 Cor. 11. 14; 12. 7. 'Era': the Greek word so rendered generaly means a limited portion of time—term, age, period, epoch.

[176] 'Exuberant of (rich in) spirit': for the word πνεῦμα, see n. 3. Cf. Rom. 12. 11, 'aglow with the Spirit'; Acts 18. 25, 'with a spirit full of zeal.' 'Every form of hypocrisy': see n. 187.

[177] This looks like an application of the principle laid down in Matt. 7. 6: *Nolite dare sanctum canibus*, etc. Cf. M. J. Lagrange, *Evangile selon saint Matthieu* (Paris 1927) 146 f. Sensual indulgence indisposes the mind for the Gospel truths; recall how Felix dismissed St. Paul when the latter spoke of 'justice and chastity': Acts 24. 25. Barnabas may be referring to the Nicolaites (cf. Apoc. 2. 6, 15).

[178] Cf. Isa. 66. 2.

[179] Cf. *Didache* 4. 4 and n. 31. The Greek is ambiguous; either 'do not waver in your decision' or 'do not doubt that the Lord's promises will be fulfilled.'

[180] Exod. 20. 7. 'Than yourself': perhaps, with a reminiscence of John 15. 13, 'more than your own life.' See n. 6 and *Didache* n. 20. '*More* than yourself': this seems to go beyond the Gospel requirement (Matt. 19. 19); but the word generally rendered 'soul' or 'life' is apt to stress the lower side of human nature. Barnabas probably means to say: 'Do not let personal and selfish interests (your own dear self) prevent you from loving your neighbor *as yourself*.' In other words, 'do not be selfish.' This agrees well with what follows, where every vice named is a violation of this principle. The word ψυχή is sometimes quite broadly used as almost = *person* (e. g. Acts 27. 10).

[181] See *Didache* n. 28.

[182] Cf. Prov. 21. 6.

[183] See *Didache* 4. 10 and n. 35. 'Private property': Acts 4. 32. 'Pure': the Greek word often connotes sexual purity. If this is here intended, the expression 'as far as you can' may be an exhortation to voluntary continence, as recommended in Matt. 19. 12.

[184] Deut. 32. 10; Ps. 16. 8. The 'saints': the Christians; cf. Acts 9. 13; Rom. 12. 13; etc. Barnabas finds two advantages in visiting one's fellow Christians; if one has the gift of instructing others, one may comfort the 'afflicted'; if one is a laborer, one may help the needy by almsgiving. The *Didache* (4. 2) mentions another advantage: one may be refreshed by the discourses of the saints.

[185] Cf. Deut. 4. 2; 13. 1; 12. 32.

[186] Cf. Deut. 1. 16, 17; Prov. 31. 9. 'Confess your sins': cf. B. Poschmann, *Paenitentia secunda* (Theophaneia 1, Bonn 1940) 85-97.

Poschmann shows (87) that it is beyond the author's purpose to go into any detail regarding penance, and that he merely mentions a few means of obtaining remission of sin (here, confession; in 19. 10, almsgiving).

[187] 'The Black One': see 4. 10 and n. 36. 'Hypocrisy': a wide term which includes many varieties (sham, pretense, make-believe, cant, simulation, affectation, *formalism*, insincerity, etc.). It is probable that the word here simply stands for 'Judaism' and 'Judaizing tendencies.' See *Didache* 8. 1 and n. 51. This latter acceptation is in keeping with the general subject of this epistle.

[188] Cf. Rom. 12. 9.

[189] Cf. Ps. 4. 3; Isa. 1. 23.

[190] Cf. Wisd. 12. 5. 'Destroyers of God's image': by abortion. See *Didache* 5. 2 and n. 43.

[191] Cf. John 12. 8; Gal. 6. 9 f.; 2 Thess. 3. 13.

[192] Cf. Isa. 40. 10; Apoc. 1. 3; 22. 10.

[193] 'Your own advisers': do not take advice from the Jews (the 'hypocrites'). Hold fast to your Christian faith.

[194] Cf. Isa. 54. 13; John 6. 45; 1 Thess. 4. 9; 1 John 2. 27.

[195] 'The fair vessel': the expression recalls 'our fair creation' in 6. 12. St. Paul uses the word 'vessel' of the human body (2 Cor. 4. 7); of men (Rom. 9. 22; cf. Acts 9. 15); of a wife (1 Thess. 4. 4; cf. 1 Peter 3. 7). Cf. above, 7. 3 and 11. 9. The adjective καλός meant, in classical times, 'fair, beautiful'; later it could mean 'good of its kind, excellent,' as 'the Good Shepherd' (John 10. 14), 'the good (kind, gracious, noble) Rewarder' (above, 19. 11), and even 'good, dear," as an epithet of admiration and affection. See E. R. Smothers, 'Καλός in Acclamation,' *Traditio* 5 (1947) 40 ff.

[196] A last reminder of the writer's purpose announced in 1. 8. As the letter began, so it ends—on a note of 'peace.' This is typical Pauline style (Rom. 1. 17 and 16. 12; 2 Cor. 1. 2 and 13. 11; etc.). Pauline, too, is the closing expression 'with your spirit.' Cf. Gal. 6. 18.

ST. POLYCARP

THE EPISTLES TO THE PHILIPPIANS

INTRODUCTION

[1] See *The Epistles of St. Clement of Rome and St. Ignatius of Antioch*: ACW 1 (1946) 96-99 and 90-95.

[2] See P. N. Harrison, *Polycarp's Two Epistles to the Philippians* (Cambridge 1936) Ch. 14: 'Echoes from the Ignatian Epistles.'

[3] Harrison, *op. cit.* 122, says: 'The brief sentences before us (that is, 13.2 of the covering note) may securely be regarded as contemporary and decisive "external" testimony to the genuineness of our Ignatian Epistles collectively. In attesting this collection they attest a fact of first-rate importance in the literary history of that period.'

[4] See Harrison, *op. cit.*, the long Ch. 5 (27-72): 'History of Criticism.'

[5] See Harrison's important work noted above. For the 'fusion' of early documents, see the same writer's remarks, *ibid.* 20-24.

[6] While the reviewers of Harrison's book generally found his theory of two letters acceptable, some objected that too long a span of years had been placed between the two letters. Thus, C. J. Cadoux (*Jour. of Theol. Stud.* 38 [1937] 270) thinks that the second letter should be dated 'not earlier than the spring following the first letter, but also not later than a couple of years after Ignatius's death.' See also A. Puech, *Rev. de l'hist. des rel.* 119 (1939) 96-102; H. D. Simonin, *Rev. des sciences phil. et théol.* 27 (1938) 258-60; also E. J. Goodspeed, *A History of Early Christian Literature* (Chicago 1942) 25.

[7] See, for example, the opening sentences in the Ignatian letters, and, above all, the elaborate *captatio benevolentiae* in Clement of Rome, ACW 1.9-11.

[8] See Harrison, *op. cit.*, Ch. 16 (172-206): 'The False Teachers at Philippi.'

[9] See 12.1 and n. 89. He humbly confesses that he is not so well versed in the Scriptures (the Old Testament, probably) as the Philippians.

[10] See 9.1 and n. 65.

[11] This touching letter to an apostate has been preserved by Eusebius, *Hist. eccl.* 5.20.

[12] See Harrison, *op. cit.* 3. See *The Martyrdom*, Intro. n. 12. Cf. Jerome, *De vir. ill.* 17.

[13] See *Martyrium Polycarpi* 9. 3.

[14] See *ibid.*, Intro. 87.

[15] See Harrison, *op. cit.* 28 ff., and A. Lelong, *Les Pères Apostoliques* 3 (2nd ed., Paris 1927) l-li.

TEXT

THE FIRST EPISTLE

[1] 'Both you and Ignatius write': this may mean: 'You write, as also Ignatius has written,' that is, to the Philadelphians (10. 1), the Symrnaeans (11. 2), and to me (*Pol.* 7. 2). A strong *esprit de corps* bound the Asian Churches into one large community of fellow feeling and of solidarity of interests. Cf. 1 Peter 5. 9.

[2] See Intro. n. 3.

[3] For this rendering, see n. 88 to the second letter. 'Those who are with him': note the use of the present tense. Ignatius, at the time of writing, is supposed to be still living. See Intro. 71.

[4] 'Reliable information': the news of Ignatius's martyrdom would naturally first come to Philippi, and from there be conveyed to Smyrna. This natural desire to learn how the great 'athletes of Christ' (see Clement of Rome 5. 1 and Ignatius, *Pol.* 1. 3 and 3. 1) had attained their immortal crown led to the writing of the *Acta Martyrum*, which are an important part of early Christian literature. They are the forerunners of our modern journals dealing with the foreign mission fields.

THE SECOND EPISTLE

[1] The same expression occurs in Ignatius, *Philad.* inscr. Polycarp speaks here as a bishop (cf. Ignatius, *Magn.* 15; *Smyrn.* 12. 2; *Pol.* inscr.) surrounded by his presbyters (so again in 11. 3; 13. 2; 14). In the early Church, bishops, presbyters, and deacons ordinarily acted as a collective body. See Ignatius, *Trall.* 3. 1 and n. 14: ACW 1 (1946) 132. Elsewhere in this letter the use of 'I' is adhered to: 3. 1; 9. 1; 11. 1-3; 11. 4-12. 1; 13. 1; 14. 1. It was natural that in course of time the personal responsibility of the head of the Church should come to assert itself (quite in accordance with St. Paul's action, e. g., in 1 Cor. 5. 3-5).

[2] 'The Church of God': St. Paul and the Apostolic Fathers only

occasionally speak of 'the Church of Christ.' Cf. the inscr. to Ignatius, *Philad.* and *Smyrn.* 'As a stranger': Christians are exiles in this world. See Clement of Rome, inscr. and n. 2: ACW 1. 103 f.

³ Cf. 1 Peter 1. 2; Jude 2.

⁴ The early Christians had a very lively and practical conception of the doctrine of the Mystical Body. See Clement of Rome, n. 113: ACW 1. 111 f.; Ignatius, *Magn.* n. 1: *ibid.* 125 f. A Christian *as such* cannot act, even in 'worldly' matters, except 'as a member of (united with) Jesus Christ.' Cf. Ignatius, *Ephes.* 8. 2, and John 15. 5.

⁵ An echo of Phil. 2. 17; 4. 10.

⁶ 'The images': Ignatius and his fellow prisoners. Of the latter we know nothing but their names (9. 1). A martyr is an 'image,' copy, imitator, follower, of Christ. See below, n. 64, and Ignatius, *Trall.* n. 7: ACW 1. 131. 'The True Love': cf. 1 John 4. 16; also Ignatius, *Rom.* 7. 2. Perhaps, however, Polycarp is thinking of Christ's true love for us (see John 15. 12), or of our genuine love for God, Christ, and the neighbor (see below, 3. 3).

⁷ 'Diadems': cf. Ignatius, *Ephes.* 11. 2. 'The elect': of God (cf. Matt. 24. 31); of Christ (cf. John 15. 16).

⁸ See Clement of Rome 1. 2: ACW 1 (1946) 9. For another sense of πίστις, see below, 4. 3.

⁹ Lit., 'from primitive times' (Lightfoot); the days of its first planting. See Phil. 1. 5; 4. 15, and compare Acts 15. 7; 21. 16. 'Celebrated': see Rom. 1. 8.

¹⁰ This is probably the sense of εἰς here. But in the Koine ἐν and εἰς interchange somewhat freely; hence, possibly, 'brings forth fruit *in* Jesus Christ' (in the well-known Pauline and Ignatian sense: see Ignatius, *Magn.* n. 1: ACW 1. 125 f.); see n. 4 above; besides, if εἰς can be pressed, Polycarp may mean that your faith 'brings forth fruit *into* Jesus Christ,' with an echo of Eph. 4. 13: Christian life aims at 'building up the body of Christ' until we 'attain to (εἰς) the full measure of the perfection of Christ.' To grow in virtue is 'to grow *into* Christ.' See n. 28.

¹¹ The Greek is graphic: 'who endured to go as far as death and meet with it face to face.' 'The throes' or birth-pangs 'of death': see the commentaries on Acts 2. 24; Pss. 17. 5 and 114. 3. Cf. Ignatius, *Rom.* 6. 1. The quotation following is from 1 Peter 1. 8. Christ 'died for our sins': an important point in Polycarp's soteriology; see n. 91.

[12] The rendering 'many desire to experience' takes for granted that many pagans and Jews actually desired to become Christians; of this, however, we have no knowledge. To remove this inconvenience, we might read a conditional sense into the participle εἰδότες and, by consequence, into the indicative ἐπιθυμοῦσιν, making πολλοί the subject: 'a joy which many would like to experience if *they* were assured, etc.' The modal force of the indicative is occasionally met with in ancient and Koine Greek. Lelong (*op. cit.* 111) and others join εἰδότες to πιστεύετε, as in the text above.

[13] Eph. 2. 5, 8, 9. 'You have been saved': virtually, that is, by your call to Christianity and by baptism. This call was independent of 'works' or 'actions.' See the following note.

[14] Cf. 1 Peter 1. 13; Eph. 6. 14; Ps. 2. 11. 'Therefore': because you have received the grace of baptism, *therefore live* as befits you (Eph. 4. 1 ff.) and 'ratify God's calling and choice of you' (2 Peter 1. 10). 'In truth': either subjectively, 'with sincerity,' or, better, objectively, 'as the Truth, Christ, demands.' See 3. 2 and n. 27. Note the context.

[15] As St. Paul had warned the Philippians against Judaizing influences (Phil. 3. 1-4), so Polycarp warns them against 'that (Judaistic) dabbling in fantastic lore,' 'that idle curiosity about trifles,' 'that worthless speculation' about genealogical registers, which belonged either to 'Israelitish families, or Rabbinical fables and fabrications' or to the aeons of the Gnostics, or, finally, to the heathen mythologies (cf. R. F. Weymouth, *The New Testament in Modern Speech* [5th ed., Boston 1943] 499). The next sentence makes it clear that the purity of the faith of the Philippians was endangered. An idea of this ματαιολογία (or ματαιότης in 7. 2) may be formed from some of the Apocrypha. Cf. Matt. 24. 12; 2 Cor. 2. 17. Note that the expression 'leave untouched' ('have nothing to do with'; 'leave on one side') has been chosen in preference to 'abandon' because it is not certain that the Philippians had actually succumbed to the temptation.

[16] 1 Peter 1. 21; cf. Eph. 1. 20 and Heb. 8. 1. See Clement of Rome 59. 2.

[17] Cf. Phil. 2. 10; 3. 21; 1 Cor. 15. 28.

[18] Cf. Ps. 150. 6 (5). The New Latin Psalter has 'omne, quod spirat.' See also Isa. 57. 16.

[19] Cf. Acts 10. 42 (2 Tim. 4. 1; 1 Peter 4. 5).

[20] Cf. 2 Cor. 4. 14; 1 Cor. 6. 14; Rom. 8. 11. For points of Polycarp's eschatology, see 2. 1 f.; 5. 2; 7. 1; 9. 2; 11. 2.

13 *

²¹ See Clement of Rome 33. 1 and n. 95: ACW 1. 110; Ignatius, *Ephes.* 14 and n. 34: *ibid.* 123. 'Avarice, love of money': we are being prepared by the writer for what he has to say about Valens and his wife in 11. 1. Cf. 4. 1; 4. 3; 6. 1; 11. 1; 11. 2. Some of Polycarp's expressions point evidently to special circumstances, dangers, or vices, existing at Philippi, but unknown to us. The expression 'blow with blow' has been taken to indicate 'a state of discord within, and scandal about, the Church at Philippi. . . . It has even come to blows.' See Harrison, *op. cit.* 168.

²² 1 Peter 3. 9.

²³ Matt. 7. 1 f.; cf. Luke 6. 36-38; Clement of Rome 13. 2.

²⁴ Matt. 5. 3, 10; Luke 6. 20. 'The humble souls': the kind of men whom St. Paul describes in 1 Cor. 1. 26-28. In the Psalms the words *pauper, egenus, miser, oppressus,* and *humilis,* are constantly used to denote the pious, law-abiding, God-fearing Jew. In our current renderings of the adjective πτωχός the idea of 'poverty' has been over-stressed: 'Ce ne sont pas ceux qui n'ont pas d'argent, mais les personnes pieuses qui se sentent désenchantées et opprimées dans le monde' (M. J. Lagrange, *Evangile selon saint Matthieu* [Paris 1929] 82).

²⁵ Compare Ignatius, *Ephes.* 3. 1. The word δικαιοσύνη (here rendered 'the practice of holy living'), which abounds in shades of meaning varying with the context, has unfortunately, through centuries of repetition, been forced into the strait jackets of 'justice' and 'righteousness.' A glance at Knox's translation of its 95 occurrences in the New Testament shows what a wealth of connotations is hidden in it. See nn. 31, 40, and 65, and Barnabas n. 5.

²⁶ See 2 Peter 3. 15.

²⁷ See Acts 16. 12. The word βέβαιος means: firm, fast, stable, constant, valid, inviolable; hence here 'authoritative.' See Ignatius, *Smyrn.* 8. 1: ACW 1. 93.

²⁸ Lit., 'to be built up (edified) toward the faith.' Since the purpose of the Church is to 'build up the body of Christ' (Eph. 4. 12), a Christian's growth in virtue may be described as 'a building up' (*aedificare*: see below, 11. 4 and 12. 2). Cf. Ignatius's elaboration of this metaphor in *Ephes.* 9. 1. See above, n. 10.

²⁹ Cf. Gal. 4. 26, where this is said of the 'heavenly Jerusalem.' Regarding the early Christian personification of faith as a mother, see the study by J. C. Plumpe, *Mater Ecclesia. An Inquiry into the Concept of the Church as Mother in Early Christianity* (Stud. in Christ. Ant. 5, Washington 1943) Ch. 2.

[30] Since faith, being 'the mother of us all,' takes first place, love cannot precede it; hence προαγούσης and ἐπακολουθούσης are best taken as distinctions of rank, in agreement with 1 Cor. 13. 13 (cf. also Ignatius, *Ephes*. 14. 1). The sequence in 1 Thess. 1. 3 is different. In Col. 1. 4 f., hope is conceived either as a step toward, the wellspring of, love (though certainly not as the motive of love), or else as prompting St. Paul to feel thankful for the graces mentioned.

[31] 'Engrossed in these': lit., when a man 'is within the limits of faith, hope, and love'; when he comes under their influence and is actuated by them. 'The commandment': see Matt. 19. 17; 22. 38; John 15. 10; Gal. 5. 14; 1 John 2. 5. 'Justification': compare the use of this word in 2. 3; 3. 1; 4. 1; 5. 2; 8. 1; 9. 1, 2. See n. 25.

[32] Cf. 1 Tim. 6. 10. An even more forceful lesson is read into this text if the word rendered 'beginning' is taken to mean 'gist' or 'sum.' Thus in Mark 1. 1 the rendering 'summary' is more appropriate than 'beginning.' The Greeks used this word also to denote 'the primal substance' out of which the world is made. In Ps. 110. 10 ('The fear of the Lord is the *beginning* of wisdom') the Hebrew rendered ἀρχή in the Septuagint may mean 'sum' (Cf. J. A. Van Steenkiste, *Liber Psalmorum* [3d ed., Bruges 1886] 976). Those 'who minister in the temple' or 'serve the altar' (1 Cor. 9. 13) are peculiarly exposed to temptations to greed and love of money. See below, 11. 1, 2. Here, however, the admonition is not exclusively aimed at church officials.

[33] 1 Tim. 6. 7; Job. 1. 21.

[34] Cf. Rom. 13. 12; Eph. 6. 11, 13. 'The armor of a holy life (innocence, right-doing)': cf. Rom. 6. 13; 2 Cor. 6. 7. See above, n. 25.

[35] Lit., 'to walk in the way, etc.': a metaphor familiar to Greeks and Semites alike; see *Didache* 1. 1.

[36] The subsequent injunctions suited to certain states of life are modelled on smilar exhortations in St. Paul (Eph. 5. 21; Col. 3. 18 ff.). Cf. Clement of Rome (1. 3 and esp. 21. 6-8). For the Gentile, Jewish, and early Christian ethical codes, see E. G. Selwyn, *The First Epistle of St. Peter* (London 1947) 101-109; 421-39; 471-88.

[37] In the primitive Church, widows were given special care and accorded special honors. For references to 'widows' in Clement of Rome and Ignatius, see ACW 1, Index *s. v.* After undergoing certain tests, they could be enrolled as deaconnesses. See K. Prümm,

Christentum als Neuheitserlebnis (Freiburg i. Br. 1939) 366 ff., and T. Schermann, *Die allgemeine Kirchenordnung des zweiten Jahrhunderts* (Paderborn 1914) 1.202 ff.

Since these women were bound by a special pledge or promise, the word πίστις seems here used in a technical sense: let widows be discreet, not 'in the faith of the Lord,' but, rather, 'in matters concerning their *fidelity* to the Lord.' Their πίστις was their 'plighted troth.' But the usual sense of 'faith' need not be wholly excluded. In the history of early Montanism, if at no other period, women were known to be particularly liable to exaggeration or even fanaticism in religious matters.

'Discreet': the Greek word means 'sober, of sound mind, reasonable, moderate, temperate, not given to fanaticism.' The context seems even to imply self-control in sexual matters; hence 'chaste.'

Polycarp here coins a happy phrase that has been much admired: widows are 'God's altar,' because 'elles devaient prier sans cesse' and 'elles vivaient des offrandes des fidèles' (Lelong, *op. cit.* 115). For later references, also as applied to virginity, see Lightfoot, *op. cit.* 329 f. God 'inspects everything for blemishes': see Clement of Rome 41.2.

[38] 1 Cor. 14.25.

[39] Gal. 6.7.

[40] Following the precedent of St. Paul (1 Tim. 3.8-10, 12, 13), the Apostolic Fathers were greatly interested in the proper conduct of deacons. See Ignatius, *Magn.* 6.1; *Trall.* 2.3; etc. (mentioned 39 times in all). They must be blameless 'in the sight of (confronted with) His just demands'; for δικαιοσύνη, see n. 25. 'God's servants': see Ignatius, *Smyrn.* 10.1. Note the weakened and wider sense of διάκονος, applied to Christ a little farther on.

[41] Lit., 'walking (living) conformably to *the real state of things* so far as Christ is concerned.' What Christ (the διάκονος of all men: Rom. 15.8; Matt. 20.28; Mark 9.35) did is the only *true*, correct, and therefore ideal, standard by which deacons must judge their conduct and obligations. In the New Testament and later the word ἀλήθεια has often this objective sense (like its opposites *mendacium* and *vanitas* in Ps. 4.3 and elsewhere).

[42] Cf. Rom. 8.17; 2 Tim. 2.12. For πολιτεύεσθαι, see Phil. 1.27; Clement of Rome 21.1. Note the proviso: as in Luke 18.8; *Didache* 16.2.

[43] For special injunctions to young men, see 1 Peter 5.5; Titus 2.6.

44 Cf. Gal. 5. 17; 1 Peter 2. 11.

45 1 Cor. 6. 9 f.

46 'And obey': young men must obey presbyters and deacons, who had, of course, inculcated sexual purity. The term ἐπίσκοπος, 'bishop,' does not occur in the body of this epistle; but we know from other early Christian literature that 'presbyter' and 'bishop' were at times used indiscriminately; see my n. 125 to Clement of Rome: ACW 1. 112; also Ignatius, *Magn.* 9. On the other hand, St. Paul, writing to the same community (1. 1), speaks of 'bishops and deacons,' and omits any mention of 'presbyters.' It is a reasonable conjecture, therefore, that in the present epistle the term 'presbyter' may include 'bishop' (cf. Lelong, *op. cit.* 117) and that the term 'deacon' may include 'presbyter.' That the term 'deacon' was capable of a wider sense is clear from its application to Christ, the High Priest (see 5. 2 and n. 41). For the fluidity of the terms 'bishop' and 'presbyter' in St. Paul, see the note by M. Meinertz, on Phil. 1. 1, in *Die Gefangenschaftsbriefe des heiligen Paulus* (4th ed., Bonn 1931) 129. It would not be absurd to conjecture that Valens was the bishop of Philippi. See n. 78.

47 Cf. Acts 23. 1; 1 Tim. 3. 9; 2 Tim. 1. 3.

48 'What has gone astray': some, referring to Ezech. 34. 4, supply the noun 'sheep.' But the Greek neuter may denote persons, as in John 6. 37 (cf. also Matt. 1. 20 and Luke 1. 35; 19. 10). Here the reference is no doubt to Valens, his wife, and their partisans. 'The sick': cf. Matt. 25. 26, 43; 'the widows': cf. James 1. 27 and above, n. 37; Ignatius, *Smyrn.* 6. 2; *Pol.* 4. 1. We have here a chapter from pastoral theology, a reflection of the pastoral duties stressed in Ignatius's letter to Polycarp.

49 Cf. 2 Cor. 8. 21; Rom. 12. 17.

50 Cf. Rom. 14. 10, 12.

51 Cf. 2. 1; Ps. 2. 11; Heb. 12. 28.

52 'To us': that is, the Smyrnaeans (Polycarp was a disciple of the Apostles: Irenaeus, *Adv. haer.* 3. 3. 4) and the Philippians: Acts 16. 12. Polycarp recognizes the principle of *tradition* in the preaching of Christian doctrine; note that he puts the Apostles on the same level with Christ. The chain of transmission is unbroken: God the Father—Christ—the Apostles (and before them the Prophets). Among the Apostles St. Paul is mentioned by name in 3. 2 and 11. 2. According to the *Didache* the right to teach is vested not only in the visiting 'prophets' and 'apostles,' but also in the resident officials called 'bishops' and deacons' (see Ch. 11: 'who render you the sacred service of teachers and prophets'; see *Didache* n. 94). The most clear-cut statement of this principle is found in Clement of Rome 42. For Ignatius of Antioch, cf., e. g., *Ephes.* 11. 2. The same doctrine is implied in Papias's inquiries made of the 'presbyters': see Papias, Fr. 2. 3; and in Barnabas's statement about the Apostles in 8. 3 of his Epistle.

'The Prophets': for the high esteem in which they were held by the Fathers, see ACW 1, Index *s. v.* 'Seducers': the noun σκάνδαλον is sometimes predicated of persons; cf. Matt. 13. 41; 16. 23; 1 Cor. 1. 23. Polycarp, no doubt, means the Docetists and their leader Marcion. 'For a mask': see Ignatius, *Ephes.* 7. 1. This statement is explained in the next paragraph.

[53] Cf. 1 John 4. 2-4.

[54] Cf. 1 John 2. 18, 22; 2 John 7; 2 Thess. 2. 5. 'The testimony of the Cross': John 19. 34 f.; 1 John 5. 6-8. To Polycarp the Cross is a witness against the Docetists. See Ignatius, *Ephes.* 9. 1; 18. 1; *Trall.* 11. 2; *Philad.* 8. 2; *Smyrn.* 1. 1., 2.

[55] Cf. John 8. 44; 1 John 3. 8.

[56] For τὰ λόγια, here rendered 'the Gospel,' see Clement of Rome 62. 3 and n. 179: ACW 1. 116.

[57] Evidently the heresy referred to is Docetism, dating from the time of the Apostles, and held in one form or another by most of the numerous Gnostic sects. It denied Christ's human nature and therefore attacked the Incarnation as well as the Redemption by His Passion and death on the Cross. That it proved a dangerous enemy of the primitive Church is constantly stated or implied in the Ignatian Epistles (see ACW 1, Index *s. v.*). The designations 'Antichrist' and 'first-born of Satan' indicate Polycarp's abhorrence of the archenemy and his grave concern in the purity of the Philippians' faith. That his outburst is directed against Marcion seems well-established; see, above all, Harrison, *op. cit.* 172-206, "The False Teachers at Philippi." At the time of writing, the errors of Marcion had not yet reached their final formulation. See also Papias, Fr. 13.

[58] 'The senseless speculation': see above, 2. 1 and n. 15.

[59] Cf. 1 Peter 4. 7.

[60] Cf. Matt. 6. 13, a second reference to the Lord's Prayer; the preceding petition, 'Forgive us our debts as we also forgive our debtors,' is alluded to in 6. 2.

[61] *Ibid.* 26. 41; Mark 14. 38.

[62] 1 Tim. 1. 1. 'The Pledge': this term is generally applied to the Holy Spirit; see 2 Cor. 1. 22; 5. 5; Eph. 1. 14. It is sometimes rendered 'guarantee,' sometimes 'foretaste.' 'Our Hope, etc.': note again an important point of doctrine, and cf. nn. 11 and 91.

[63] 1 Peter 2. 24, 22. See Ignatius, *Smyrn.* 2.

[64] Cf. 1 Peter 2. 21. After exhorting the readers to the practice of Christian virtue in general, Polycarp now takes a higher flight and makes a final appeal to their loyalty to Christ 'who endured *everything*' (a hint at His death for us). He carried His patient endurance 'to the limit' (see 9. 1) to set us an example of what we should be ready to do for Him. For the idea of being one's 'imitator' and its application to Christian conduct, see Ignatius, *Trall.* 1. 2 with n. 7: ACW 1. 131; also above, n. 6. Both our 'imitation' of Christ and our 'patient endurance' in imitation of Him reach their climax in martyrdom. See n. 65. The writer's insistence on 'patient endurance,' copied from the New Testament (32 instances; the corresponding verb ὑπομένειν occurs 17 times), runs through the Apostolic Fathers (19 and 30 instances, respectively). The idea of martyrdom as the crown of a Christian life is expressed as early in the New Testament as Matt. 10. 22.

[65] Polycarp now shows that *the* great and paramount *lesson in holiness* which a Christian has received is to hold himself in readiness for martyrdom. 'The lesson in holiness': the same somewhat vague expression occurs in Heb. 5. 13, where the writer takes the readers to task for 'having become like children who need milk, instead of solid food'; those that still need milk 'do not understand the lesson of holiness.' This lesson is appropriately called λόγος, since it is 'the word' of God laid down in Holy Writ. See n. 27. Both this passage from *Hebrews* and the context in Polycarp's epistle favor the interpretation of δικαιοσύνη just given. For the range of its connotations, see above, n. 31 and Barnabas n. 5. The Greek verb here rendered 'carry out' seems to mean 'to obey one *in authority*'; hence almost 'to be loyal to one and show this loyalty by obedience,' as a soldier who obeys his commander. The applicability to a martyr is obvious.

[66] See n. 6. These men were not members of the Philippian community. 'Your own community': cf. Phil. 1. 7, 28-30. 'The other Apostles': such other *missionaries* as were known to the Philippians, whether they were apostles in the narrower or the wider sense. See *Didache* n. 70.

[67] Cf. Phil. 2. 16; Gal. 2. 2. The aorist ἔδραμον indicates that Polycarp, when writing this letter, knew of Ignatius's martyrdom.

⁶⁸ See Clement of Rome 5. 4, 7.

⁶⁹ Cf. 2 Tim. 4. 10.

⁷⁰ Cf. 2 Cor. 5. 15; 1 Thess. 4. 14; Ignatius, *Rom.* 6. 1.

⁷¹ A conflation of various passages: 1 Cor. 15. 58; Col. 1. 23; Rom. 12. 10; 13. 8; 1 Peter 2. 17; John 13. 34; 15. 12, 17.

Polycarp's views of a virtuous life may be gathered from 3. 3; 5. 2; 10. 1 (faith); 10. 1; 10. 2 (charity); 10. 2 (good example); 6. 2 (forgiveness); 8. 2; 9. 1 (patient endurance); 12. 1 (meekness); 11. 1, 2, 3, 4 (forbearance and moderation); 4. 1; 6. 1; 11. 1, 2 (avarice); 12. 3 (prayer).

⁷² Cf. 2 Cor. 10. 1. 'Give precedence': Rom. 12. 10.

⁷³ Cf. Prov. 3. 28.

⁷⁴ Cf. Tob. 4. 10 f.; 12. 9. 'Submit': Eph. 5. 21; 1 Peter 5. 5.

⁷⁵ Cf. 1 Peter 2. 12; Matt. 5. 16.

⁷⁶ Apparently quoted from Ignatius, *Trall.* 8. 2, who had quoted it freely from Isa. 52. 2 (see the instructive note by J. B. Lightfoot, *op. cit.* 2. 172). The Latin *vae*, like the Greek οὐαί, is an interjection of grief or of denunciation; as 1 Cor. 9. 16 ('It would go hard with me' [Knox]; 'poena mihi imminet' [Zorell]). It does not seem to express downright malediction, except perhaps in Apoc. 9. 12; 11. 14.

⁷⁷ 'You are practicing': or, if the verb is in the imperative, 'which you yourselves must practice.'

⁷⁸ Nothing further is known about this man. Valens and his wife may have been guilty of 'some sordid and dishonest money transaction, as in the case of Ananias and Sapphira.' Cf. Lightfoot, *op. cit.* 3. 341. 'His office': *locum* = τόπον; cf. ACW 1. 113, 134, 144.

'Be pure': the Latin version reads *casti*, which is assumed (by Zahn, Lightfoot, Funk, etc.) to stand for ἁγνοί, 'chaste,' in the original. Although some of the older interpreters (e. g., Jacobson) saw here an indication that Valens had involved himself in some unchaste affair, modern critics agree that the entire context shows that the presbyter's scandalous behavior had something to do with avarice; and avarice was, in effect, a sort of religious impurity (see n. 81). Harrison, *op. cit.* 167, understands the words 'be pure and true' to be a warning, addressed to all, 'to refrain from avarice and keep *true* chastity. It would seem that either Valens, or someone who shares with him the responsibility for the present trouble. ..as been thinking to hide, or make up for, his love of money by a great show of what he calls chastity.'

⁷⁹ 1 Thess. 5. 22.

[80] Cf. 1 Tim. 3. 5.

[81] Cf. Eph. 5. 5 (also Col. 3. 5), where avarice is termed *idolorum servitus*. Idolatry in turn had been condemned in the Old Testament (cf. Ezech. 16. 20 ff.) as 'fornication.' Hence a theologian such as St. Augustine could seriously consider both idolatry and avarice as causes for separation in marriage, the Lord having excepted fornication when He inculcated the indissolubility of the marriage tie. Cf. Matt. 5. 32. See Augustine, *De Serm. Dom. in Monte* 1. 12. 36; 16. 46, and the observations in ACW 5 (1948) nn. 90 and 124. For 'idolatry,' see Barnabas n. 170.

[82] Cf. Jer. 5. 4 and 1 Cor. 6. 2.

[83] An obscure passage. The words may mean: 'who in the early days (of Gospel preaching) were his letters of recommendation' (cf. 2 Cor. 3. 2). See Lightfoot, *op. cit.* 3. 342 f. The Philippians were praised in St. Paul's letter to them (Phil. 1. 3-9).

[84] Cf. 2 Thess. 1. 4. The Smyrnaeans came into the Church after the conversion of the Philippians.

[85] Cf. 2 Tim. 2. 25.

[86] Cf. 2 Thess. 3. 15. 'Be considerate': in view of the wide-spread controversy which later disturbed the Church regarding the treatment of the so-called *lapsi* (persons who had fallen away from the faith or otherwise given great scandal), it is interesting to see that Polycarp stood for leniency. Compare Clement of Rome 56. 1 and 57. 1; also Ignatius, *Ephes.* 10. 1, 2.

[87] 'Diseased': a medical term; or, 'subject to suffering'; 'frail.' Cf. Acts 26. 23; Ignatius, *Ephes.* 7. 2; *Pol.* 3. 2. For the expression 'the whole of your community,' see 1 Cor 12. 26 f.; Clement of Rome 38. 1 and n. 113, 59. 2 and n. 165: ACW 1. 111 and 116.

[88] The Church, as 'the Body of Christ' (Eph. 1. 23), is a living organism. Her purpose is to 'build up' (*aedificare*) this mystical union with Christ, by teaching the members (1 Cor. 14. 4), by forming in them Christ's image (Gal. 4. 19). There must be no 'diseased' members in this body, and none must be suffered to wither and be thrown away (John 15. 2, 6). Besides being in a healthy condition, the Church must preserve her numerical integrity: none must be lost and others, as yet outside her fold, must be incorporated (see below, 12. 2). These are commonplaces among the Fathers.

Polycarp goes one step farther. He says: by doing this, that is, by reclaiming any stray members (and incorporating fresh members: 12. 2), 'you promote your personal spiritual growth.' Here is an intimation which eventually brought into being the active and the contemplative orders of the Church. The former are busy with the outer world, but *thereby* foster their own inner growth; the latter are busy with forming the inner man, but *thereby* influence the outer world for good. See I. Herwegen, *Sinn und Geist der Benediktinerregel* (Einsiedeln 1944) 12. As he says: 'The inner and the outer world must co-operate in producing the perfect man.' Compare Luke 10. 42.

[89] Cf. Clement of Rome 53. 1; Ignatius, *Ephes.* 14. 1.

[90] Cf. Ps. 4. 5 and Eph. 4. 26. The first part is generally rendered: 'be angry, and sin not.' The New Latin Psalter renders: 'Contremiscite, et nolite peccare.' Polycarp, of course, quotes the Septuagint.

[91] Cf. Heb. 6. 20; 7. 3. 'Further your growth': see nn. 28 and 88. Here we have Polycarp's Christology in a nutshell; cf. his prayer in *Martyrdom* 14.

[92] Cf. Acts 8. 21; 26. 18; Col. 1. 12. 'Are yet to believe': 1 Tim. 1. 16. Inward growth must keep pace with outward expansion. See n. 88.

[93] Cf. Gal. 1. 1; Col. 2. 12; 1 Peter 1. 21.

[94] Eph. 6. 18; 1 Tim 2. 1. 'The saints': the faithful. See n. 15a to Ignatius, *Magn.* 4: ACW 1, 127.

[95] Cf. 1 Tim. 2. 2 and the celebrated passage in Clement of Rome 61; also n. 175: ACW 1. 116 f.

[96] Cf. Matt. 5. 44; Luke 6. 27. Cf. *Didache* 1. 3.

[97] Cf. Phil. 3. 18.

[98] Cf. John 15. 16; 1 Tim. 4. 15; Matt. 5. 16.

[99] Cf. Col. 1. 28; 2. 10; James 1. 4; Matt. 5. 48.

[100] Crescens, the bearer of this letter, was perhaps also Polycarp's amanuensis (see Ignatius, *Rom.* n. 28: ACW 1. 136). The whole tone of this postscript seems to indicate that it belongs at the end of this second letter, and not at the end of the covering note. For, otherwise, what is the meaning of *in praesenti* (for the Greek ἄρτι: 'recently, lately, once before') if it does not imply that Crescens had on an earlier occasion brought the covering note to Philippi and during his stay there edified the whole community?

[101] Compare the similar greetings in Ignatius, *Pol.* 8. 3; *Trall.* 13. 2; *Smyrn.* 13. 2 ('Farewell *in the grace* of God').

THE MARTYRDOM OF ST. POLYCARP

INTRODUCTION

[1] Still one of the best accounts of the problems posed by these *acta* and of the literature published is that by O. Bardenhewer, *Geschichte der altkirchlichen Literatur* 2 (2nd ed., Freiburg i. Br. 1914) 669-71; cf. also 1. 161-63.

[2] Or Marcianus. The manuscripts show both forms of the name: see 20. 1 and J. B. Lightfoot, *The Apostolic Fathers. Part 2: S. Ignatius, S. Polycarp* (2nd ed., London 1889) 3. 398 f.

[3] See A. Lelong, *Les Pères apostoliques* 3 (2nd ed., Paris 1927) lx. See n. 15 on the text.

[4] The so-called *Acta Martyrum* are not, however, usually presented in epistolary form, as the present account is. On the subject, cf. H. Leclercq, 'Actes des martyrs,' *Dict. d'archéol. chrét. et de lit.* 1. 1 (1924) 373-446.

[5] See n. 46 on the text.

[6] See below, nn. 5, 24, 56, 58 on the text.

[7] Irenaeus states (*Ep. ad Flor.* = Eusebius, *Hist. eccl.* 5. 20) that as a youth he had often seen Polycarp and heard him tell of his intimate acquaintance with the Apostle John (cf. the note following). The same witness reports (*Adv. haer.* 3. 3. 4) that on a visit to Rome the aged bishop of Smyrna converted many heretics; also that on one occasion he encountered the archheretic Marcion (cf. below, the account in the Moscow manuscript). See also n. 10.

[8] Irenaeus (*Adv. haer.* 3. 3. 4) writes simply that the appointment was made 'by Apostles,' while Tertullian (*De praescr. haer.* 32. 2) states that according to the records of the see of Smyrna the honor was conferred by the Apostle St. John.

[9] See Polycarp, *Phil.* Intro. n. 3.

[10] Cf. Irenaeus, *Ep. ad Vict.* = Eusebius, *Hist. eccl.* 5. 24. 16; Eusebius, *ibid.* 4. 14.

[11] P. N. Harrison, *Polycarp's Two Epistles to the Philippians* (Cambridge 1936) 5, sums up Polycarp's important place in the Asian Churches as follows: "He was the neighbor and colleague of successive bishops of Ephesus, the friend and perhaps the host of Ignatius, the companion of Papias, the first and most uncompromising opponent of Marcion (outside Marcion's home-Church and country), the revered teacher of Irenaeus's boyhood."

[12] Cf. Clement of Rome 64: ACW (1946) 49. This appendix is perhaps a postscript added by the author of the *Martyrdom*.

[13] Cf. Bardenhewer, *op. cit.* 2. 671.

Text

[1] The best commentary on this expression, so unusual to us, is found in Chs. 5 and 6 of the *Ep. to Diognetus*. See also Clement of Rome, inscr. and n. 2: ACW 1. 103 f. Lit., 'a Church that is in a state of pilgrimage' (in the sense explained in Heb. 13. 14); hence, as it were, 'God's pilgrim Church at Smyrna.' The noun παροικία ('settling in a strange place' or 'in a foreign country') came to be a common term for a Christian community in any place. From it our word 'parish' is derived. See E. G. Selwyn, *The First Epistle of St. Peter* (London 1947) 118.

[2] The early Christian communities took a lively interest in each other's affairs; their catholicity of outlook and the consequent brisk inter-diocesan exchange of news are abundantly illustrated by the Ignatian letters. See e. g., Ignatius, *Philad.* 10. 'The Catholic Church': see below, n. 46.

[3] Cf. Jude 2; see also 1 Peter 1. 2; 2 Peter 1. 2.

[4] 'Sealed the persecution': compare the same Greek word in Matt. 27. 66; Apoc. 20. 3. Here 'to seal' means 'to close, as it were, by a seal.' After Polycarp's martyrdom the Smyrnaeans seem to have enjoyed a respite from persecution.

[5] The writer is particularly interested in Polycarp because of the resemblance between his martyrdom and the Passion of Christ, which is 'the martyrdom narrated in the Gospel.' Christ, too, was a 'martyr' (a 'witness' to the truth); see John 18. 37; Apoc. 1. 5; 3. 14. H. Delehaye, *Les passions des martyrs et les genres littéraires* (Brussels 1921) 27 ff., shows that the idea of resemblance between Christ's Passion and the sufferings of the martyrs was familiar to the early Christians. There is a special point in noting that Christ and Polycarp 'waited to be betrayed'; Quintus's self-intrusion (see Ch. 4) was disastrous. Some of the points of resemblance noted in the narrative are somewhat remarkable, though not strange enough to pronounce them legendary.

[6] Cf. Phil. 2. 4.

[7] This idea is taken up in many later *acta martyrum*: cf. Eusebius's account of the martyrs of Lyons and Vienne, *Hist. eccl.* 5. 1. 51, 56; *Passio SS. Perpetuae et Felicitatis* 4; *Acta Pauli et Theclae* 24; etc.

[8] Compare 11. 2 below. 'The unquenchable fire': cf. Matt. 3. 12; etc.; also Ignatius, *Ephes.* 16. 2. 'Eternal life': Matt. 25. 46.

[9] 1 Cor. 2. 9; Isa. 64. 4; 65. 16. 'Already angels': that is, no longer subject to the infirmities of the flesh, but already disembodied. Cf. Hermas, *Vis.* 2. 2. 7 and *Sim.* 9. 25. 2; Tertullian, *De res. carn.* 26; 62.

[10] This subject is not actually expressed in the Greek. Some editors (Zahn, Funk, etc.) inserted 'the tyrant'; but this is supported only by the authority of a scribe and, moreover, is anachronistic, since such appellatives for proconsuls and other presiding officials were not used in the *acta* until a later date. Lightfoot, *The Apostolic Fathers. Part 2: S. Ignatius, S. Polycarp* (London 1889) 3. 368, suggests that 'the Devil,' mentioned in the sentence immediately following, is the subject to be supplied.

[11] 'Over any of them': that is, of the group of twelve mentioned in 19. 1; or, 'over all of them,' if we include the unfortunate Quintus mentioned in Ch. 4. For the view that the sufferings of the martyrs were the work of the Devil, see Ignatius, *Rom.* n. 18: ACW 1. 136. See below, 17. 1.

[12] Lucius Statius Quadratus, who was also a rhetorician. See below, 21.

[13] Cf. Ignatius, *Rom.* 5. 2.

[14] The charge of atheism was commonly leveled against Christians: cf. Justin, *Apol.* 1. 6, 13; Athenagoras, *Leg.* 3 ff. To be an atheist, not to believe in the pagan gods, was a crime against the Roman state religion. See n. 27 below.

[15] Quintus's self-intrusion was not 'according to the will of God' (see above, 2. 1); Polycarp's conduct was in harmony with the Gospel teaching: Matt. 10. 23; John 7. 1; 8. 59; 10. 39; Acts 13. 51; 17. 14. It may well be that the reference to Quintus's nationality is not without some significance. Zahn (*Ignatii et Polycarpi epistulae, martyria, fragmenta* [Leipzig 1876] 138 f.) pointed out that his impulsiveness and ardor are native qualities identical with the religious fanaticism and exaggerated asceticism that marked Phrygian Montanism a decade or two later. Again, as Lightfoot (*op. cit.*, 369) remarks, the present incident illustrates the proverbial cowardice of the Phrygians; cf. Tertullian, *De an.* 20: 'comici Phrygas timidos illudunt.' But Phrygians could also die heroically for their faith; thus the physician Alexander among the martyrs of Lyons: Eusebius, *Hist. eccl.* 5. 1. 49-51. 'To offer incense': see n. 25.

[16] Compare Cyprian's flight from Carthage during the persecution of Decius in 250. The same martyr was also said to have had a vision foretelling him his impending execution; cf. Pontius, *Vita Caecil. Cypriani* 12.

[17] And this is what he himself had urged: *Phil.* 12. 3. It is noteworthy that this account frequently touches upon the subject of prayer and contains several prayers and doxologies.

[18] That is, at the farm he had just left. 'Of his own household': cf. Matt. 10. 36. The Jews, too, were eager to do away with Christ: Matt. 26. 5. See above, n. 5. 'Herod': another point of resemblance between Christ's Passion and Polycarp's martyrdom.

[19] See n. 5 and compare Matt. 27. 62; Mark 15. 42; John 19. 31.

[20] Cf. Matt. 26. 55.

[21] Cf. Matt. 6. 10; Acts 21. 14.

[22] Ancient Christianity prayed standing and facing the East. Cf. Matt. 6. 5. See the remarks by J. C. Plumpe, ACW 5 (1948) 198 n. 29.

[23] See n. 46.

[24] Note again the parallel to an incident in Christ's Passion. 'A great Sabbath': see below, n. 56.

[25] The expression 'Lord Caesar' was offensive to Christians because it seemed to imply that Christ was not 'Lord' (see Phil. 2. 11; also 1 Cor. 12. 3). Cf. Tertullian, *Apol.* 34: 'I am of course willing to call the emperor " Lord " in the common acceptation of the term and only when I am under no constraint to call him " Lord " in place of God.'

'Offering incense': this is Lightfoot's attractive suggestion (see *op. cit.* 3. 376 f.) in place of 'offering sacrifice.' Besides the excellent references he gives (Porphyry, *De abst.* 2. 58; Josephus, *Bell. Iud.* 7. 3. 3; etc.), cf. 3 Kings 12. 33. For the general custom of offering incense to emperors, cf. Tertullian, *Apol.* 30; Arnobius, *Adv. nat.* 7. 36; Pliny, *Ep.* 10. 97; etc. 'And what goes with it': that is, such other tokens of worship as accompanied the offering of incense; or, *saying* such other things as they were accustomed to say, as in 9. 2.

[26] 'A voice was heard from heaven': that is, from God; or, less probably, 'a voice rang out in the sky.' See John 12. 28. For the text, see Jos. 1. 6, 7, 9; Deut. 31. 6, 7, 23; Ps. 26. 14; 30. 25.

[27] 'The Fortune of Caesar': the Roman goddess Fortuna was the special protectress of the emperors. See W. F. Otto, in *Pauly-Wissowa's Real-Encyclopaedie* 17 (1912) 36 ff.; for her identification

with the *genius* of the emperors, see *ibid*. 1164 ff. 'The atheists': note the use of this term in two different senses here and later in 9. 2. See above, n. 14.

²⁸ See Polycarp, *Phil*. Intro. 73.

²⁹ The usual formula of Christians confessing adherence to their faith. See, e. g., the replies given by the martyrs of Lyons and Vienne, in Eusebius, *Hist. eccl.* 5. 1. 19, 20; *Passio SS. Perpetuae et Felicitatis* 6. 4. For the first appearance of the word 'Christian,' see ACW 1. 127 n. 15a.

³⁰ Being rather well-disposed toward the venerable Polycarp, the proconsul wants him, by a set appeal, to incline the crowd in his favor, so that he could release him. This recalls Pilate's ineffectual efforts to release Jesus (John 19. 12); see above, n. 5.

³¹ 'To render honor to magistrates': cf. Rom. 13. 1, 7; 1 Peter 2. 13. See also the noble prayer for state officials set down by Clement of Rome 61, and my remarks: ACW 1. 116 f. 'In so far as it does not harm us': that is, not conflict with our conscience.

³² Here Polycarp evidently extends a gentle invitation to the proconsul ' to change to what is good,' to become a Christian.

³³ 'The Jews living at Smyrna': see Apoc. 2. 9. Polycarp, it seems, was 'the angel of Smyrna' mentioned in the verse preceding. See n. 37.

³⁴ Here called Asiarch. This Roman official was the head or president of the *Commune Asiae*, a confederation of the principal cities of the Roman province of Asia. His authority in matters of religion is indicated below (21), where he is called the high priest; he also presided at games. Cf. the long excursus by Lightfoot, *op. cit.* 3. 404-15.

³⁵ This type of sport (*venationes*), normally held in the amphitheatre, involved any kind of exhibition or contest in which wild beasts took part. Usually beasts were pitted in battle against one another or against professional beast fighters, the *bestiarii*. During the persecutions, their place was taken by Christians, who, because addicted to a forbidden religion, were treated like criminals. Since the program of such 'hunting' was filled for that day, the Asiarch said he was not empowered to introduce an additional number.

³⁶ See above, 5. 2; also John 18. 32.

³⁷ See above, 12. 2, and below, 17. 2 and 18. 1. The part often taken by Jews in fomenting persecution of Christians, is succinctly stated by Tertullian, *Scorp.* 10, speaking of Jewish Synagogues as 'fountainheads of persecutions' (*fontes persecutionum*).

[38] For this solemn formula, see Apoc. 4. 8; 11. 17; 15. 3; 16. 7; 21. 22.

[39] See Ps. 58. 6; Judith 9. 12, 14. 'The saints who live under your eyes': the Christians. Cf. Luke 1. 75.

[40] Cf. John 12. 27.

[41] Cf. Matt. 20. 22, 23; 26. 39; Mark 10. 38, 39. 'Your Anointed': cf. Luke 2. 26; 9. 20; 23. 39.

[42] Cf. 5. 29. 'In soul and body, in virtue of, etc.': a terse expression of the Christian belief in the resurrection and of its cause.

[43] Cf. Ps. 19. 4.

[44] See J. A. Kleist, "An Early Christian Prayer," Orate Fratres 22 (1948) 201-6.

[45] The words 'a dove and' seem to be a later addition. In the early Church the dove was a symbol of the soul of a saint just leaving the body.

[46] The earliest occurrence of the expression 'the Catholic Church' is in Ignatius, Smyrn. 8. 2, written some forty years before The Martyrdom of Polycarp: "Where the bishop appears, there let the people be, just as where Jesus Christ is, there is the Catholic Church." See ACW 1. 93; and my remarks, ibid. 141 f. The writer of The Martyrdom uses the term in the same sense as Ignatius. It occurs in inscr.; 8. 1; 16. 2; 19. 2. The text in 16. 2 is not quite certain. Most of the Greek manuscripts and Eusebius (Hist. eccl. 4. 15) speak of 'the Catholic Church at Smyrna'; but the old Latin translation and the Moscow Greek manuscript use the word 'holy' in place of 'Catholic.' If the expression 'the Catholic Church at Smyrna' is genuine, it means that group of Smyrnaean Christians whose belief was the same as that of the universal Church and, therefore, orthodox, in opposition to the doctrines of local heretical or schismatic innovators. It follows that the writer of The Martyrdom used the same language that a modern Catholic writer uses when, for example, he speaks of 'the Catholic Church at St. Louis.' To him the expression means that group of Christians, living at St. Louis, whose faith is the same as that of the universal Church and, therefore, orthodox. For a thorough discussion of the references to 'the Catholic Church' in Ignatius and in the Martyrium Polycarpi, see G. Bardy, La théologie de l'Eglise de saint Clément de Rome à saint Irénée (Unam sanctam 13, Paris 1945) 64-67.

[47] It appears that here we have an indication—the first testimony of this kind in early Christian literature—that the remains or 'relics'

of martyrs were venerated. The devout Smyrnaeans 'took up the bones' of Polycarp and interred them in a decent place (18. 2 f.), where the Christians assembled each year on the anniversary of his death to praise God for the saint's heroic defense of the faith. See P. Séjourné, " Reliques," *Dict. de théol. cath.* 13. 2 (1939) 2318 ff. Note in the following the precision with which the writer distinguishes between the worship of God and the veneration of relics: 'Him we worship—as being the Son of God; the martyrs we love—as being imitators of the Lord.' That a memorial Mass was celebrated at Smyrna on the anniversary, is conjectured by F. J. Dölger in a reference to the passage below (18. 3): IXΘΥΣ 2 (2nd ed., Münster i. W. 1928) 567 f.

⁴⁸ Alce must have been a Christian at Smyrna, probably the same person to whom Ignatius sent greetings: *Smyrn.* 13. 2; *Pol.* 8. 3.

⁴⁹ Cf. 1 Peter 3. 18.

⁵⁰ Lit., 'he placed it in the middle': made is accessible to all, or, in the context, withdrew it from private ownership; he confiscated the body in the name of the State.

⁵¹ This is the oldest record of the ancient Christian concept which regarded death (and especially a martyr's death) as a birth, and the day and anniversary of death (especially of a martyr) as a birthday; but the underlying sentiment, that death is in reality a passage to life, is already indicated in Ignatius of Antioch, *Rom.* 6. 1 ('The *birth* pangs are upon me'), 2. 2 ('May I *rise* in His presence'), and 7. 2 ('There is in me a *Living* Water'). In the Roman Martyrology the word *natalis* (*dies*) denotes the day of a martyr's death. See the very interesting discussion of this subject by A. C. Rush, *Death and Burial in Christian Antiquity* (Stud. in Christ. Ant. 1, Washington 1941) Ch. 4: "Death as a Birth. The Day of Death as *Dies Natalis*." 'The heroes': see Clement of Rome, n. 25: ACW 1. 105.

⁵² One of these was Germanicus, mentioned in 3. 1.

⁵³ Christ is called 'the Shepherd of our souls' in 1 Peter 2. 25.

⁵⁴ Marcion composed the account; Evarestus, mentioned later, committed it to paper. 'To the brethren farther on': see n. 2.

⁵⁵ 'The seventh day before the kalends of March': the 22nd (or, in a leap year, the 23rd) of February. See the discussion of the problem in Harrison, *op. cit.* 269-83.

⁵⁶ 'A great Sabbath': an obscure expression; according to Lightfoot (*op. cit.* 1. 711), the writer seems to mean 'any sabbath which

coincided with a festival or other marked day in the Jewish calendar.'

[57] A striking addition, perhaps used to avoid mentioning the reigning emperor. Compare Luke 3. 1.

[58] In 1. 1, the writer had spoken of Polycarp's martyrdom as being 'of the type narrated in the Gospel.' He—or, more probably, a second writer—now exhorts the readers to make Christ's teaching, expressed in the Gospel, their rule of life; and ends by saying that it was 'thus,' that is, in accord with the Gospel, that Polycarp suffered martyrdom.

[59] Perhaps the same man that is mentioned by Eusebius, *Hist. eccl.* 2. 25. 6. Nothing is known of Socrates or Isocrates.

[60] A writer of the second half of the fourth century. See above, Intro. 89.

[61] The idea of being 'gathered' into the kingdom of Christ is familiar from the Old and the New Testament; see *Didache* n. 60.

[62] Cf. Irenaeus, *Ep. ad Flor.* = Eusebius, *Hist. eccl.* 5. 20. 6.

[63] Cf. Irenaeus, *Adv. haer.* 3. 3. 4. 'The first-born of Satan': see Polycarp 7. 1 and n. 57.

PAPIAS

INTRODUCTION

[1] All things considered, the opinion of J. Donovan, "Earliest Witness of the First Two Gospels," *Ir. Eccl. Rec.* 25 (1925) 237, seems well-founded: Papias 'was probably born as early as A. D. 61, hardly later than A. D. 71.' See also J. V. Bartlett, 'Papias's "Exposition": its Date and Contents,' in H. G. Wood, *Amicitiae Corolla. A Volume of Essays Presented to J. R. Harris* (London 1933) 17: 'Papias was probably at least forty years old by the end of the first century.'

[2] See Irenaeus, *Adv. haer.* 5. 33. 4 = Fr. 1. 4.

[3] See Fr. 13. 2.

[4] See Fr. 2. 1; for the title, see below, n. 6 on the text.

[5] See Fr. 1.

[6] See Fr. 2. 13.

[7] The Greeks regarded with suspicion the written word as contrasted with the spoken or living word. See Plato, *Phaedr.* 275 D ff. The written word 'has no power of adaptation; it speaks in one voice

to all; it cannot answer questions, meet objections, correct misunderstandings, or supplement its own omissions' (S. H. Butcher, *Some Aspects of the Greek Genius* [3d ed., London 1904] 188).

[8] Cf. Frs. 2. 9 and 11. 2. See n. 15 on the text.

[9] The preposition παρά does not require this interpretation.

[10] Note the particles καί (after που) and τε (after ἅ): 'both—and, in particular.'

[11] J. Donovan, *art. cit.* 240, suggests 'the Presbyter' or 'the grand old man.' See 2 John 1 and 3 John 1.

[12] The addition of τοῦ Κυρίου μαθηταί shows the writer's joy in being able to add to his list of distinguished informants two men who were actually disciples of the Lord—surely a privilege for any Christian in the year 100 or thereabouts.

[13] Some scholars (Swete, Colson, etc.) had already expressed the feeling (mainly from the use of ἔνια) that something like 'completeness' must be included in the word τάξει. A most welcome confirmation of the sense here attributed to it came from H. J. Cladder, 'Cerinth und unsere Evangelien,' *Bibl. Zeitschr.* 14 (1917) 317 ff., who, by a study of the teachings of Cerinthus, provided the historical setting for this fragment.

[14] See J. A. Kleist, 'Rereading the Papias Fragment on St. Mark,' *St. Louis Univ. Stud.*, Ser. A: Humanities 1 (1945) 1-17. There pertinent modern literature on the fragment is indicated.

TEXT

[1] Irenaeus states that certain promises made by Christ (Matt. 26. 29; Luke 14. 14) and the blessings invoked upon Jacob by Isaac (Gen. 27. 28) will be realized at the end of the world, when Christ returns to reign on earth for a thousand years, "when, too, creation, etc." Similar dreams were entertained by Talmudic writers in their comments on Isa. 65. 17; Jer. 31. 8; Ezech. 17. 23; Osee 14. 8. See F. X. Funk, *Patres apostolici* I (Tübingen 1901) 346-49; T. Zahn, *Forschungen zur Geschichte des neutestamentlichen Kanons und der altkirchlichen Literatur* 6 (Leipzig 1900) 152 ff. 'Liberated': from the curse pronounced on the earth by God in Paradise (Gen. 3. 17) and from 'the tyranny of corruption' (Rom. 8. 21).

[2] 'Presbyters': men of the primitive age; not men so termed in Fr. 2. 3. 'When the Lord taught': we marvel how such fantastic notions could be attributed to Our Lord, or how 'Apostolic interpretations' (see below, Fr. 2. 12) could be so grossly 'twisted.'

3 'Spring up': grow spontaneously, without aid or cooperation from man. On chiliasm, see Frs. 9 and 10; Barnabas 15. 5; G. Bardy, "Millénarisme,' *Dict. de théol. cath.* 6. 2 (1929) 1760-63; J. P. Kirsch, 'Millennium and Millenarianism,' *Cath. Encycl.* 10 (1911) 307-10. Cf. Barnabas n. 160.

4 'Measures': a measure (*metretes*) was about 10. 5 gallons. One grape, therefore, yields 262.5 gallons—'un linguaggio fantastico' (Bosio, *op. cit.* 255).

5 Irenaeus did not copy the account given above in 2 and 3 directly from Papias's work, but merely repeats what some 'presbyters' had heard from John; yet he goes on to say: 'And then he (Papias) adds'! See Funk's (*op. cit.*, 348 f.) adjustment of the passage. He thinks verse 5 should follow directly verse 3.

6 'The Lord's Gospel': this sense of λόγια has been definitely established by J. Donovan, *The Logia in Ancient and Recent Literature* (Cambridge 1924). See *id.*, 'Earliest Witness of the First Two Gospels,' *Irish Eccl. Rec.* 25 (1925) 237-44; also ACW 1 (1946) 117 n. 179; J. P. Christopher, ACW 2 (1946) 104 f. n. 64.

7 'The presbyters': see n. 2 and the Introduction 107. The particle καί before ὅσα merely reinforces the preposition σύν in συγκατατάξαι.

8 'The longest accounts': perhaps a reference to heretical teachers, such as the Gnostics (Funk 351).

9 'The Truth': see John 14. 6; 18. 37; 1 John 3. 19.

10 The Apostles are here called 'the Lord's disciples,' as so often in the Gospels. See Intro. n. 12. For another interpretation, see Funk, *op. cit.* 352.

11 'I ascertained': to be supplied from the preceding sentence. Note τε: 'In particular, I ascertained.' Little is known about this Aristion. He may have been one of the 'seventy-two disciples' (Luke 10. 1). He was the teacher of Papias (see Fr. 2. 7 and 14). It has been surmised that he was the author of the closing verses of the second Gospel (16. 9-20). See Zahn, *op. cit.* 6. 217 ff.; O. Bardenhewer, *Geschichte der altkirchlichen Literatur* 1 (2nd ed., Freiburg i. Br. 1913) 448 f.

'What they *had* to say': that is, at the time when I asked them; or, '*have* to say,' that is, even now at the time of recording the interview. Papias's direct question was: 'what do you *have* to say?'

12 Papias does not mean to disparage the Gospels. See Intro. n. 7. Whether he means any other writings besides the New Testament we have no means of knowing.

[13] 'The man whose statements Papias had heard partly from his own lips and partly through the medium of other disciples of his, and then recorded in several parts of his work, is a Jewish Christian by the name of John, who had removed from Palestine to Asia Minor. This man was, according to the unanimous tradition of the second century, the Apostle John' (T. Zahn, *Einleitung in das Neue Testament* [3rd ed., Leipzig 1907] 211.

[14] It was only about 260 that Dionysius of Alexandria ventured to guess (οἶμαι) that there must have been two Johns in Ephesus at the same time, both known as 'presbyters,' '*since it is said* (φασίν) that there were two tombs at Ephesus, and that each of the two is said (λέγεσθαι) to be John's' (Eusebius, *Hist. eccl.* 7. 25. 16). Eusebius died about 340. See J. Donovan, 'The Elder John and other Johns,' *Irish Eccl. Rec.* 31 (1928) 337-50; 'The Papias Presbyteri Puzzle,' *ibid.*, 37 (1931) 124-37; 'The Papias Tradition and the Ephesian Legend,' *ibid.* 38 (1931) 482-500.

[15] Not the Apostle Philip, but 'the Evangelist,' one of the seven deacons in the Church of Jerusalem (Acts 6. 5), who preached the Gospel in Palestine (Acts 8. 5-40) and later in Caesarea (Acts 21. 8). According to one report (Eusebius, *Hist. eccl.* 3. 31. 3), he finally settled, with his daughters, in Hierapolis. For the term ἀπόστολος (omitted by the Syriac translator!), see *Didache* 11. 3 and n. 70.

[16] Acts 1. 23 f. Compare Fr. 11. 2.

[17] See nn. 1 and 3. 'The Apostolic interpretations': see, for instance, Apoc. 20. 4. Among the early defenders of chiliasm were Papias, Pseudo-Barnabas, Justin Martyr, Irenaeus, the Montanists (Tertullian), and others. See below, 2. 13, and above, n. 2.

[18] 'The presbyter': as Eusebius understood this term; or, "The Grand Old Man,' an affectionate reference to the aged Apostle, perhaps current among his disciples. See Intro. 111. Mark became St. Peter's 'interpreter' by writing his Gospel, which was in substance the memoirs of St. Peter. There are, however, other possible explanations of this somewhat ambiguous term. I may refer the reader to my commentary in the article referred to above (Intro. n. 14). See J. Donovan, 'The Papias Presbyteri Puzzle,' *Ir. Eccl. Rec.* 37 (1931) 124-137. The questions raised by this extract are fully discussed by M. J. Lagrange, *Evangile selon saint Jean* (5th ed., Paris 1936) xxix ff.

[19] The interpretation of this extract hinges on the meaning assigned to the phrase which is generally rendered 'though not in

order' (οὐ μέντοι τάξει); see Kleist, art. cit. 13-16. In reality, John means to say that Mark did not write 'with full detail,' 'without gaps in his narrative.' See Intro. 111. The rendering verbatim, given in the text above, is that which τάξει has in Modern Greek.

²⁰ The Hebrew language spoken in Syria and Palestine at the time of Christ was Aramaic. In Acts 21. 40, St. Paul 'parla en araméen, la seule langue qui pût être comprise de tout le monde' (M. J. Lagrange, op. cit. xix). In Papias's time our Greek Matthew was already in existence; cf. below, 12. 2.

²¹ Eusebius apparently means the pericope generally printed (though not found in the best ancient manuscripts) as John 8. 1-11. The Gospel according to the Hebrews was a Jewish-Christian apocryphal writing. See M. J. Lagrange, 'L' Evangile selon les Hébreux,' Rev. Bibl. 31 (1922) 161-81; 321-49; M. R. James, The Apocryphal New Testament (Oxford 1924) 1-8.

²² Not the apologist Apollinaris, bishop of Hierapolis, but Apollinaris of Laodicea, the learned heresiarch (Apollinarianism). Cf. Zahn, Forsch. 6. 262-65; Bardenhewer, op. cit. 3 (2nd ed., 1923) 285-91. The text following is from Acts 1. 18.

²³ This fragment deals with the end of Judas's career. The heinousness of his conduct toward Our Lord stirred the imagination of the early Christians into lively activity and gave rise to grotesque legends (φασίν, twice) and pictorial representations. Evidently this information did not originate with 'the presbyters.' The most recent consideration of this fragment will be found in R. B. Halas, Judas Iscariot. A Scriptural and Theological Study of his Person, his Deeds, and his Eternal Lot (Cath. Univ. of Amer. Stud. in Sacred Theol. 96, Washington 1946) 165-70. History also reports a heretical sect—Cainites—who venerated Judas and followed a Gospel of Judas (Irenaeus, Adv. haer. 1. 28. 9)!

²⁴ Here the meaning of several Greek words is not obvious. The sense of the passage seems to be this: as we would say that a man, after a career of crime, 'ended in the penitentiary,' so, Papias says, Judas 'ended in his own place, as they express it.' In Acts 1. 25, St. Peter said that Judas 'went to his own place,' meaning, of course, 'the place of torment' (Luke 16. 28); and so the Christians, speaking of Judas, would appropriate this expression, and say: 'After an agony of pain and punishment, he finally went " to his own place." ' We do not know where Judas hanged himself or where he was buried. A more popular expression would be: 'he went to the place where he belonged.'

[25] Papias seems to mean that some of the angels—before the fall, of course—were charged with the orderly arrangement of the earth, but that, after their fall, this charge was frustrated. Cf. Heb. 1. 14 ('the spirits apt for service' [Knox]). See H. Pope, 'Angels as Divine Agents in Governing the World,' *The Cath. Encycl.* 1 (1907) 477 f.; also E. Schneweis, *Angels and Demons according to Lactantius* (Stud. in Christ. Ant. 3, Washington 1944) Ch. 3: 'The Angels in the Scheme of Divine Providence.'

[26] The author refers to Gregory of Nazianzus (d. about 390) and Cyril of Alexandria (d. 444).

[27] John the Apostle (John 13. 25).

[28] Pantaenus and his pupil Clement were the celebrated heads of the catechetical school of Alexandria. Ammonius was a contemporary of Clement's pupil, Origen. Eusebius (*Hist. eccl.* 6. 19. 10) states that he wrote a work entitled *Harmony between Moses and Jesus.* Incidentally, Eusebius thought that this Ammonius and the famous Neoplatonist philosopher Ammonius Saccas were one and the same person (cf. Bardenhewer, *op. cit.* 2. 198-202).

[29] 'Pre-conciliar': supposing the reading συνόδων. Lightfoot reads συνῳδῶν and renders: 'who agree with each other.' The first council, that of Nicaea, was held in 325. 'Hexaëmeron': the history of the six days of the Creation (Gen. 1).

[30] 'Allegorically': lit., 'spiritually,' that is, in the spirit of prophecy, in a sense higher than the literal and obvious one.

[31] 'Guilelessness' or 'guiltlessness,' 'innocence.' 'By them': the early Christians (Funk 365); cf. Luke 18. 16.

[32] Cf. Clement of Alexandria, *Paed.* 1. 6. 32.

[33] Cf. Irenaeus, *Adv. haer.* 5. 33. 3; cf. above, Fr. 1.

[34] See Irenaeus, *ibid.,* and Fr. 1. We may compare Rom. 14. 17.

[35] 'The theologian': this title was given to the Apostle during the Arian controversies. See T. Zahn, *Die Offenbarung des Johannes* (Leipzig 1924) 91.

[36] See Fr. 2. For § 1 of the present fragment the author is indebted to Eusebius, *Hist. eccl.* 3. 39 and 25.

[37] The epitomist here erroneously attributes the words 'the theologian and his brother' to Papias. See Zahn, *loc. cit.;* Funk, *op. cit.,* 366 f. The reference is to John the Baptist and the Apostle James, bishop of Jerusalem.

[38] 'Passed the scrutiny': Barsabas and Matthias were *judged fit* by the Apostles to fill the place of the traitor Judas: Acts 1. 23-26.

[39] See Fr. 2. 9. Manaemus may be identical with Manahen mentioned in Acts 13. 1. 'Till Hadrian's time': see below, *Ep. to Diognetus*, Intro. n. 11.

[40] That is, Patmos; cf. Apoc. 1. 9; Tertullian, *De praescr. haer.* 36; Eusebius, *Hist. eccl.* 3. 18. It was here that the Apostle composed the *Apocalypse*. See M. Meinertz, *Einleitung in das Neue Testament* (4th ed., Paderborn 1933) 324.

[41] Of twenty-seven manuscripts of Georgius's *Chronicon*, only one, the Codex Coislinianus here cited, carries the testimony attributed to Papias (§ 2) and Origen (§ 3). It is undoubtedly an interpolation. Moreover, the other twenty-six manuscripts contradict the statement that John died a martyr's death, saying that 'he died a peaceful death' (see Funk, *op. cit.* 368 f.; also above, n. 37).

[42] Cf. Mark 10. 38 f.; also Matt. 20. 22 f.

[43] Cf. Origen, *Comm. in Matt.* 16. 6 (GCS 40. 485 f.), which passage was misunderstood by the interpolator.

[44] 3. 1.

[45] '*Exotericis*': some take this to be an error for *exegeticis*.

[46] The reference to Marcion in this context is perhaps a confusion of an incident related by Irenaeus (*Adv. haer.* 3. 3. 4) concerning the Apostle St. John and the heresiarch Cerinthus, with the story of the encounter between Polycarp and Marcion (see Irenaeus, *ibid.*; also above, Polycarp n. 57; *Mart. Pol.* Mosc. MS. 3). In the final sentence 'He' (*Is*) seems to refer to Marcion as subject. Moreover, since it is extremely doubtful whether the curious statements in § 2 actually refer to Papias, the editors of the fragment either omit them (Lightfoot stops after the words 'at the dictation of John') or bracket them (as is done here, following Funk and Bihlmeyer).

THE EPISTLE TO DIOGNETUS

INTRODUCTION

[1] Christ wanted brotherly love to be the distinguishing mark of His disciples. See the commentaries on John 13. 34 f. ('a new commandment') and 35 (the badge of true discipleship). Cf. also 1 John 3. 11, 23; 4. 7, 11 f.; 2 John 5. Compare the common observation of the pagans, as reported by Tertullian (*Apol.* 39): 'Look, how they love one another,' and that of Minucius Felix (*Octav.* 9. 2): 'They love one another almost before they know each other.'

² The *Epistle of Barnabas* was written for the express purpose of warning a Christian community against Jewish propaganda. See above, 31.

³ L. B. Radford, *The Epistle to Diognetus* (London 1908) 32. Much useful information will be found in this volume.—Chapters 11 and 12 have often been attributed to Hippolytus of Rome; cf. O. Bardenhewer, *Geschichte der altkirchlichen Literatur* 1 (2nd ed., Freiburg i. Br. 1913) 320.

⁴ Concerning the differences in style, rhythm, etc., see J. L. Jacobi, 'Zur Geschichte des griechischen Kirchenliedes,' *Zeitschr. f. Kirchengesch.* 5 (1882) 198-200.

⁵ See *Poet.* 1450b, 26; cf. L. Cooper, *Aristotle on the Art of Poetry* (Boston 1913) 28.

⁶ *Eph.* 1. 23.

⁷ The integrity of the Epistle is briefly discussed by L. B. Radford, *op. cit.* 31-38. P. Godet, 'Diognète (Epître à),' *Dict. de théol. cath.* 4. 2 (1924) 1368, notes 'le caractère semi-poétique du morceau (11 and 12), qui décèle un fragment d'homélie.'

⁸ Classical scholars have not been chary in their admiration for the style of this epistle. 'The *Epistle to Diognetus* is one of the most brilliant things ever written by Christians in the Greek language' (E. Norden, *Die Antike Kunstprosa* 2 [Leipzig 1923] 513 n. 2. U. v. Wilamowitz-Moellendorff adopted the epistle into his well-known *Griechisches Lesebuch* (text: 1. 2. 356-63; commentary: 2. 2. 225-27).

⁹ For further particulars, see Bardenhewer, *op. cit.* 1. 321-23; Radford, *op. cit.* 21-31.

¹⁰ See F. Ogara, 'Aristidis et Epistolae ad Diognetum cum Theophilo Antiocheno cognatio,' *Gregorianum* 25 (1944) 74-102.

¹¹ See Andriessen's recent series of studies in *Recherches de théologie ancienne et médiévale* 13 (1946): 'L'Apologie de Quadratus conservée sous le titre d'Epître à Diognète' (5-39; 125-49; 237-60); 14 (1947): 'L'Epilogue de l'Epître à Diognète' (121-56). The author offers a summary of his findings in *Vigiliae Christianae* 1 (1947) 129-36: 'The Authorship of the Epistula ad Diognetum.' He points out that the only extant fragment of the *Apology* of Quadratus, preserved by Eusebius, *Hist. eccl.* 4. 3, answers completely to what we should expect between verses 6 and 7 of Ch. 7: 'But the proofs of our Savior's power were ever-present, for they were genuine: those who were healed, those who rose from the dead,

who were not only seen when they were cured and rose, but were constantly present, not only while the Savior was on earth, but also for a considerable time after His departure, so that some of them even lived till our own times.' Compare Papias, Fr. 11. 2.

[12] Cf. W. Weber, *Untersuchungen zur Geschichte des Kaisers Hadrian* (Leipzig 1907) 168 ff. Tertullian, *Apol.* 5. 7, speaks of Hadrian as 'omnium curiositatum explorator.' Some expressions in this Epistle seem to indicate that Easter was the time when it was presented to Diognetus: 11. 5, 'today' and 'announces seasons'; 1. 9: 'the Passover.'

[13] Cf. Andriessen, 'The Authorship . . . ,' 133 f. A. S. L. Farquharson, *The Meditations of the Emperor Marcus Antoninus* (Oxford 1944) 271, identifies the Diognetus named by the emperor as his painting master. E. J. Goodspeed, *A History of Early Christian Literature* (Chicago 1942) 147, says: 'Diognetus was the tutor of Marcus Aurelius, and he may be the individual ostensibly addressed in the opening lines.'

[14] Even so one wonders how a pagan could be supposed to form a clear idea of certain Christian doctrines (as, for example, the atonement) from the vague way in which the author refers to them.

[15] See *Martyrium Polycarpi*, nn. 14 and 27.

[16] See n. 18 on the text.

[17] The apologies of Aristides and Quadratus were not altogether lost on Hadrian. During his reign the Christians were treated with greater leniency, and in some parts of the empire persecution ceased altogether. See A. Ehrhard, *Urkirche und Frühkatholizismus* (Bonn 1935) 143.

[18] See Radford, *op. cit.* 8.

TEXT

[1] 'Diognetus': lit., 'sprung from Zeus'; first used by Hesiod, the word was later frequently applied as a name to persons of high nobility. Its application to Hadrian, both as emperor and as an Athenian *archon*, is appropriate. See Andriessen, *art. cit.* 133 f. 'Christians': this name was current in Rome about the middle of the first century; cf. Ignatius, *Magn.* 4 and ACW 1 (1946) 127 n. 15a. For its origin, see E. Peterson, "Christianus," *Miscellanea Giov. Mercati*, vol. I (Vatican City 1946) 355-72.

[2] 'Superstition': this is probably the meaning of the Greek word here. See n. 13. Elsewhere it occurs in the sense of 'religion' or

'the quality of being religious'; cf. Acts 17.22 and 25.19. See P. J. Koets, 'Δεισιδαιμονία': A Contribution to the Knowledge of the Religious Terminology in Greek (Utrecht 1929). It is not necessary to assume that Diognetus had actually asked these questions in writing or by word of mouth. His general interest in religion may have prompted the writer to formulate them as they stand.

³ 'This new blood': as we speak of 'fresh blood' when we mean new members admitted to a family or society. Others render 'new race' and refer to Tertullian's 'tertium genus dicimur' (Scorp. 10). 'New spirit': lit. 'pursuit,' 'practice.' See also Radford, op. cit. 52 f. The adjective καινός recalls Acts 17.19. For a general survey of Christianity from the point of view of its 'newness,' see K. Prümm, Christentum als Neuheitserlebnis (Freiburg i. Br. 1939).

⁴ Diognetus is to be initiated in the Christian mysteries (see 4.6; 7.1-2; 8.10; 10.7; 11.2, 5); hence the need of a previous purification, as in the Eleusinian mysteries. Similarly St. Peter opens his second doctrinal section (1 Peter 2.1) with the significant ἀποθέμενοι: 'lay aside; renounce.' See n. 18.

⁵ Cf. Eph. 4.24; Col. 3.10. 'A hearer': in the technical sense of 'follower; disciple; pupil.' 'Also': also, even, of Christianity, as you are now of the mystery cults.

⁶ This is a commonplace among the early apologists; cf. the passages collected by E. H. Blakeney, The Epistle to Diognetus (London 1943) 36 f. The writer's exposure of these crudities, if meant seriously, is itself a little crude; or does he write with a touch of humor? The criticism is somewhat softened by the frequent use of ὑμεῖς, which includes the great mass of pagans. See n. 73.

⁷ Cf. Ps. 113.16; 134.15-18.

⁸ This sentence may be read as a question, as here translated, or as a statement: 'Therefore, you do not prove that it has sensation.'

⁹ The participle λογιζόμενοι may be conditional: 'if they realized or reflected.' 'Exactly as if': their punctiliousness in offering sacrifices leads the writer to suspect that they actually believed God needed this worship. His intention here is to show the resemblance between the Jewish and the pagan attitude of mind. He speaks in the present tense: in Hadrian's time the orthodox Jews regarded the old religion as still in force.

¹⁰ Cf. Exod. 20.11; Ps. 145.6; Acts 14.15.

¹¹ In 3.2, however, the author admitted an essential difference between the two kinds of worship.

[12] The writer forgets that the Jews offered sacrifices, etc., in obedience to God's express commandment (see n. 16); or else he holds (as Barnabas did; see n. 16 on his Epistle) that these regulations were from the start not meant to be taken literally. The phrase δοκούντων παρέχειν belongs to both groups, and the verb παρέχειν means, in the context, 'to make a real *offering*,' one in which something is '*given*' (see above, 2. 4).

[13] 'Their superstition': such it was after the death of Christ or, at least, after the destruction of Jerusalem. See n. 2.

[14] See Barnabas's wholesale condemnation of the Jewish 'fast days and new moons' (Barnabas 2. 5). Certain Jewish festivals were regulated by the moon. We have a relic of this reckoning in the celebration of Easter, which occurs on the Sunday that falls upon, or follows, the 14th Nisan of the Jews, that is, the first full moon after the vernal equinox (March 20).

[15] It was not the Mosaic Law but its misinterpretation by the Pharisees that forbade an act of kindness on the Sabbath. See Mark 3. 4 and Luke 6. 9.

[16] Circumcision *was* a mark of election, in the sense that by it one became a member of the Chosen People; Gen. 17. 10 ff. The writer is unfair in his criticism of Jewish practices.

[17] Men specially posted scanned the horizon for the first appearance of the moon. The 'days' referred to are especially Friday and Saturday: the former ended when three stars had become visible. When only two stars were seen, it was still twilight, and it was only a doubtful sin (breaking the Sabbath) to be found working.

[18] Note this first occurrence, in the present epistle, of the important key word μυστήριον (*mysterium*). See 7. 1; 7. 2; 8. 10; 10. 7; 11. 2; 11. 5. Here it stands for Christianity's full spiritual content and efficacy—the 'secret' of its supernatural control over the life of the soul. Since Hadrian was initiated in all the mystery cults, the reference to Christianity as a 'mystery religion' was well calculated to direct his attention to the new worship.

[19] Cf. John 1. 18.

[20] This thought is elaborated in Ch. 7. "Inquisitive men': both the noun and the adjective are emphatic. Inquisitiveness was a well-known trait of the Athenian character; cf. Acts 17. 21, 23. 'A doctrine of human origin': Stoicism, Epicureanism, etc.

[21] In trying to win Diognetus for Christianity, the author's main reliance is, apart from the absurdities of idol-worship, on the moral

argument drawn from the wholesome effect of Christian life on the minds of contemporary society. The idea of impressing outsiders favorably by one's conduct rested on Matt. 5. 16 and was a prominent feature of early Christian teaching. Cf. 1 Thess. 4. 12; Col. 4. 5; 1 Peter 2. 12; 3. 1 (the conduct of a Christian wife may succeed in convincing a heathen inquirer even when the spoken word has failed); 1 Tim. 2. 2-4; Titus 2. 5; Polycarp 1. 3.

[22] 'Aliens': sojourners; pilgrims; strangers; visitors. See my note 2 on Clement of Rome: ACW 1. 103 f. Cf. 1 Peter 1. 1; 2. 11. 'The idea of Christians as sojourners in the world came to be felt as so expressive of their condition that παροικία became a common term for a Christian community in a place; hence our word "parish"'; see E. G. Selwyn, The First Epistle of St. Peter (London 1947) 118. The rendering 'but only as aliens' is modelled on the Greek; but the particle ὡς should be expanded so as to make the words mean 'but only as considering themselves aliens.' 'They put up with everything': with every indignity, disability, inconvenience, occasioned by their being foreigners. The clause 'Every foreign land, etc.' rivals, in beauty of diction, the best in all Greek literature.

[23] References to the pagan practice of exposing children abound in pagan and early Christian literature. See H. Leclercq, 'Alumni,' Dict. d'archéol. chrét. et de lit. 1. 1 (1924) 1288-1306. Abortion and infanticide are specially stigmatized in the Didache (2. 2) and in Barnabas (20. 2). 'Their board, not their bed': the pagans believed that at the common meals of the Christians the grossest immoralities were practiced. Cf. Tertullian, Apol. 39. 11: 'Omnia indiscreta apud nos praeter uxores.'

[24] Cf. 2 Cor. 10. 3; Rom. 8. 12 f. 'Hold citizenship': their real home is in heaven: Phil. 3. 20. 'They obey the laws': 1 Peter 2.13 ff. 'They rise above the laws': they go beyond the requirements of the laws; their ideal of life is higher than that of the law of the land. The practice of perpetual virginity, for example, was well established in the early Church. See below, n. 62.

[25] Compare the series of pointed contrasts in 2 Cor. 6. 8 ff. 'They are unknown': nobody takes the trouble of ascertaining their religious convictions. They are known as 'Christians,' and the very name is enough to condemn them. See the opening paragraph in Tertullian's Apology.

[26] Cf. 2 Cor. 6. 10. The noun ἀτιμία may have a legal connotation: 'the deprivation of privileges, esp. of civic rights.'

[27] Cf. 1 Cor. 4. 12. 'As evildoers': see 1 Peter 2. 12; Matt. 5. 10-12. Nero made the Christians the scapegoats for his crimes. See Tacitus, *Ann.* 15. 44. 'They rejoice': see 1 Peter 4. 13, 14; Matt. 5. 12; James 1. 2.

[28] 'The Jews make war': the present tense (see n. 9) affords no certain clue to the date of composition. The reference may be to the Bar Kochba insurrection, in Hadrian's time, in which many Christians were slain. 'At a loss to explain': they can assign no reason for their enmity; they would not, of course, admit that the lives of the Christians were a constant rebuke to them. Christ predicted this 'hatred' and gave the reason for it: John 15. 18 ff.; 1 John 3. 13; 1 Thess. 2. 15 f. and *Martyrium Polycarpi* 12. 2.

[29] This statement of the place and task of the Christians in the world has been justly admired. 'Here we have already, in germ, a Greek philosophy of history, discussing the place and task of Christendom in the world' (G. Hahn, *Die Kirche der Märtyrer und Katakomben* [Freiburg i. Br. 1939] 236. We may compare Matt. 5. 13 ('the salt') and 15 ('the light of the world').

[30] Compare the same expression in John 17. 14.

[31] 'Invisible': while visible in its existence, membership, and effects, the Christian religion is invisible; grace and the Church's life-giving principle are, as such, not visible to the eye. See n. 67.

[32] An echo of Eph. 5. 29.

[33] 'The flesh': note the double sense of the word: the body, and its unruly passions. Cf. Eph. 5. 28 f. 'Loves the flesh': the union of body and soul is natural.

[34] Aristides, *Apol.* 16. 6: 'The world stands by reason of the fervent prayers of the Christians.' See Justin, *Apol.* 2. 7. Compare the Church's solemn prayer, recorded by Clement of Rome (59. 2-61). God was willing to spare Sodom if ten just men were found in it. (Gen. 18. 32). God saved the entire ship's company for the sake of St. Paul when the latter sailed to Italy (Acts 27. 24). The world must last at least till 'the full tale of the Gentile nations is complete' (Rom. 11. 25 Knox). 'As in prison': an allusion to Plato (*Phaed.* 62B)?

[35] Cf. 1 Cor. 15. 42; etc.

[36] As Tertullian puts it: 'Etiam plures efficimur, quotiens metimur a vobis: semen est sanguis Christianorum' (*Apol.* 50. 13).

[37] The life of the Christians is unique because their faith is unique.

[38] The word λόγος occurs repeatedly in this document. In 10. 2,

it means 'reason'; elsewhere it may mean 'word,' 'teaching,' 'the (Gospel) message,' or 'the Word,' 'the Logos,' as in John 1. 1. Other titles of honor are given to Our Lord in 9. 6.

³⁹ 'Some subordinate': on the classes or orders of angels and their office as God's agents in governing the universe, see the commentaries on Eph. 1. 21 and Col. 1. 16. See Papias, Fr. 4 and n. 25. 'Whether angel': Geffcken (cf. Hennecke, *op. cit.* 622) renders ἄγγελον with 'messenger' (*Boten*).

⁴⁰ 'Architect': demiurge; a neutral term applicable both to God (so Plato) and to inferior beings. Cf. Heb. 11. 10. The early Fathers did not shrink from appropriating current philosophical terms to express Christian ideas. See ACW 1. 108 n. 68. 'By whom He created': see John 1. 3.

⁴¹ 'By whom—whose—from whom': similar summations of the glories of Christ or of the gifts of God bestowed on man are found in Clement of Rome (35.2; 36. 1, 2). See n. 66. 'He created the heavens': see the brilliant exposition in Ch. 20 of Clement of Rome's letter.

⁴² 'Inscrutable counsels': see Clement of Rome 20. 5 ff.; the writer means the laws of nature. In speaking to a pagan, it was important to say that the marvels of the cosmos were created by, and dependent on, one personal God, and were, besides, a work of love. See n. 43.

⁴³ With this clear-cut exposition we may profitably contrast the vagueness of expression in the *Hymn of Cleanthes*, which markes the height to which Stoic philosophers were able to rise.

⁴⁴ This section recalls John 3. 16 ff. 'As God—as Man to men': a highlight in the writer's Christology. 'Coercion': cf. Irenaeus, *Adv. haer.* 4. 64. 3. God does not coerce men to save their soul.

⁴⁵ Cf. Mal. 3. 2 f. 'His coming': at the end of the world (see Matt. 24. 27). In 7. 9, the same term (παρουσία) means Christ's 'abiding presence' in the Church.

Regarding the break which follows this text, an early editor (F. Sylburg) of the Epistle conjectured that the author continued: The Christians believe in this coming of Christ at the end of time with such firm conviction that nothing can daunt them. The conjecture has met with approval (cf. Radford, 71); however, see above, Intro. 130 and n. 11.

⁴⁶ That is, Christ. The Incarnation is in many respects God's most wonderful self-revelation: Heb. 1. 2. 'Pretentious': lit., 'trustworthy,' said ironically.

⁴⁷ So Heraclitus, while Thales attributed such primacy to water.
⁴⁸ Cf. John 1. 18.
⁴⁹ Cf. Mark 10. 18. 'A great purpose': cf. Eph. 3. 9. 'As a secret': *ibid.*
⁵⁰ Epicurus believed that, while the gods enjoyed perfect bliss, they were totally unconcerned about the happiness of men. 'He granted us all things at once': perhaps a reminiscence of Wisd. 7. 11 or Rom. 8. 32. 'Which none of us, etc.': the author is preparing the reader for the μυστήριον; see n. 18.
⁵¹ Lit., '*during* the previous time'—from the fall of man down to the Incarnation. 'Unbridled desires': cf. Titus 3. 3.
⁵² Cf. John 3. 5.
⁵³ Note the accusative of time in the pronoun ὅν.
⁵⁴ Cf. Titus 3. 4 f.
⁵⁵ God the Father 'lifted the burden of our sins'; how He did it is explained in the next sentence. The pronoun αὐτός, in the sense of 'uninvited, voluntarily, of one's own accord,' is common Greek. It emphasizes initiative. So, again, in the sentence following: 'Of His own accord He gave up His Son.'
⁵⁶ Cf. Rom. 8. 32. 'As a ransom': see Matt. 20. 28; Mark 10. 45; 1 Tim. 2. 6. We wonder whether Diognetus could form any clear idea of the atonement from this brief statement.
⁵⁷ Cf. 1 Peter 3. 18.
⁵⁸ 'There is no doubt that he (the author) held the doctrine of salvation through the righteousness of Christ' (Blakeney, *op. cit.* 14); nor is there any doubt that he believed righteousness, grace, and virtue to be real inward endowments of the justified soul. Note the opening sentence in 7. 2 ('firmly established it in their hearts') and the exposition in 10. 2-6. None of the Apostolic Fathers held the doctrine of a purely imputative righteousness.
⁵⁹ 'Not to be solicitous': this comes as a sort of anticlimax in the present connection, but was a much-needed reminder for a heathen; cf. Matt. 6. 32, 33; Col. 3. 1 f.
⁶⁰ 1 John 4. 9, 19.
⁶¹ 'Imitator': see Ignatius, *Trall.* 1 and ACW 1. 131 n. 7. Cf. 1 John 3. 16; also Blakeney, *op. cit.* 80.
⁶² Gal. 6. 2 ('Bear the burden of one another's failings'; Knox). In this way, again, Christians 'go beyond the laws' (see n. 24). 'The *god* of the recipients': such an expression would not sound strange to Jews or pagans; cf. John 10. 34.

[63] 'Then': not until then, not until you have come to *know* and *love* the true God; 'you will realize': lit., gaze at, behold, with a sense of wonder; 'that God lives in heaven': you will see and judge of earthly things, in the midst of which you live, as God in heaven sees them; aided by this divine light, 'you will in good earnest discourse on the mysteries of God,' which are not revealed to 'outsiders' (see Mark 4. 11). For the Greek idiom ἄρχομαι with the present infinitive, see J. A. Kleist, *The Gospel of St. Mark* (Milwaukee 1936) 154-61.

[64] 'Forever': since μέχρι τέλους (Heb. 3. 14) and εἰς τέλος (Matt. 10. 22) are sometimes used interchangeably, and since εἰς τέλος sometimes means 'forever,' it seems advisable to assign this latter sense to μέχρι τέλους here, instead of rendering 'to the end' and supposing that, in the opinion of the author, the damned will eventually be annihilated. 'For conscience' sake': see Matt. 5. 10.

[65] True mysticism is above, not contrary, to reason. 'What has been handed down': tradition as a rule of faith is again emphasized in 11. 6. See n. 70. 'Reckoned as trustworthy': see John 15. 15.

[66] 'He was, etc.': see n. 41. 'In the beginning': cf. John 1. 1; 1 John 1. 1; 2. 13 f. 'Appeared new': in the Incarnation. Christ was Man, born in time, yet proved Himself to be God from all eternity. 'The saints': the Christians. 'Accounted a Son (or, the Son)': Ps. 2. 7; Matt. 3. 17. 'Today': this 'would be a vivid touch if it meant the anniversary of His vindication as the Son of God' (Radford 82). The mention of wax-tapers in 12. 9 may be another reference to Easter Day.

[67] 'Grace': from what follows, it is clear that the author thinks of grace as a divine influence and the spring of multiple activity in the Church. Note the combination 'Church . . . and grace': the Church, the outward visible institution founded by Christ for the salvation of men; grace, the sum total of the invisible powers entrusted to the Church of that purpose (see n. 31); hence, 'the grace of the Church' (6): the grace which is at home in the Church, and the treasure confided to the Church. The author feels that he owes the pagan inquirer an explanation of the hidden springs of that Christian life (Col. 1. 6) which he has so eloquently described above. In stating some of the activities of grace, he seems to personify this subtle influence and is, perhaps, thinking of its Mediator, Christ (who is called 'Grace' in the *Didache* 10. 6), or of its Dispenser, the Holy Spirit (Gal. 5. 25; etc.).

15 6

⁶⁸ Grace 'grants understanding': such as neither pagan nor Jew possessed (see above, 2-4); 'reveals mysteries': this effect would naturally attract a pagan desirous of mystical experiences (cf. Eph. 6. 19); 'announces seasons': in the Church, festivals and times of sorrow are announced, not by moon and stars (as in the Jewish calendar; see 4. 5), but by grace (the Holy Spirit?—see John 16. 13); 'glories in believers': in those who have πίστις (see 8. 6); grace (Christ?) 'glories' in the growing number and holiness of the faithful (cf. Matt. 11. 25 ff.); they are Christ's 'crowning glory' (John 17. 10), just as the Thessalonians were the Apostle's 'glory and joy' (1 Thess. 2. 20); 'gives freely to seekers': Luke 11. 9. Will the addressee (Hadrian?) prove himself a true 'seeker' (ὑπερεσπουδακότα)?

⁶⁹ The blessings just mentioned must be secured by fidelity to the baptismal vows and by adherence to the Apostolic tradition. See nn. 65 and 70. For πίστις, 'fidelity,' see Polycarp 4. 3 and n. 37.

⁷⁰ That is, do not teach or prescribe more or less than was handed down from the Apostolic times (referred to a little later as 'Apostolic tradition'). The commentators quote Jerome, *Ep.* 63. 2: 'To me nothing is more important than to preserve Christ's authority and not to deviate from the lines laid down by the fathers' (lit., 'not to shift the bounds set by the fathers': *patrum transferre terminos*).

⁷¹ This is another pregnant pronouncement, a *multum in parvo*. The genitive νόμου may be objective or, better, subjective (like the other genitives): either 'fear of,' 'reverence for the Law,' or, 'the fear (of God) inculcated by the Law.' The verb ᾄδεται seems to indicate that the author is thinking especially of the psalms used in the liturgy (cf. Ps. 118. 54), and that he regards 'the fear of God' (so awe-inspiring to the Jew!) as a matter for jubilation to a Christian.—The noun χάρις denotes 'the inspiration' as well as 'the office or function' of the prophets (both old and new); see Rom. 12. 6. 'The grace of the Church': see n. 67. The phrase 'is exultant' (Luke 1. 41, 44; 6. 23) suggests that the author regards 'grace' as something personal (Christ? the Holy Spirit? the whole Church so richly blessed?). See nn. 67 and 72.

⁷² 'Grieve (or, distress) this grace': cf. Eph. 4. 30. 'Whomsoever He chooses': an apologetic reference to the author's own boldness in undertaking so difficult a task as the communication of the teachings of the Logos. See John 3. 8.

⁷³ In the Greek there is a change to the plural number. Some-

times Diognetus is addressed personally, sometimes as the representative of the whole pagan world. See n. 6.

[74] Cf. Gen. 2. 9; 3. 24; Joel 2. 3. '*They* rear in themselves': the writer is not here speaking of the Church as a paradise of delight, but of every Christian soul endowed with 'knowledge and life.' It is important to bear this in mind in interpreting 12. 8, where such a soul is referred to as 'Eve' and 'a virgin.' 'Then'—that is, as long as knowledge and life flourish in the soul—'Eve is not seduced and a virgin can be trusted' (that is, to remain pure and undefiled); the blessings showered upon this soul are imperishable and never lost as were those granted to Eve in Paradise.

[75] Cf. Gen. 2. 9. Note the author's important association of 'knowledge' with 'life.' To produce its happiest and ripest fruits, the Christian religion must be 'known' (understood, appreciated) and 'lived.' This γνῶσις has nothing to do with the pretensions of Gnosticism. See Barnabas n. 8.

[76] Cf. 1 Cor. 8. 1.

[77] *Ibid.*, 9. 10.

[78] 'For you': note the personal touch in the singular number. 'Your heart, etc.': 'In other words, Christian wisdom must be the spring of action, and Christian life the realization of truth' (Westcott, quoted by Radford 87). The word χωρέω means 'to have capacity for,' 'to make room for,' 'absorb,' 'grasp,' 'assimilate.'

[79] Those who had themselves initiated in the pagan mysteries, were eager to know how they could be 'saved.' A Christian, the writer says, who knows God and lives accordingly, and is a faithful member of the Church, enjoys many advantages: salvation is pointed out to him; there are men qualified to teach him; the celebration of Easter comes in due season; the Church displays her liturgy; and, above all, Christ, the Logos, delights in teaching the saints. The word 'salvation' has a mystical ring. 'Wax-tapers': the reading here adopted is κηροί (not καιροί). See n. 66.

INDEX

INDEX

abortion, 16, 62, 157, 183
Abraham, 30, 49, 50, 57
accursed, 63; Christ as, 25, 166
acta martyrum, 88, 185, 197
Acta Pauli et Theclae, 198
Adam, 45; first and Second, 173
adultery, 16, 18, 64
aedificare, 188, 195
Aelianus, 177
agape, 7, 158, 159, 162
Agent, the, 38, 168. See Black
　One, Devil
ἄγγελος, 176. See angel(s)
ἅγιον, τό, Holy Communion, 160
ἁγνός, 194
Alce, 98
aliens (Christians), 139, 215
allegorical interpretation of Scrip-
　ture, 33, 34, 35
alms, 13, 16, 24, 80, 155, 156
Altaner, B., 151
Ammonius, 120; A. Saccas, 209
Anastasius of Sinai, 120, 121
Andrew, St., Apostle, 115
Andrew of Caesarea, 120
Andriessen, P., 131, 211
angel(s), 62, 91, 97, 120, 141,
　199; bad, of Satan, 50, 62, 181.
　See ἄγγελος
anger, 13, 16, 79
Anicetus, Pope, 73, 87
Anselm, St. 168
Antichrist, 79, 165, 170, 192
anti-Semitic bias, 6
Apelles the Marcionite, 131

Apocalypse, 33, 120, 122, 158,
　161
Apollinaris of Laodicea, 119, 208
Apollos, 131
Apostles, 3, 5, 15, 43, 79, 80, 99,
　145, 146, 147; = missionaries,
　22, 161
Apostolic Church Order, 5
Apostolic Constitutions, 5
ἀπόστολος, 207
appetites, natural, 40
Aristides the apologist, 131, 216
Aristion, 107, 116, 122
Aristotle, 129
Arnobius, 200
Arnold, A., 159
arrogance, 16
Asiarch, 201
aspersion, baptism by, 3
astrology, 16
atheism, etc., 94, 132, 199
athlete, God's, 87
Athenagoras, 199
ἀτιμία, 215
augury, 16
Augustine, St., 12, 155, 168, 179,
　195
αὐθάδης, 156
avarice, 16, 64, 72, 76, 81, 195.
　See covetousness

baptism, baptismal water, etc., 3,
　4, 6, 19, 20, 30, 53, 158; re-
　birth in, 155